First Confession

CHRIS PATTEN

First Confession

A Sort of Memoir

ALLEN LANE
an imprint of
PENGUIN BOOKS

ALLEN LANE

UK | USA | Canada | Ireland | Australia
India | New Zealand | South Africa

Allen Lane is part of the Penguin Random House group of companies
whose addresses can be found at global.penguinrandomhouse.com

First published 2017
002

Copyright © Chris Patten, 2017

The moral right of the author has been asserted

Set in 10.5/14 pt Sabon LT Std
Typeset by Jouve (UK), Milton Keynes
Printed in Great Britain by Clays Ltd, St Ives plc

A CIP catalogue record for this book is available from the British Library

ISBN: 978-0-241-27559-7

www.greenpenguin.co.uk

MIX
Paper from
responsible sources
FSC® C018179

Penguin Random House is committed to a
sustainable future for our business, our readers
and our planet. This book is made from Forest
Stewardship Council® certified paper.

To my family and my cardiologists

Contents

I

Politics and Identity

From far, from eve and morning
And yon twelve-winded sky,
The stuff of life to knit me
Blew hither: here am I.
                    A. E. Housman, *A Shropshire Lad*

The things that make me different are the things that make me.
                    A. A. Milne, *Winnie-the-Pooh*

A Chinese anthem, written in 1100 BC, warned against three foolish things: first, deep sleep in an unknown house; second, setting out to sea in a borrowed junk; third, not to lag behind when the elephant approaches a new bridge. To which sound advice, over 3,000 years later, one might add a fourth foolish thing – writing a political autobiography, particularly if it is a memoir of the conventional sort. The author poses as the person she or he wanted to appear to be: a somebody, not too dreary, right about everything or, if not absolutely right, then heroically wrong. The more honest examples of the genre may concede some surprise at the public heights to which the author has been lifted by what he or she knows better than anyone else are pretty modest talents.

There may also be the admitted discovery that as you ascend you feel much the same as you did when you started the climb. I recall a former boss when I was in my twenties, Jim Prior, a Suffolk farmer, a friend of Ted Heath and a Cabinet minister, opining wistfully on one occasion as he opened his ministerial red box with its gold-embossed coat of arms, 'I used to think before I got into the Cabinet, that if ever

I

I made it, I would seem a very different person. But it's all just the same.' So it is, at least for the normal and sane.

At their worst, conventional political memoirs, often produced more for buying and selling than reading, seem written almost straight out of the office diary with occasional forays into *Rough Guide* geography lessons. 'Afghanistan is a poor country surrounded by mountains': thus the tone and style of Hillary Clinton's door-stopping contribution. It is not only Hillary's way. A regular part of these autobiographies is the tittle-tattle about backstairs dramas – who said or did what to whom? Which minister's wife was a lousy cook? Who served bought mayonnaise out of a jar? What colour boxer shorts was the Prime Minister wearing? Maybe all this adds to sales and gives some welcome relief from the heavy-handed justifi-cations for every controversial twist and turn over the decades of a career. But can you actually remember the parliamentary row over the Chimney Sweeps Bill of twenty years ago? Do you want to remem-ber it? How much do people want to recall about even the most harrowing and dramatic events? Perhaps it is just as well that they usually turn the page or the channel and get on with life. Overall, what do you learn from this literary species about political motiva-tion, about the reasons for a political career, about the onion skins of a politician's personality, about the point of it all, about who she or he really is, staring every morning into the bathroom mirror before the shaving gel is dabbed or the powder is applied?

The discouragements are formidable. But it occurred to me that to track down myself would enable me to discuss an issue that had begun to intrigue me, namely the relationship between politics and identity, the things that had shaped me and whether and how they had come to reflect my life and opinions. As I wrote, the question of identity moved from the wings to centre stage, and roiled politics and nations on both sides of the Atlantic. Were the changes taking place fundamental and lasting? Or were they the unhappy result of a com-bination of haphazard events and of a random mixture of personalities? Trump, Farage and Le Pen appeared to be joined politically and cul-turally at the hip. Were technology and migration producing similar effects from Vienna to Virginia? Had the hollowing out of political parties left a void to be filled by duplicitous hucksters? Was the crash of 2008 to blame, or were the causes of whatever was happening more subtle, and more a result of perceived threats to the identities of groups and individuals? Had political debate been infantilized by changes in the way people received information? Had reason been dethroned, or had it never really enjoyed pre-eminence? Occasionally I thought I could begin to detect the stink of decline on the breeze, even the reek of decadence. So I wanted to try to answer some of these questions by exploring who I am, and what made up my own identity.

One of the most fundamental questions about political life – or political science, as some like to call it, as if it were one – is 'Who are we?' With what pattern of loyalties do we identify? Which narratives, memories and experiences shape our behaviour? Do we always find ourselves caught in the same threads of that spider's web? Can we move about from one strip of the silky trap to another? All of which raises a preliminary question. 'We' is simply the collection of 'I's. So who am I? What makes up my identity? Genetics, nature, nurture play a major role. But in addition, as with everyone else, my identity in part reflects choices I make. It is also in part the result of influences over which I have little or no control. 'Know thyself' was Socrates' challenge, a challenge both to personal memory and to honesty. Here, perhaps, is the beginning of a justification for writing in this rather different way about my life.

How much does any of us remember? Some train their memories like a classical rhetorician. That was the advice given to Charlemagne by Alcuin, an English scholar and poet at his court: do what Cicero did, learning the skills of public oratory, for which a good memory is invaluable. However, Alcuin noted that to have a good memory it is important to avoid drunkenness. When I first entered Parliament, where alcohol is occasionally consumed, I trained myself to speak for long periods without a text. When the time came, I was able as a minister to speak from the Despatch Box in the House of Commons in a big debate with just a few sketchy notes, often enabling me to get away with defending a bad cause simply because of presentation. I recall, in one debate about the wretched poll tax, an Opposition speaker on the other side of the Despatch Box muttering in a rather worried voice to a colleague, 'He hasn't got any notes.' Over the years, my ability to pull this sort of trick has deteriorated, though I do not think drink is the villain, and I can still master a brief pretty quickly. Tony Judt, the fine and brave historian and essayist, created what he called a 'memory chalet' to trigger his recollections, as motor neuron disease closed inexorably in on him, switching off one light after another until all was dark. The chalet provided a storage cupboard for his well-stocked mind. It was presumably modelled on the 'memory palace' of images which Matteo Ricci, the sixteenth-century Jesuit missionary to China, used to teach his pupils through mnemonics, and which has been brilliantly recorded by Jonathan Spence in his book on Ricci.

How much, though, do we choose what we remember? Do we simply remember what we wish, good or bad? It does not necessarily help to have kept a diary. Some diaries are admittedly so comprehensive that they acquire an additional authenticity. How can this not be the whole person? Pepys takes us from the navy's accounts, to the Stuart court, to his table, to the lavatory and notably to bed with such attention to detail that we think we must know the real Samuel. But do we? And what of a diarist of our own times like Alan Clark? Clark constructed a tale in which he was not only of course the central character – a mendacious philanderer – but a major figure in the politics of his times. Read Clark and you are led to believe that one of the dominant issues in British politics in the 1980s was when and how he would ascend to Margaret Thatcher's Cabinet. But this Mr Toad's journey – 'Poop poop!' goes Alan's flashy limousine – was never headed to Downing Street except in his own entertaining fictions. Was his night-time sex life perhaps as riddled with fiction as his daytime politics? Demonstrating how the silliness of a doubtless very clever judge could cause maximum distress to two honourable politicians and their families, a Lord Justice of Appeal spent years in the later years of the Major government trying to decide during an inquiry into arms sales to Iraq whether he should believe Alan Clark's word or that of Nicholas Lyell and William Waldegrave. Most of their colleagues in the House of Commons would have taken about five minutes to conclude that Clark was being as honest as usual, but Sir Richard Scott took a great deal longer to come to this blindingly obvious conclusion.

I have kept a diary at one or two periods of my life, in Hong Kong, for example, and reading it now enables me to see a little more clearly what was happening twenty years ago without condensation on the rear window. But I emerge from it too well. I am who I want to seem: affable and relaxed under pressure, even gay in the old-fashioned sense. Was it really like that? Did I just shrug off the mandarins' and businessmen's stilettos as they were aimed at the back of my smart (made by Sam of Kowloon) suits? I rather doubt it. But I had to pretend that I did not care a jot, go on whistling and crack a few deadpan jokes.

Why do I find myself thinking so much about identity? The primary reason is that now I look back I realize how much of my public and private life has been spent dealing with the politics of identity, whose wild and carnivorous beasts have torn so many societies to pieces and unleashed so much havoc. Today they threaten to do even more damage on two fronts. The world is safer than it was when the West and the Soviet Union snarled at each other from behind their silos of nuclear weapons, and when wars on most continents played surrogate for Washington and Moscow (only 'small' wars, unless they visited *your* town or village), but today's random violence with alleged religious roots and a malevolent hostility to anything which seems alien and particularly Western causes mounting worry. While he is probably thinking partly about every sort of conflict, civil and economic as well as violent, Pope Francis exaggerates a little when he sees a world in flames. Yet, in many regions, the fires really are raging. Unsurprisingly many share the Pope's view of our civilization's proximity to apocalypse as jihadists bomb lawyers in a hospital at Quetta, as they continue their bloody campaign in Lebanon, Yemen, Turkey, Bangladesh and Saudi Arabia, as an elderly priest is slaughtered on the steps of his altar, as innocent European citizens are mown down from Nice to Westminster. Identity politics, not ideological, strips our world of its certainties and even some of the quite comforting old uncertainties of great power politics, such as the insane balance of mutually assured destruction. On top of this, the growth of identity nationalism – 'America First', 'pure-blooded Frenchmen', 'take back control' – threatens the survival of the institutions of global governance and economic order which have given the world a hugely beneficial infrastructure of rules and co-operation for more than half a century. We appear to be prepared in the West to forget the habits of working together which we once took for granted.

Let me demonstrate how my own career has often brought me into contact with the present or the past horrors of identity politics. It is a public life which has taken me hither and yon. One evening the chairman who was introducing me as an after-dinner speaker began: 'Lord Patten has had a chequered career.' Just how 'chequered' has it been?

My great-grandfather was an economic migrant from Ireland in the first half of the nineteenth century. I was brought up as a Catholic in 1950s England, when Catholics were regarded as a little bit odd, a tad foreign. I went as a student to America in the 1960s, when race riots, anti-Vietnam protests and the Civil Rights Movement dominated political life there. I worked by chance in a New York political campaign that trampolined me away from an intended career in the BBC and into politics and eventually an uncomfortably marginal parliamentary seat at Westminster. Later came my first ministerial job, which took me to Northern Ireland. I remember the first time I saw a blown-up body, one foot rather deftly blasted to the top of a laurel bush. I had seen dead bodies before – my father, mother and step-father, all groomed for the coffin and worms by a funeral parlour – but they had all been in one piece. I returned to the Province thirteen years later to try to take the police out of the cauldron of political acrimony. I worked closely for Margaret Thatcher and John Major. Indeed, I recall once being asked in Siena by a group of ladies from Yorkshire if I would agree to be photographed with them collectively and one at a time. It took for ever. As they moved on to their next Duomo, I heard one say to the others, 'He's so nice, that Mr Major.' I used to be confused with John fairly regularly. It cannot be my shape.

After losing my parliamentary seat in Bath, I went as Governor to Hong Kong. Some suggested when I was there that my arguments about civil liberties, the rule of law and democracy showed how little I understood, and how ignorant I was in denying the proposition that there is a civilizational clash between the Christian West and the Confucian East. After that I was sent as a Commissioner to Brussels in 1999. My departure for the EU was regarded by some as an unpatriotic act. I found myself for much of the time there dealing with the problems of Palestine and Israel, and the residue of violent conflict in the Balkans. Was there something about being an Orthodox Serb Christian or a Croat or a Bosnian Muslim which made it inevitable that you would want to kill the others?

How much of my own identity is the result of confronting the extremes of identity politics? Have I simply used my experiences to buttress a set of prejudices that were already in place and are mostly the progeny of a belief that, once you turn your back on moderation, all is soon lost? You cannot be moderately moderate in safety. Indeed, you need paradoxically to be immoderate when you are standing up for moderation. But is all this the result of accumulated objective experiences and judgements? Is it genuine? Am I fooling others and lying to myself and to them because I believe this is what they will like? Most of us hide parts of ourselves in dark burrows like John le Carré characters, manipulating others by showing them what we think they want or expect to see. Above all, most of us want to seem to be someone whom others will like or admire.

There are some contributors to my identity which do not appear in the introductions favoured by the chairman at meetings. I am white, very happily married, and have three daughters – Kate, Laura and Alice – and eight grandchildren. I have been in love with the same person, Lavender, for over forty-six years. I subscribe to the view that one is only as happy as one's least happy child. My grandchildren provide the principal reason for such optimism as I have about the future, partly because I assume that there must be lots of other grandparents with similar views about the grace of their own grandchildren. As our older generation falls by the wayside, they carry on, our genetic stake in the future of humanity. I believe in God and an afterlife. I am a Christian, a Catholic. I have a British passport and think that I have been lucky to live in Britain during what must have been (at least until now) the happiest, healthiest and most peaceful period in British history. I am a patriot in an English sort of way, not Podsnappian, though inconveniently I do get a lump in my throat when singing 'I vow to thee, my country'. I believe that Britain has been diminished in economic and geo-strategic ways during my lifetime. On the other hand, I had no doubt until recently that it was a nicer, more tolerant country than it used to be. I hope this is still true, although doubts accumulate. I was a scholarship boy from the deep middle (certainly no higher) of the London, suburban middle class. I am an Atlanticist and a pro-European. I was shocked by the result of the EU referendum which will make us poorer (especially those who are already poor) and less influential for good in the world. Above all, I am appalled by what it says about the state of our democratic politics and saddened that it took the unparliamentary device of a referendum to demonstrate this. I am liberal on economics and social issues. On questions like gender equity, sexual preference, gay marriage and capital punishment, I tick most of the boxes on a tabloid newspaper's hate list. But as my wife noted, 'No day is entirely wasted if you have been attacked by a tabloid.' I am a Conservative of a rather old-fashioned sort: while there is not much noblesse about me, I strongly believe in 'noblesse oblige'.

My favourite painting is *The Surrender at Breda* by Velázquez; it shows grace and magnanimity in action. My favourite story is the parable of the prodigal son in St Luke's Gospel, though I have more than a sneaking sympathy for the dutiful son who stayed at home, too. My favourite films are *The Producers* (the original version) and *Some Like It Hot*, which of course has the greatest last line in any movie – 'Well, nobody's perfect.' My favourite piece of music is the canonical quartet from Beethoven's *Fidelio*, 'Mir ist so wunderbar', and my favourite passage in English literature is the last paragraph of George Eliot's *Middlemarch*. The second half of the very last sentence of *Middlemarch* pulls together the principal theme of this, perhaps the greatest, English novel: 'the growing good of the world is partly dependent on unhistoric acts; and that things are not so ill with you and me as they might have been, is half owing to the number who lived faithfully a hidden life, and rest in unvisited tombs'. Exactly. All that is me. I'm not making any of it up; at least, I don't think I am.

These are my compass points, my comfort blankets. Here is what makes me feel at ease, happy and secure. But a sense of identity does not always do that, or do that for everyone. While it can push and pull strongly in constructive directions (consider the peaceful nationalism of a Catalan or Scot) elsewhere it can and does also cross a line into territory that denies civic humanism and common decency. This is especially true when it exaggerates its own uniqueness. It can goad you into belligerence. It can trap you in history's cage, and bad history at that. It can increasingly define you not by what you are for, but by what you are against. It can turn victimhood into a way of life, or more likely of death. It can make you into a fanatic – Christian, Jewish, Muslim, Hindu, Buddhist, nationalist or vegetarian. It can squeeze all the wonderful complexity out of life, paint all the greys black, white and blood red, eviscerate all the 'not quites' and 'yes buts'. It can turn young Irish Republicans into bombers and hunger strikers, and their Unionist fellow citizens into assassins. It can recruit apparently normal young men from plural societies to become torturers and murderers, making the trip from East London or Yorkshire to Syria to cut off other men's heads and rape their wives and daughters. It can open concentration camps in what was once Yugoslavia. It can arouse a young man from forested Artigat in rural south-west France to travel to Toulouse and kill Jewish children, or excite other young French men and women from the Paris *banlieues* to gun down journalists and to butcher their contemporaries in that city of light. It can drive people from their own country, whether in Asia, the Middle East, Europe or the United States, to embrace death themselves in order to kill others. The list goes on and on, and every time the catalyst is above all a corruption and hardening of the idea of identity.

It is curious that identity politics has become such a threat to our security and stability at exactly the moment that globalization and technology appear to be flattening borders, and bringing us closer together. The threat is seen in slightly different ways in poorer countries and in more developed ones. Some in less well-off countries assume that globalization is a Western bid for economic and political hegemony, that it will impose a Western model on everyone. The advance of China and other Asian countries does not give much support to this argument. What is true, however, is that globalization has left some whole countries, and larger groups in other countries, far behind in their development with the gap between their living standards and those of the better off increasing. While not everyone can win the race, there should be fairer rules in trade, for example, about how it is conducted, and more investment in education in poor countries. There are also aspects of globalization that appear to be monopolized by developed, usually Western, societies. One reason why campaigns against AIDS and other diseases have run into difficulties in Africa is that science, and even medical science, is so strongly culturally associated with the Caucasian West. Add to these issues of inequity a worry that globalization can lead to the sort of standardization that again favours the rich West, and you can certainly detect issues that contribute to identity politics. Nativism has become more alluring with its simple answers, the rhetoric of control, and triumph of ill-remembered histories, as international co-operation is thought to have failed, even to have become a menace.

The consequences of identity politics are readily globalized. Terror can be financed by credit cards and transported by aeroplanes. Destroying the institutions of one state can, as we know, result in flows of migrants which threaten the cohesion of others. Mass immigration produces a backlash. Europe provides a home to almost 80 million international migrants mostly from Africa and the Middle East. In Britain even migrants from elsewhere in Europe are thought to be unsettling and the forerunners of many more from further afield. In America about 14 per cent of the population are foreign born compared to 5 per cent in 1970. This is where identity politics becomes a sharper threat to us, in Europe and even in America, encouraging our plural democracies to turn in on themselves and embrace a Hobbesian agenda in which international co-operation on traditional liberal lines becomes the casualty. Our memories of what a fiercely nationalist world was like in the first half of the twentieth century become scummed. Our instincts to protect ourselves tell us to shut gates, pull up drawbridges, distrust all those others whose different identity menaces us. Victimhood begets victimhood; a denial of common humanity echoes and reverberates across countries and continents.

Many in the West do not feel at all that they are the winners in globalization's competitive climate; they think that less well-off countries have unfairly stolen a march on them, grabbing their jobs and picking off their industries. This was plainly a major factor in Mr Trump's victory in the US presidential election, the triumph of one strong personality over two political parties that had become cut off from their roots. In the US much of the anger focused on free trade; in Europe the EU plays surrogate for this aspect of international behaviour. Both Trumpites and Europeans, in parties of the embittered on the left and the right, reject the post-war narrative of international co-operation, economic development and a non-violent domestic political tussle between parties that were broadly in favour of more state action and those who believed the opposite. There was a general consensus about the balance required to make an equitable form of welfare democracy work. That sort of politics is today assaulted by loosely organized populism, a refusal to engage in a rational discussion based on long-accepted facts and assumptions, which feeds off a sense of alienated identity.

Populism denies the fundamental importance of the virtues and institutions of restraint which make democracy acceptable and effective for a whole community. The rule of law, constitutional checks and balances, the recognition of the rights of minorities and not just of majorities, an instinct for compromise – all these are being subordinated to a belief in the popular will. And the popular will means 'my' people not 'your' people. So, for instance, the people whom the British Parliament and government must obey today do not include any of the 48 per cent who voted to stay in the EU. 'The people' who are in complete charge are the other 52 per cent. In America, 'the people' are not even the majority, because the aggregate popular majority voted for Hillary Clinton. Populism is government by 'my' people, and forget about nuance or consensus, let alone magnanimity.

The right frets about the loss of old (frequently imperfectly recalled) certainties; the left feels trapped in a downward economic spiral. Sometimes both sentiments collide and connive. Local identities are drowned in global tides. Looking east, some American and European populists see an unlikely hero in Vladimir Putin, the bragging and assertive demi-tyrant who has reinvented the nastier sorts of nationalism in a great country that under him today is sometimes, alas, little more than a gangster state on the highway to economic degradation.

The rise of economically motivated populism creates a paradox. Some of the most effective answers to it would involve policies that would customarily horrify those (on the Republican right) who most benefit from the populist hostility itself. In America, for example, it is true that free trade and the huge success of manufacturing exporting industries in emerging markets like China, India and Mexico have made some US companies unprofitable and have therefore contributed to the loss of jobs. It is worth asking whether firms that are uncompetitive because of cost or product quality should or could survive indefinitely – presumably at a cost through subsidies to the state, or to the consumer. But to protect domestic markets from competitive free trade overall hurts the poor more than the rich, not least because of the rise in costs. So what is the best answer for those who lose their jobs?

It is partly for government to help them through socially redistributive tax-and-spend policies, especially labour market schemes like retraining. The US spends 0.1 per cent of its GDP on labour market policies, as compared with 0.6 per cent in OECD countries as a whole. Whether Mr Trump's billionaire cabinet and Tea Party supporters will embrace policies that will address, in an economically and socially sensible way, the impact of a growing lack of competitiveness in the 'rustbelt' states that voted Republican seems very doubtful. In addition, Mr Trump is likely to discover sooner or later the number of American multinationals that export part of what they produce to emerging markets, like Mexico, where they are completed and sold back into the USA.

In Europe, similar questions arise. Recent high levels of European immigration in parts of England, which have sustained economic growth, plainly increased the size of the Brexit vote there. One answer would be to increase levels of social spending in those areas; this has been done successfully in Denmark. But Conservatives show little sign of being prepared to embrace this sort of redistributive economics. As their opponents argued in the 2017 General Election, they are unlikely to abandon the espousal of fiscal rectitude and more cuts in social spending. So Europe is too often blamed for the consequences of dramatic failures of economic and social policy. As for Labour, its leadership has had difficulty connecting to the mainstream political agenda.

Things are made worse by social media. Yes, the internet and social media can link people across oceans and continents and open their minds and eyes to things to which they previously had little or no access. Immediate access to information and knowledge of all kinds can do and often does immense good. But there is a darker side to this. The internet can promote fragmentation by allowing those with a very strong sense of a single identity to connect with others who have a similar outlook. The interaction between them then turns on a sense of identity enhanced even further, to the detriment of other connections and wider interests of people with different points of view. The vulnerable, the angry and those who feel oppressed connect with those like themselves; they exploit one another's grievances and weaknesses. Before long, they are setting off to join Isis or (in too many tragic cases) shooting up their classrooms. It also enables many people to receive their news in a very selective and politicized way – sound bites and factoids, tablet e-papers,

Fox, Twitter and so on. Their existing worries are aggravated and their instincts made much more extreme. Glance at the news headlines and reporting of the Breitbart News Network whose chairman, Steve Bannon, was made Mr Trump's strategic adviser in the White House. Breitbart has been accused, with good reason, of xenophobia, racism and misogyny. No wonder that Bannon's appointment was applauded by the Ku Klux Klan. Breitbart is associated with the 'alt-right' in America and in Europe, where so-called identitarians in France, Germany, Austria and elsewhere link racist groups through their websites across the continent. The skinhead right is joined to allegedly more respectable right-wing groups which call for a *reconquista* in Europe, recapturing the continent for white Europeans from high-breeding immigrant hordes. Are British tabloid newspapers much different? The headlines from one during the weeks before the referendum tell a familiar tale: 'Migrants spark housing crisis'; 'Britain's wide-open borders'; 'Deadly cost of our open borders'; 'Britain's broken borders'; 'How many more can we take?' A few high-minded campaigners for Britain to leave the EU still claim that the outcome had nothing to do with immigration, race and the stoking of xenophobia.

St Augustine wrote: 'When regard for truth has been broken down or even slightly weakened, all things will remain doubtful.' Balanced analysis by the media commands little attention beyond the despised so-called elites. In a society where facts are made up to be exchanged by tweet or over a beer in the saloon bar, bigots become more articulate: so much more material is being fed to them. There is not much of a market for 'on the one hand, on the other'. We seem to be threatened once again by perturbed demons similar to those in Matthew Arnold's great mid-nineteenth-century poem 'Dover Beach', written as faith seemed to be assaulted by science. Today it is corrupted faith transmitted by technology that threatens certitude and peace, and offers no help for pain.

> And we are here as on a darkling plain
> Swept with confused alarms of struggle and flight,
> Where ignorant armies clash by night.

This is why I want to write about identity, beginning with my own, rather than produce a conventional political autobiography. Along the way I hope I may explain a little about why I embarked on the odd, demanding and occasionally satisfying political life; how important the political adventure was in the balance of what I have done; how and when I realized like others that most political careers usually end in minor or major failure; and how I remain more strongly attached than ever to the idea – even after the world-shaking events of 2016 – that liberal values constitute the best hope for a decent future and the strongest basis for what is still the honourable adventure of politics. Explaining how this person we used to recognize, but have now probably forgotten, emerged for a time into the spotlight of modest celebrity and then faded out of it will also, I hope, give a few insights into what has happened in Britain and the world during my lifetime. I hope above all that in trying to describe myself honestly, without memories being too blurred or occluded by small vanities, I will be able to add a little to the arguments for an immoderate defence of liberal order and a counter to the violence of narrow identity.

Because I have written this book around the things that have shaped me, it does not simply follow the time-line of my years from childhood to old age. I begin, however, conventionally, with my family background and my education, concluding that chapter with some thoughts on social mobility. I then travel to America as a student and go on to discuss that great country's impact on who I am today, and for that matter who you are too. Then I discuss why I am a Conservative and what sort of Conservative I am. I write about my early years in Conservative politics and my life in Parliament. I describe the three leaders I have served: Heath, Thatcher and Major. In Northern Ireland I confronted identity politics at their most ferocious. In Hong Kong, I encountered some ludicrous arguments about the impact on our identities of alleged civilizational differences, especially involving China. I discuss my experiences as a European Commissioner in Brussels (for example, dealing with the Balkans) and explain why I think Britain voted to leave the EU, comparing the reasons for this vote and for the election of President Trump. I look at my Poobah years in Oxford, the BBC and Rome. I conclude, I hope not too gloomily, thinking about religion, violence and death, a visitor eventually at every hearth.

So here it is: my first confession, for which I hope the penance will not be too severe.

2

Mass and Privet

Parish of enormous hayfields
Perivale stood all alone,
And from Greenford scent of mayfields
Most enticingly was blown
John Betjeman, 'Middlesex'

... the Church was my first book ... my introduction to
ceremony, to grace and sacrament, to symbol and ritual.
John McGahern, *Guardian* (8 April 2006)

'Why waste your money looking up your family tree?' Mark Twain
asked. 'Just go into politics and your opponent will do it for you.'
Fortunately, in contemporary British politics there has never been
much effort to discredit public figures by disinterring the sins of their
bloodline. A distant relationship to Oswald Mosley is not to be recommended, but other than that there is less muck-raking about
heredity in Britain than in America. Perhaps that reflects the fact
that politics on the allegedly class-ridden, European side of the Atlantic is less dynastic than in the 'land of the free'. Our dynasties are
constitutionally confined to palaces these days to which the public,
who pay for them, are admitted from time to time to have a look
around.

I only really became interested in my roots because of my growing
sense that many of those with whose contribution to the public realm
I had to contend created trouble for the rest of us by their sense of
single-blooded loyalty to some cause or other. This self-identification
was invariably far from the whole story. Anglo-Irish relations, at the

worst of times, were a bleak example. The history and culture of the people of our archipelago – Britain and Ireland – are inextricably intertwined, individuals and families. Thinking of my years in Northern Ireland, the very names of politicians – the Norman French Fitzgerald and Molyneux, the Scottish Paisley, the English Adams – showed this and contrasted oddly from time to time with the views of those who bore them. So I went hunting for my own ancestry, knowing that like that of so many who hold a British passport on my father's side it lay in Ireland. At least six million people who live in the United Kingdom today have at least one Irish grandparent. Go back further than grandparents and the numbers soar.

My own great-grandfather, Patrick, was born in 1829, in County Roscommon. His name seems to have changed from Patton to Patten, which may have been a clerk's error rather than a deliberate exchange of letters by Patrick himself. At some time in the 1840s, like a million others, he fled Ireland's potato famine. They left behind a million dead with heavy fatalities in the town, Boyle, in which he lived. The population of this little town, near Lough Key and the Curlew Mountains, is smaller today than it was when Patrick left. Suitably, the Irish Museum of the Famine was established in Roscommon. Patrick headed east for Britain and established himself initially in Haslingden, near Rossendale in Lancashire, just north of Manchester. He worked first, as he described on the census form, as a chair-bottom maker, presumably repairing cane chairs. But he soon progressed to become a weaver, married into a Yorkshire family of weavers, and eventually became a tailor. Patrick and his wife, Mary, had four daughters and one son, my grandfather Joseph (born in 1860), who became a teacher and married a fellow Irish member of the profession, Annie Nolan. By the turn of the century, before the 1902 Balfour Education Act brought Catholic schools into the state-funded system, they were running St Alban's School in the Ancoats district of Manchester, a community that contained many Italian immigrants, was often served by Italian parish priests and was famous for making ice-cream for Mancunians. The Italians, mainly from southern Italy, Lazio and Campagna, and the Irish, helped to rescue the Ancoats slum from crime and violence.

Discovering this fairly typical nineteenth-century story of immigrant diasporas bravely leaving behind hardship, disease and starvation and making a new and successful life in a foreign country is one of the high points of so many family histories of the time, histories which remind us how time collapses. There is much else you discover or imagine as you work your way through census reports and parish records. There is the huge gulf between public and private life, a salutary reminder for those who spend most of their lives in politics of how little it seems to make an impact on the daily life of most people, except when it implodes in bloodshed or privation. What some critics deride as public apathy is simply normal people getting on with making the most of their opportunities and trying to cope with the small disasters that bombard most lives; this is the heroism of muddling through. Digging deeper into my family history, on both of my parents' sides, I have also come to a deeper sense of how much in any family we hide from one another – not just from the future, which in any event many feel can best look after itself. How judgemental can we be about the small hypocrisies, the harmless vanities, the casual domestic cruelties, the heartless selfishness that are part of every family history? How can we pronounce from our vantage point and from a contemporary moral stance about behaviour in the past? The best we can do is try to be better and kinder ourselves; to remember how much it is sheer courage that usually gets people through disappointment and heartbreak; and to recognize how the greatest disruption to our well-ordered plans is often love, occasionally regretted but usually embraced and invariably transformative.

Joseph and Annie sound and look from contemporary photographs and records like a very loveable couple: all that headteachers should be, he with juniors, Annie with infants. They were well-fed and comfortably built. They had two daughters, and then, after a gap of fifteen years, a son, Francis, my father, in 1909. The two girls, Evelyn and Maud, taught the violin and the piano and had a millinery shop in the Stockport Road, where the family also lived. My father, who went to the Xaverian College, was inevitably an altar boy, with the best cotta and cassock from the ecclesiastical outfitters Cassertelli's. He also had a state-of-the-art, three-spring cricket bat, which seems to have taken pride of place, scarcely surprisingly, over the violin which his sisters taught him.

My grandfather was remembered, not just for his work with the children of Ancoats, Ardwick and Gorton for whom he helped to organize summer camps in the Peak District, but also for his stylish dress sense, not always a characteristic of teachers. He sounds a bit of a dandy – well-cut dark suits, silk cravats secured by a diamond pin, figured waistcoats, a splendid gold watch chain and an ebony walking stick. That Edwardian flair – attained even by someone as stout as Joseph – is not something that passed down to his grandson.

I wonder what the reaction of my grandparents was during the Anglo-Irish turmoil of the 1910s and 1920s. Were they proud of the Republicans who stormed Dublin's Post Office in 1916? What did they believe was the motive – a simple Republican gesture of defiance or an attempt as well to halt the payment of pay cheques to Irishmen serving in the British Army in the war? Deep down did they question (or even hate) the British colonial power that made martyrs of the rebels? They probably kept their heads down and went to mass to pray for the souls of the faithful departed. I asked my father once about their attitude. He could see the point I was making and seemed a bit concerned that he did not know the answer. He was only a small child in 1916, but had never subsequently asked his parents about their attitude to the Irish fight for independence. Dad was a kind, charming and affable man, and like my mother did not much care for an argument. That makes it all the more surprising to me that he defied his parents – as must surely have been what happened – when, having forsaken the violin and taken up the drums at school, he turned down a place at Manchester University and went off to join a band that played gigs on the Isle of Man in the summer, and travelled around the country during the rest of the year. Would his successfully aspirant parents have been so broad-minded in the 1930s to wish him well on his way? Did they buy him a set of drums for the house in Stockport Road? Were they loving liberal parents ahead of their time? Perhaps they were; maybe they had more than their ration of genial Irish kindness. I never met them. I wish I had. They both died in the 1930s, Joseph in the year that my father married, 1938. That leads to the next part of a story that tested parental attitudes.

My mother, Joan Angel, was born in 1915 in Exeter. Her own mother, Clara, had been born in Taunton in 1876 to parents who were tailors. By the age of five, Clara was living according to the census as 'a visitor' in Exeter; presumably this was some kind of fostering arrangement when her parents moved to London with a tailoring and drapery business. By the age of fifteen, my grandmother was working as a draper's assistant and went on to become a milliner. She married Percy, who was as good-looking as she was herself; he clearly took after his extremely beautiful mother, Ellen, mother of six and self-declared head of the household. As a small child, I met two of Percy's sisters, Aunt Meg in Exeter and Aunt Gwen, who lived in Teignmouth. Gwen was a companion to another old lady, called Aunt Pan. I once embarrassed my mother and sister when very young by commenting loudly over tea and scones in Teignmouth on the old ladies' smell.

Percy went to work as a clerk at Heavitree Breweries, an independent brewer of which by the time of his retirement he had become company secretary. So far, I guess, so normal. But then there is an uncomfortable surprise. Percy and Clara had three children, not, as my sister and I had always thought, two. Our lovely Aunt Ina, who managed to be cheerful despite a life which was shot through with disappointment and illness, was born in 1905, and my mother ten years later in 1915. I have now discovered that two years after Ina, Percy and Clara had a son, Colin Marcus. Why did we never know that we had an uncle? Ina at least must surely have known, though perhaps the age difference explained why his existence was never known by my mother. We can only guess at what happened. Colin died in a hospital for the mentally handicapped in Dawlish on the Devon coast in 1945. What was the nature of what the census calls the 'incapacity' from which he suffered? Was it both an excessive burden and an embarrassment for my grandparents? Today I guess that most families would be more likely to confront a tragedy like this more openly: better days, but how can I judge? As a family – my parents, sister Angela and I – used to go regularly to Dawlish, renting a flat on the front for our summer holidays. Had my mother known, even if her brother was long since dead, would she not have felt rather awkward about the coincidence of pleasure and family tragedy?

It was a long way from Joan's clearly happy childhood. My mother was a very beautiful woman, throughout her life, who much enjoyed her nickname, 'Bella'. She was curvaceous, and a little more than curvaceous in late middle age, with head-turning good looks: lovely eyes and mouth, a pretty laugh and a radiant smile. As a young woman she must have been dazzling and certainly took Exeter's amateur dramatics by storm. She even got favourable mentions in national publications like *The Stage*. A professional repertory company, Malvern Players, offered her a place in their troupe. Her parents refused to let her go; acting was regarded then as beyond louche. Anyway, they were delighted that she seemed to be heading for a local life of comfort and provincial prestige. The beauty got engaged to the son of a well-off local businessman. Then disaster struck. My mother went to a dance at the Rougemont Hotel in Exeter, where the drummer in the band was my father. Love's percussionist beat the retreat from an engagement and genteel prosperity in Exeter. She had fallen in love with an Irish Catholic drummer. Oh dear, the turmoil! Colm Tóibín could do justice to the story. On top of everything else, in order to marry the man, she informed her parents that she had to abandon their (fairly lightly held) religious views and become a Roman (the word would have been stressed) Catholic. Her mother did not speak to her for weeks and she received nothing in her father's will.

My maternal grandfather died in 1938, six years before my birth, but I did know my maternal grandmother, the only one of all my grandparents with whom I spent any time. She lived until 1967 and died aged ninety-one, fired up into old age by regular glasses of Guinness and pale ale. She had forthright opinions on most issues, especially the monarchy (she used to stand for the National Anthem after the Queen's Christmas message on television) and politics (she was far and away the strongest Tory in the family; at elections she ran committee rooms and acted as a teller for the Conservatives in Exeter). But I never heard her utter a word on any religious matter; nor can I ever recall her setting foot in a church. I suppose it was the sheer foreignness of being a Roman Catholic, and perhaps a bit of prejudice about Irish immigrants, that must have been the cause of her difficulty with my parents' marriage.

Gran was very kind to us when my sister and I went to stay with her at her terraced house in Exeter. The garden smelt of honeysuckle, that lovely evergreen 'Halliana' with biscuit-coloured flowers. There were tiny new potatoes from the vegetable patch fried in bacon fat for breakfast and big, fat loganberries for tea. She had a ripe collection of mildly vulgar Devonshire sayings and toasts. There were no echoes there of Luther's 'A Mighty Fortress is My God'. Despite his unsuitability, Gran came to love my father. Everyone did. He was too loveable for his own good.

My parents had my sister, Angela, the year after they were married, in 1939, and then in 1941 my father went off as a Royal Air Force officer to the Middle East, running the gauntlet of the German submarines and bombers to get there. He spent most of the war in Palestine and Lebanon, a country he loved for its sophisticated and tolerant mix of religions and nationalities. For their safety Mum took Angela to live in Exeter with her own mother. That lasted until the Baedeker raids of 1942 when Luftwaffe bombers devastated the centre of the city, fortunately missing the cathedral, in retaliation for the RAF's increasingly effective targeting of German cities like Lübeck. My great-grandmother seems to have been one of the casualties of the German attacks, and died shortly after, two years to the day before I was born. The flattening of the heart of Exeter (where the post-war rebuilding did the city few favours) prompted my mother and sister to move up to the Lancashire coast to live in a holiday house owned by my father's sister Maud and her husband, who was a prosperous potato merchant – an appropriate business for a scion of the great famine. It was in that coastal town, Thornton-Cleveleys, that I was born on 12 May 1944.

After demobilization, my father used his contacts in the music business to get a job with a publisher of popular sheet music in London, in what was called Tin Pan Alley. It was in the West End, which my mother always referred to as 'in town'. Dad brought the family down to London and my parents bought a new house built on the borders of Greenford and Southall in Middlesex to the west of the city. By a few yards and licks of paint we were in Greenford, a suburb which had grown up around the new arterial road to Buckinghamshire and Oxford, the Western Avenue, and just south of the Underground Central Line and the older Metropolitan Line, connecting Baker Street with Amersham and the real countryside. Greenford had once boasted market gardens, elm trees and the Brent River wandering, as John Betjeman wrote, 'Wembley-wards at will'. Its proximity to a new road system and an old canal had attracted factories like Rockware glass, and Lyons and Hovis bakeries, and the construction of several housing estates. These provided a new generation of Londoners, either side of the Second World War, with the spurious notion that they were moving out to the country beyond Ealing, the queen of suburbs as its residents liked it to be called. The sense of countryside was reflected in the use of mock Tudor beams in semi-detached houses and the preserving of green spaces like Horsenden Hill, where in later years I used to go with school friends for a surreptitious smoke during lunch hours or on our way to our games field.

Our first Greenford house was in Hillside Road in a new terrace of housing, bought in those days for well below a thousand pounds. The houses lacked any touch of rural pastiche, except an inglenook brick fireplace in the front room. They were plain and rather ugly, surrounded by larger 'semis' built before the war. Most of the residents when we moved there in 1947 were young families like us. My two friends next door, Robin and Kevin, were the sons of a civil servant, who commuted into central London like my father, starting with two bus rides to get to the Central Line station at Greenford. At the top of the road, there was a turning circle for cars, not that there were many in the street. Robin, Kevin and I used to play cricket there when we got older, using an old stink pipe as a wicket.

I spent most of my years at primary school living there. Gradually during the 1950s and 1960s the ethnic composition of the road changed as large numbers of Indians and Pakistanis moved into Southall, initially recruited, so it was believed, by a former British Indian Army officer for his own factory. They were also attracted by work elsewhere, for example at Heathrow Airport, opened and developed as London's main airport in 1946. Though there have been racial tensions over the years, I do not recall any trouble or much evidence of prejudice when the population's culture and ethnicity began to change so dramatically, with Sikhs, Muslims and Hindus moving into the area. According to the census the largest number of residents in Hillside Road and the surrounding streets now is from

India or the Indian diaspora. I cannot remember a single prejudiced comment about colour or religion from either of our parents. It would have been easy to imagine such attitudes emerging as Asian communities transformed Greenford. Going back to the street today, two things stand out. First, many of the front gardens have been dug up and covered with hard standing for cars, hebe and hortensia replaced by Hondas. Second, many of the 1940s houses in our terrace have been done up, with smart porches and Georgian front doors. Houses like ours, with a sliding door between what we called the lounge and the dining room, sell for over £300,000 these days.

I walked to school, at first looked after by my sister. The journey was just over a mile and took about half an hour at our snail's pace. We used to go down an alley opposite our house alongside the playing field of Greenford Grammar School. In the summer the wire fence on one side was covered with belladonna, which we knew as Deadly Nightshade. My sister told me that it was smeared on the tips of arrows to make them certain killers, and that the Roman Emperors picked it in order to murder their opponents. She would pretend to eat a few of its black berries and then do a Sarah Bernhardt death scene in the alley, a regular piece of dramatic acting which never failed to terrify her nervous younger brother.

Our route took us through Greenford's older residential areas, eventually bringing us out at the covered market in the Broadway. This is where Mum came to buy fish every Friday morning. There was a Sainsbury on one side of the Broadway with sales staff in white overalls and hats in the days before it became self-service. Mum used to get bacon there, sliced very thin when it was streaky so that it would crisp nicely for weekend breakfasts. There was a baker which I think was called Liszt's, like the composer. Their paper bags, with perhaps an iced bun inside for tea, carried the slogan, 'Good Flavour Always Finds Favour'. How true! Further down was Burton's Tailors, which had kitted out Britain's servicemen on their demobilization after the war. Above the tailor was a billiard hall, but no one we knew ever set foot in it. At the traffic lights by the pub, we crossed the road where I was once almost knocked over. The car actually touched me. I remember my mother giving me a lecture, the point of which was not to look both ways before crossing, but always to wear clean underpants in case an accident ever hospitalized me. Then we passed a sweetshop, where we bought our first post-rationing allowance in 1953 – Flying Saucers, Gobstoppers, Lemon Sherbets, Fry's Chocolate Creams. Finally, after a Post Office building, there was the parish church and the primary school, which was named after it: Our Lady of the Visitation.

Catholics in Greenford had initially been looked after by Benedictine monks, but an order of missionaries – the Pallotine Fathers – took over the growing community including many Irish and Polish families, building a small red-brick church in 1937. The school followed in 1948 and a new and far larger church (like an aircraft hangar, my mother always thought) was constructed in the late 1950s. I do not know why the church and school were named after one of the most charming scenes in the New Testament, described early in St Luke's Gospel. Shortly after the Annunciation, Mary goes to visit her much older and hitherto barren cousin Elizabeth, perhaps in now sad and divided Hebron in the Palestinian hill country, to give her the extraordinary news about her role as Mother of God. As Mary enters the room to greet Elizabeth, the older woman's baby – who is to become John the Baptist – leaps in her womb, cleansed of original sin. The scene provides many of the words of the most frequently enunciated Catholic prayer, the Hail Mary, and the most beautiful prayer, the Magnificat. This meeting is used as the subject matter for many great Renaissance paintings, including two by Ghirlandaio, my favourite of which in the Louvre depicts not only three very beautiful young women – Mary, Salome and Mary of Cleopas – but an exquisitely graceful and serene, much older Elizabeth.

We moved from Hillside Road to Courthope Road not long before I transferred to secondary school. Our new house, quite close to the station, was in what my mother regarded as the best road in Greenford. It was not in Ruislip or Northwood, let alone the centre of Ealing, in any of which she would have preferred to live, but it was definitely a step up. Now I can see that it was in the middle of the world of Lupin Pooters whimsically described by John Betjeman. The regimental symmetry of the houses along the arterial Western Avenue is replicated in the estates either side as far down as Perivale, with its Hoover Art Deco factory building striped with bright Aztec and

Mayan colours (which is now the most magnificent Tesco supermarket). Betjeman saw the roofs of Perivale as a line of trawlers in a
Cornish gale. I have never quite seen that myself, but he was correct
in writing that once you could smell the scent of mayfields in Greenford. In Courthope Road, where small boys would not have dared to
play cricket in the street, you also caught the smell of laburnum,
nicotiana and privet in the summer. A flower-filled, weed-free front
garden was the nearest we now came to the rural charms of Middlesex. Two doors down from us a very serious gardener with a face
like a polished apple grew magnificent dahlias, the scarlet Bishop of
Llandaff on duty every summer on either side of his garden path. I am
not sure what the real bishop would have made of the girlie maga-
zines that our neighbour kept in his potting shed, which my father
was shown to his embarrassment every time he borrowed weed-killer
or a hoe.

At the corner of our road was the Conservative Club, once plainly
a farmhouse. It was the battle HQ of the local party, who fought a
titanic struggle against Labour every election in our marginal constituency of Ealing North, a few hundred votes either way deciding
the result. Ealing South, by contrast, was a pretty safe Conservative
seat. The club was also a boozer, somewhere I imagine between the
average saloon bar and a golf club. We never set foot in it. My parents
voted Conservative, took the *Daily Express* every day in the years
when it was a very good right-wing newspaper, and once put a Tory
sticker in the window. But their political views were understated and
moderately felt. They might have been mildly surprised if I had turned
out to be a socialist, but would not have regarded it as any sort of
treason. Anyway, the Conservative Club stood on duty at the end of
the road, a sentinel for the worthy values of suburban England.

Travel was by foot, bus or Tube, or, from the time when I was in
junior school and onwards, in our car. Walking to school was often a
perilous business in the winter. There were regular peasouper fogs,
and in December 1952 there was the great London smog, which killed
upwards of 12,000 people. I do not suppose it did much good to our
lungs, but of course I had the bigger risk of the Deadly Nightshade to
worry me. Buses became an important part of my life when we moved
to Courthope Road. I got the 92 bus into Greenford and, when I

changed to a secondary school in Ealing, then caught the 97 from outside the Playhouse cinema. Once in Ealing, buses like the affable 65 wandered off to all sorts of more salubrious destinations like Kew, Richmond and Barnes. My father always aspired to ownership of a Rover or a Jaguar, though he never quite made it. But we did once have a Lanchester saloon, which we took on our first foreign holiday to Paris and Luxembourg, where my father was pursuing his developing interests in music publishing with the popular radio station. There was something about the car which required the petrol to be put into the tank very slowly. At the first garage at which we stopped in France my sister, who had just started learning French at secondary school, was told by my father to instruct the attendant 'to fill her up gently because she blows back'. Reasonably enough she threw a strop. My father would have found it hard to credit that the engineering which was created for these beautiful cars with their fluid flywheels is now owned by an Indian company, Tata, which no longer manufactures them.

Those of us like my sister and me who had such happy childhoods should be able to sue for deprivation of literary royalties. No horror stories of abuse, no beatings, no lack of love, no real shortage of anything needed to keep me happy, no serious illness. The only thing I ever used to bother about was a bit of loneliness, particularly in my early teens. Greenford was a bus journey from my friends at school. I had to look after myself quite a lot since I was too idle to cycle and, later, too nervous to ask for a motor scooter. I am grateful that I had always had some imagination. For years in my primary school all that I needed for entertainment in the garden was a bamboo cane or a cricket bat and ball. With the cane, I would, when young, wander about imagining myself the King of Spain intent on the conquest of more of Europe than Napoleon ever seized. Later, throwing a squash ball against our garage doors and trying to hit the rebound, I would play whole Test matches from Cape Town to Brisbane. I do not believe I was ever on the losing side.

Far better than the garage door was my father, who had been a pretty good cricketer at school and who followed the fortunes of Lancashire county cricket team. He was enlisted as part of my preparations for international stardom at every opportunity. My mother tried to protect him from my demands, usually in vain, and cricket became one of the central aspects of my relationship with him. At just before 7 p.m. on summer evenings I would wait at the front gate and as soon as he came around the corner on the road from the Central Line station I would wave my bat and holler. The poor man would hardly have time to take off his Windsor-knotted tie and suit jacket before he was persuaded into the back garden either to face my express bowling or to have his own slow off-breaks swatted into the herbaceous borders. When I bowled myself, I used to start my run-up from the fence at the bottom of the garden, sprint up the path between the Victoria plum trees and the gooseberry bushes and hurl my thunderbolts at him from the edge of the lawn. We had to tie a net behind the stumps to protect the French windows from the balls that were missed by whoever was batting, and also to guard against the destruction of a large Yucca which was my dad's particular pride. One summer we had to lop a large branch off the flowering cherry, which, growing at silly mid-off, interrupted the flight of my father's spinners. On beach holidays in England we used to take a full set of stumps, bails, bats and balls to set up on the sand at low tide. I used to judge holidays largely on the basis of the adequacy of the beaches for pitches. One year we even took the full Test Match paraphernalia to southern Brittany and played day after day before groups of puzzled but polite French holidaymakers. When I was about fourteen or fifteen Dad encouraged me to go off by myself in the summer holidays with a copy of the little *Playfair Cricket Annual*, full of statistical tables, and a satchel with sandwich-spread sandwiches, two Kit-Kats and a bottle of made-up lemon barley water, to watch county cricket matches on the grounds of London and the Home Counties. One day I went as far as Canterbury to watch my hero, the Lancashire fast bowler Brian Statham. I got his autograph on my sandwich wrapper and then lost it on the way home.

The real highlights were being taken by my father to big sporting events. In 1957 Dad took me to Lord's to see the West Indies play the MCC. The West Indies side bristled with outrageous talent – Walcott, Worrell, Weekes, Sobers, Hall, Kanhai, Ramadhin and Valentine. The names of the last two had formed the chorus of a calypso sung after the West Indies had defeated England in 1950. I can still remember two of the five verses, ending with the words: 'With those two little pals of mine, Ramadhin and Valentine'. But the day we went to Lord's there was not much 'cricket, lovely cricket'. It was grey with just enough drizzle to keep the players in the pavilion for most of the day. No wonder Caribbean players always bowled so fast and scored runs so quickly: they must have wanted to do as much as possible while they could actually play the game before the traditional English cricketing weather set in once again.

The weather was better when, four years before that first visit to the headquarters of cricket, I was taken by my father to Wembley Stadium for the Cup Final between Blackpool and Bolton Wanderers. Having been born close by the town, I had always supported Blackpool, a commitment which was set in stone by the fact that the great right-winger Stanley Matthews played for the club. On the Bolton side there was a fine centre forward, Nat Lofthouse ('the lion of Vienna'), a big, rumbustious, typically English player. Well, typical for the time: he applauded Blackpool's winning goal, created by the great dribbler, Matthews, who had never before won a cup-winner's medal. The 4–3 victory, achieved with only two minutes of the match remaining, ensured that I remained a Blackpool fan for years. My enthusiasm even survived a cup defeat by West Ham to which my father took me. The West Ham fans caused me huge embarrassment by singing 'Bye bye Blackpool' to the tune about the departing blackbird as their team (with a young Bobby Moore) slaughtered my favourites. Over the years, my enthusiasm for Blackpool, and indeed for football as a game, diminished. Outside Spain, Latin America and occasionally Arsenal, the game did not seem so beautiful any more. There was in particular a problem that English teams seemed to have in passing the ball accurately to one another. But like other politicians (it is usually a harmless bit of gallery-playing) I sometimes pretended to an interest in football which had long since waned. Some politicians know what they are talking about when football is the topic of discussion: Kenneth Clarke is one. Others get into awful trouble when they claim an unlikely and knowledgeable attachment to a team. Tony Blair may or may not have bragged about watching Jackie Milburn playing for Newcastle, even though he was four and living in Australia when Milburn retired; he may well have been misreported as he claims. David Cameron confused West Ham and Aston Villa, forgetting that he was supposed to support Villa because his uncle was chairman of the club. I have given up any real pretence of knowing about football since two of my grandsons became passionate fans, who if asked could name the manager of Valencia and the striker of Paris Saint-Germain, and even the centrebacks of Aston Villa and West Ham. For most people 1953 was remembered principally not for Stanley Matthews but for the coronation of Queen Elizabeth II, the longest-serving monarch in British history, whose reign is synonymous with the word duty. It marked not only the beginning of Elizabeth's extraordinary reign but also the invasion of British living rooms by television. I recall sitting in our neighbour's front room to watch the solemn events in Westminster Abbey. But I am not sure that at that age, given the choice, I would have given pride of place to the abbey over Wembley Stadium.

My father was a good-looking man; like his own father he was stout and not very tall, but he was not jowly. His life in his middle years was punctuated by regular but fleeting and ineffective diets. There was definitely more talk about losing weight than doing it (why does that sound familiar?) but he did not really stand much chance of becoming slimmer. My mother cooked wonderfully well, taught by her own mother, and believed that she should give us all in large quantities what we liked to eat: pies, roasts, cakes, crumbles, butter, cream. Unusually for the 1950s, she was quite adventurous too, using onions, garlic, pasta and olive oil in the days when bottles of oil had to be bought at the chemist's. To this ample home cooking he added business lunches: persuading singers and their agents to perform the songs he was publishing invariably seemed to involve taking them to some of the best West End restaurants. Dad knew his way up and down the eateries of Dean Street and Old Compton Street. In later years he must have forgotten that having business accounts at restaurants did not mean that you had avoided payment, an easy mistake into which many fall. Who knows, perhaps it was the quality of the starters in L'Epicure that persuaded the American singer Guy Mitchell to sing one of my father's publishing hits, 'She Wears Red Feathers (and a Hula-Hula Skirt)'?

My father drank enthusiastically – wine, beer, whisky – but he was certainly not an alcoholic. On the other hand, while at work he smoked immoderately. He hardly smoked at home or on holiday, except for the occasional pipe. What he liked most about that was the paraphernalia. His cigarettes were untipped Player's Medium Cut with a bearded sailor on the packet or tin or occasionally Senior Service in a white packet displaying seagulls, a sailing ship and the phrase 'The Perfection of Cigarette Luxury'. The words 'Smoking Kills' did not appear. He would suck each inhalation of smoke deep into his lungs and let it out in a great whoosh, enough smoke to summon Apaches from miles away. This habit presumably contributed to his early death. My mother rarely smoked. When she did, on social occasions, she liked Du Maurier, in a distinctive orange box with silver markings. Neither of my parents was remotely censorious when I began to smoke myself aged fifteen or sixteen. I smoked pretty well anything bland with a tip, though I once had a crack at Gauloises Disque Bleu at university – encouraged to do so by seeing too many French films. I smoked until I was thirty-eight and gave up more or less for good in 1982. 'Tagamet for life,' said my doctor, referring to the most used drug to combat stomach ulcers, 'or give up smoking.' My last cigarette stub was cast in a disgraceful bit of vandalism into the Grand Canal in Venice. I then put on two stone in weight but at least I am still alive, fourteen years older as I write than my father was when he died.

I said I never met anyone who disliked my dad. 'Oh, Frank! What a lovely man!' they would say about him. He was great fun – always with a stock of good Jewish jokes picked up from his many friends in the music business – but, more than that, genuinely witty. He did not read much but when he did his chosen writers were American humorists like Runyon, Thurber and Perelman. His favourite one-liners were borrowed from Groucho Marx: Groucho bumping into his hostess when leaving a party early, 'I've had a wonderful evening but this wasn't it.' And a regular favourite, 'Those are my principles and if you don't like them . . . well, I have others.' Dad was kind to the point of excessive generosity. He tipped more than others, made larger contributions to church and office collections, and was always first to raise a hand to stand a round or pay for a meal. Naturally, when he poured whiskies or gins they greatly exceeded a publican's measure. He behaved like this while (I suspect) always being more strapped for cash than he could or would admit, a point not lost on my mother. His Catholicism mattered to him in a sort of tribal way. It was his heritage; he was a member of the tribe. He was not overt about it, though we did have one rather garish plaster statue of the Virgin Mary on a shelf halfway up the stairs, and there were a couple of crucifixes in bedrooms. He went to mass every Sunday, kept the other observances and was keen that the rest of us did. There was a Rosary Crusade in the 1950s, launched by an Irish-American priest, with the slogan: 'The Family That Prays Together Stays Together'. We once went to a rally in Wembley Stadium. We would very occasionally say the rosary together, but despite the infrequency of such devotion we did stay happily together. Dad used to say that good works were the best sort of prayers, and he did what he said. He belonged to the Saint Vincent de Paul Society, an organization founded in the slums of Paris in the nineteenth century to mobilize voluntary help for the poor and disadvantaged. Most Sunday afternoons he used to visit a local hospital for the mentally ill and handicapped. He made good friends with several of the patients, one in particular who believed that he was a reincarnation of Emperor Napoleon. I used to egg my father on to offer sympathy for the appalling weather in Russia during the winter.

So my father was a good and kind man, not much of an authoritarian; he only smacked me once, and that was for being rude to my mother. All this is admirable but he was not, in the world's terms, very successful; indeed I reckon he used to delude himself a little about the success that lay just around the corner. This must have encouraged my mother, perhaps too much, to dream of all the little comforts and social advances that mattered to her. But they never quite materialized: no Rover, no house in Ruislip. We never knew hardship, and enjoyed nice holidays and good (free) education, and there was very little evident tension at home. But there must have been times when my mother was sad and disappointed about expectations dashed and three-quarter promises not fulfilled. In the late 1950s my father changed his business from the publication of music to making jingles for the TV commercials which were paying for the new independent television companies. At first the business went well, but not long after I left university it folded. He was driving up and down to see his entrepreneurial nephew in Manchester in May 1968, looking for a new job, when he crashed and subsequently had the heart attack that killed him. He must have been so unhappy, driving around the country with a car full of business files, and feeling that he had let down the wife and children that he loved so much.

My father was hugely proud of me. The most unforgiveable thing I have ever done is not to have shown how proud I was of him. My relationship with him in my late teens and early twenties never really shook off the supercilious patronizing of a young smart-arse. There were good days together. He came to see me play cricket for my Oxford college in my last summer at the university, when I bowled out most of the Gentlemen of Oxfordshire almost before he arrived and there was a triumphant lunch afterwards at the Bear Inn at Woodstock. There was nothing really fractious between us, but deep down I reckoned that he was not as successful as I would have liked him to be. I have always worried that I may not have hidden this cold and harsh sentiment sufficiently, let alone prevented it from metastasizing in the first place. If only I could have grown up before he died. I have always been sad that I was never able to establish a loving adult relationship with this dear man. After his death I read through his private business correspondence, the papers in the car, trying to sort out what it was that he had left, and my mother's financial future. I followed a worrying trail from unpaid bill to rejection letter to financial demand through schemes and dreams that had come crashing down in his last few years. How worried, worried sick, he must have been behind his façade of cheerful enthusiasm. As I read all those letters I cried more than I ever have again in my life.

My sister Angela was much closer to my father emotionally than I was, even though from about the time I was a sixth-former she worked abroad. She belongs to that last generation of women who should have gone to university, but in those days only 6 per cent of our age group went into higher education and a much smaller percentage of women. From a convent school in Ealing she went to the French Lycée and jobs in Strasbourg and then Rome. She is an excellent linguist with good French and Italian in particular, the sort of person whom bad linguists describe as having a good ear, ignoring the amount of intellectual rigour involved in learning any language well. We grew up with a far less spiky relationship than is so often the case between siblings. She looked after me when I was first at school, teased me a bit and inveigled me into her extraordinary, surreal Goon-ish games of the imagination. She never displayed any annoyance or envy at the extent to which her clever younger brother was cosseted, spoilt and praised. She was also much bolder than me. When we stayed with my mother's sister, Ina, and her husband, Michael – a childless couple – in Bristol, she was always happier to ride pillion on one of his powerful motorbikes than her slightly nervous brother. She was also the first to climb a tree or go on the more adventurous rides at the fair. Funny and kind, like our father, she is a serious ecumenical Christian who has moved from devout Catholicism to devout Anglicanism, impelled by a pretty fierce intellect and a lot of usually unsatisfactorily answered questions. She married a much older man, a talented painter and potter, who made her very happy, not least because he is the only person I have ever known who quite literally did not have a bad word to say about anyone. He was a sin-free zone, proof if it were needed that original virtue lives alongside original sin.

Our mother, like other mothers, was not averse to making the occasional personal criticism. I do not mean that she was catty or unkind: she was neither of those things. But she had unshifting standards, often about things that did not always matter very much at all like dress, household tidiness, nails, and assumed or actual personal hygiene. She was judgemental about individual behaviour in a way that was pretty foreign to my father. One of her highest forms of praise was to describe someone as 'band box', neat and tidy as she was herself; indeed when she was dolled up to go out with Dad in the evening she could look film star glamorous. When she came to see me at school events, prize-givings or sports days, she was always the best-looking mum in the hall or on the touchline. The most important thing about her was that she loved our father and her children as much as a mother possibly could. She was very tactile, cuddled and kissed us all a lot, and glowed with pride about our achievements. I have mentioned her enthusiasm for upward mobility, frustrated by our father's unsatisfactory business career. She was delighted that her son, kitted out in tweed and twills with his first dinner jacket from Burton's in his suitcase, went to Oxford. Her pleasure when I became a Member of Parliament could have been sliced with one of her well-kept butter knives. I can barely imagine what she would have thought of her son, a product of the rolling acres of Greenford, being described as a Tory grandee.

A year or so after my father died my mother married his best friend, our Greenford doctor. Dad and Denis McCarthy, an Irishman from Mayo who had worked for the National Health Service since its inception, played golf and drank whisky together. Denis was a good doctor and a kind man and made my mother very happy until, at the moment of his retirement, she died of a heart attack in her sleep aged sixty-four. My last conversation with her was a result of chance. I phoned her to tell her that because a Cabinet minister, Norman St John Stevas, was unable at the last minute to appear in BBC TV's *Question Time* with Robin Day, I was being parachuted into the programme, much to the producer's displeasure. I hope that her last sight of me on the television did not contribute to her attack; more likely it was the dairy products and the occasional cigarettes. Geneticists advise us to choose our parents carefully. Mine both died ridiculously young of cardiac problems. I have been more lucky thanks to angioplasty, a keyhole bypass operation and statins. I am still here more because of modern medicine than because of self-discipline. But heredity and my dicky heart can never overwhelm my sense of good fortune that I had two parents who loved me and loved each other. Their lives could have been longer and could have been more prosperous.

As I have said, my mother became a Catholic in order to marry. I am not sure that she would ever have spent much time thinking let alone talking about religious matters, but she observed all the rites of the church that she had been obliged to join. My earliest memory of a religious observance or prayer is my dad, as he kissed me good-night, tracing the letters INRI on my forehead with his finger. INRI – 'Iesus Nazarenus Rex Iudaeorum': 'Jesus the Nazarene, King of the Jews'. These were the words that Pilate insisted should be fixed to the cross of Jesus at the time of the crucifixion. To the Pharisees cavilling that it should say Jesus had only claimed the title, Pilate responded, 'What I have written, I have written.' As he made these marks on our foreheads, my father repeated the prayer he thought had helped to keep him safe on the passage by wartime convoy to the Middle East. 'May Jesus of Nazareth, King of the Jews, preserve you from sudden and unprepared death.' I did the same with my own children and now do it with my grandchildren. Perhaps the prayer helped Dad in the wartime Mediterranean but not unfortunately on the peacetime M6.

Most of my early religious memories are based on our school and the church which was responsible for it. These were the days before Pope John XXIII and his calling of the Second Vatican Council, which first met in 1962. It did not conclude until 1965. The Council transformed the Church itself and attitudes towards it. While we were not really then a butt of popular prejudice, people were a little suspicious of us, as we seemed to want to prolong the Counter-Reformation, deny the modern world, and lock down any possibility of change in what we did and thought. We could not blame others for reckoning we were a little odd, with all that mumbo jumbo in a dead language, the smell of incense, the infallible Italian and his court in Rome, and the distancing of ourselves from others who claimed to be Christian but denied themselves the glorious certainties of the one, true faith. To some I am sure we were like Freemasons without the funny handshake and the rolled-up trouser leg. Naturally, we learned the same Bible stories as those other Christians who had protested against us and persecuted us just as we had persecuted them. But I am not sure we thought that their God was quite the same as ours, in those days before the Second Vatican Council called for the Catholic Church to be brought up to date and invited separated communities to join us in the quest for unity.

My early religious education came before all that. Sweet women teachers with twinsets and comfortable bosoms taught us the Hail Mary, the Our Father and the Rosary, and some of the simpler stories from the Bible, mainly from the New rather than the Old Testament. We learned the words of Cardinal Wiseman's hymn 'Full in the panting heart of Rome / Beneath the apostle's crowning dome', the chorus of which is the triumphalist 'God bless our Pope', repeated twice and followed by the epithet 'the Great, the Good'. There were more words in it than in the National Anthem and an unqualified ultramontane sentiment that carried the chorus over the Alps and across the main, 'from torrid south to frozen north', which clearly meant us. Each year our knowledge of the Catechism was tested, beginning with the question, 'Who made you?' The Archbishop of Westminster or one of his suffragans would go from classroom to classroom asking for the answers prescribed by the Church. One year Cardinal Griffin came but he only asked easy questions. Even the slower children in our class knew who had made them and why. Answer to the first question, 'God', and to the second, 'To know Him, love Him and serve Him in this world, and to be happy with Him forever in the next.' I always liked that answer. I was a bit riled when the Cardinal moved on without giving me the chance to show that I knew the names of all the Beatitudes.

I was an early recruit to the Guild of St Stephen, wearing as an altar boy like my father before me a cassock and cotta, scarlet beneath and white surplice with lacy frills above. The Pallotine Fathers taught us the Tridentine Liturgy; in those days the mass had to be said in Latin and girls were certainly not allowed on the altar. (In some churches abroad, for example the United States, the presence of girls is still resisted by arch-conservative bishops and priests.) We pronounced the Latin, unlike the Romans, with soft Italianate Cs and Gs, and Vs as Vs not as Ws. I used to serve mass once during the week and once on Sundays and had to fast for twelve hours before taking communion. The small vestry where we changed into our cassocks smelt of communion wine and the priest's tobacco. I knew all the words to the mass – 'Introibo ad altare Dei' – but my mother stopped me repeating them all when I pretended to say mass myself with Carr's water biscuits and a glass of squash on the dining room table at home. It made a change to be a cardinal inside the house rather than King of Spain in the garden. My mother's intervention was, I think, a reflection of her suspicion that what I was doing smacked of heresy rather than an effort to thwart any sense I might entertain of vocation for the priesthood.

One year I was chosen to lead the May procession in my scarlet and white vestments, hands devoutly and sweatily pressed together, my sticking-up straw hair plastered to my head with a dollop of glistening Brylcreem. I came at the head of two columns of would-be angels, little girls in long white dresses with blue ribbons and posies of flowers. The procession, with the parish priests and a plaster statue of the Blessed Virgin Mary carried aloft by the Knights of St Columba, started in the school hall, wound around the car park, and then ventured briefly into the street outside accompanied by a police constable with a small crowd of goggle-eyed spectators watching this exotic intrusion into Greenford life. We finished in the church with Benediction and the Rosary, and then had sticky cakes in the school hall.

Benediction, with the Blessed Sacrament exposed on the altar in a monstrance, was celebrated with some of my favourite Latin hymns – especially 'Laudate Dominum' ('Praise the Lord', based on the shortest of the psalms) and 'Tantum Ergo' (the end of a hymn by St Thomas Aquinas inviting the congregation to venerate the sacrament). At secondary school, I discovered that you could sing the 'Tantum Ergo' to the tune of 'Oh My Darling, Clementine', which some of us used to do in a quiet descant. So much of the bone and marrow of my life was learned as part of my religious education and early religious practice. The prayers and hymns I learned and the narrative which became so familiar – the miracles, the parables, the martyrs – have provided me with a cultural framework and a personal lifeboat. In an art gallery or church, I can usually remember the story behind the biblical scenes depicted and can often recall who the saints are and how hideously they died – St Lawrence, patron saint of chefs with the gridiron on which he was horrendously barbecued; St Sebastian, usually so improbably fey given all those flesh-piercing arrows that did not apparently finish him off. Why did Caravaggio's astonishing paintings of St Matthew in the French church in Rome make such an impression on me when I saw them too late in my life? The answer is partly because I remember being told the story behind the most famous of the paintings, the calling of St Matthew in his counting house by Jesus, by a Benedictine monk at secondary school. The point of the story for a Christian was the initial 'Who, me?' disinclination of Matthew to follow Jesus, hardships and all, eventually to his own crucifixion. Whenever I have been afraid, or have reason to feel grateful about the way the world has spun for me, the same prayers come to mind. I once told a friend this. He looked a shade

embarrassed and said, 'You might as well be an elderly Irish nun.'
There are far worse lives to contemplate.

Despite my gratitude for what I learned as a child, I have become
increasingly outspoken as I have got older about what has often felt
like an authoritarian anti-intellectualism in the Catholic Church. I
wish my religion was discussed in a more rational way that goes back
to its roots, to what really matters, and to the way decent people –
whether Catholic or not – live. This should not be frowned upon, as
it often is, in a Church which for centuries has honoured the ever-
questioning Thomas Aquinas. I ceased to believe in Father Christmas
at about the time I was first learning about God. I have always felt
that there should be more of an intellectual rupture between the two.
The great Parisian theologian Abelard, who was one of the most
important European thinkers of his day and who helped to inspire
the twelfth-century Renaissance, reversed the two aspects of belief
which had hitherto dominated Christian thinking. While Anselm of
Canterbury had argued 'fides quaerens intellectum' – faith seeking
understanding – Abelard believed that understanding should pre-
cede faith. I have always found that a more intellectually satisfying
position.

This became the focus of my anxiety about the great religious
crossing that baptized Catholic children subsequently make, their
first confession and communion. Pius X, a very autocratic Pope, who
was determined to try to protect the Church against the modern
world, decided that children could tell the difference between right
and wrong at the same age – about seven – as they could understand
the nature of the Eucharist. At seven I confessed my sins so that I
could receive communion. I am sure I was well taught by loving
teachers and I know that today most children are even more sensi-
tively taught (given some of the scandals of recent years). Nor did I
ever have much fear of the dark confessional box. Confession is the
subject of a wonderful story by Frank O'Connor in which a terrified
child, confused in the dark, clambers up on to the shelf designed for
a penitent's elbow so that when the confessor twitches the curtain to
find out what is happening all he can see is the child's knees.

How much did I know of good and bad when I was seven? One of
the problems is that as one got older confession became like settling

a driving offence – three points off for just breaking the speed limit, six for doing seventy in a built-up area. When did a venial sin – Purgatory, with just a bit of pain until you were absolved – turn into a mortal sin – lighting the sort of hellfire described in the famous sermon in James Joyce's *Portrait of the Artist as a Young Man*? To be fair I cannot recall when I last heard a sermon about hell, but Catholic teaching has not departed much, if at all, from the sort of gradations of alleged wickedness satirized in the very title of the Catholic David Lodge's novel *How Far Can You Go?* This inevitably became a dominant issue for boys and young men, and presumably for young women too.

Sexual behaviour, about which the celibate necessarily know less than the sexually practising, has become an obsession in debates about the Church's teaching. This must be one reason why the numbers of practising Catholics who go to confession have plummeted. Children are required to confess before communion in churches where only a small minority of adults themselves take this sacrament. Their parents must know this. For a young man growing up I can speak to the huge embarrassment of confessing to what Baden-Powell called 'beastliness'; from what I know, I doubt that he ever stopped many boy scouts from indulging in it. What was a more or less acceptable dirty thought on the purgatorial side of the dividing line between venial and mortal? What was touchable and what not? Which part of my body, or yours, crossed the frontier from Purgatory to Hell? How could I prevent something untoward happening in the night? It is not far-fetched to argue that the obsession with masturbation (allegedly 'moral disorder') and its confession must have played a significant role in the Catholic Church's disastrous history of child abuse and the wicked attempts to cover it up. 'Suffer little children . . . to come unto me; for of such is the kingdom of heaven'.

The Catholic Church, which I am happy and proud to regard as my home, has got sex badly wrong. People talk with reason about the rest of the world's obsession with sex. But the same is true of the Church. What if we had become as focused on wealth, charity, income distribution? What if we had decided in the words of the Magnificat that we needed 'to put down the mighty from their seat' and to exalt 'the humble and meek'? If it really is 'easier for a camel to go through the eye of a needle than for a rich man to enter the kingdom of God', should we not say a lot more about this than about 'beastliness' and condoms?

Some argue that to ask for any change in the teachings of the Catholic Church would be tantamount to feminizing it, an odd and very offensive criticism. It would leave the world, they say, with an Anglicanized Church, Catholic-lite. I do not understand what is wrong with asserting that the Church, which has regularly changed some of its teaching, should hold on to the essential message encapsulated in the Sermon on the Mount, while being a little more like the world it serves and understanding of the lives of those who are still practising Catholics. At least it should discuss more openly why so many faithful Catholics live patently good lives which are at odds with what is said by Church leaders about, in particular, the family, marriage, sex and love. All of which is some distance from Our Lady of the Visitation's church and primary school, where I was first taught to confess. I will return to it at the end of this book.

3

Scholarship Boy

'Here today, up and off to somewhere else tomorrow! Travel, change, interest, excitement! The whole world before you, and a horizon that's always changing.'

Kenneth Grahame, *The Wind in the Willows*

'Mr Hector's stuff's not meant for the exams, Sir. It's to make us more rounded human beings.'

Alan Bennett, *The History Boys*

It was not just the Catechism that we learned off by heart at Our Lady of the Visitation, not just prayers like the Hail Mary and the Magnificat. Like most other primary schools in those days – the 1950s – we were encouraged, no, obliged, to memorize tables, poems and correct spellings. The classes were large. A single teacher took forty or more of us all together down a path where rigour at an early age led quite quickly to the excitement of discovering bigger and broader horizons on one's own. The method was very didactic in ways that for many years went horribly out of fashion. It has been creeping back into primary schools in recent years, as it should. I am rather impressed by what my grandchildren appear to be learning these days.

What made for an even more disciplined environment was the personality of our headteacher, Mr Deasey, and the port for which we all set sail, the eleven-plus exam. This determined the sort of secondary schools to which we would go. Allegedly, we were directed to the type of schools that most suited our talents. Mr Deasey was a burly, grizzled and grey-haired man who ran a very tight ship. He was not unkind but expected punctuality and hard work from both his pupils and his staff. His son was in my class, consistently ahead of the rest of us, and doing practice eleven-plus papers for two or three years before we all had to sit the actual exam, which he of course passed with flying colours. He went to the same secondary school as me and from there on to Cambridge to study Classics. Some of what I learned at Our Lady of the Visitation has remained with me – friend and companion – throughout my life, not only the prayers and the first encounters with the New Testament. For example, I am still a whizz at mental arithmetic, turning Celsius into Fahrenheit or kilometres into miles. Above all, I was encouraged to read widely, and to enjoy what I read, and was allowed to have what were thought to be somewhat precocious tastes. Before everyone had a television set in the front room there seemed to be a view that provided you were reading a book, you were likely to be better occupied than if you were doing anything else.

I remember in particular two female teachers. Mrs Williams would sit us on her knee when we were upset; when I was aged about seven, she read *The Wind in the Willows* to me and the class, as I snuggled against her capacious bosom. I had a crush on Miss Lynch, who taught us when we were a little older. She always looked elegant, pastel-coloured cardigans and a single row of pearls or other beads. She had beautiful hands. She opened the door from Badger, Mole, Ratty and Toad to Enid Blyton's adventuring 'Fives' and 'Sevens' and even Richmal Crompton and the William stories, surely subversive stuff for eight- or nine-year-olds. I am not sure that in those days I would have known why William's father was always having trouble with his liver, or what brought down on the heads of Violet-Elizabeth's parents the patronizing disdain of their neighbours. What was wrong after all with making a fortune from 'Bott's Digestive Sauce', especially when your own father made his living trying to sell the songs of the weeping crooner, Johnny Ray? After that came a great leap forward in reading, which began at primary school and continued into my early teens. I read Jeffrey Farnol's pirate adventures *Black Bartlemy's Treasure* and *Martin Conisby's Vengeance*, in both of which much buckle was swashed. Then it was on to the great Conan Doyle historical novels of the Hundred Years War: *The White Company* and *Sir Nigel*. Distant sightings of King Edward III and the Black Prince stoked a passionate interest in the Middle Ages, just as Rosemary Sutcliffe had engendered a fascination with Rome and Roman Britain. After that I embarked on the Hornblower novels by C. S. Forester, which took the eponymous hero from his first voyage as a midshipman all the way to the House of Lords and an admiral's tricorn hat. There were more than ten Hornblower books; I read them all several times. As for comics I was bought the *Eagle* from the first edition in 1950, and followed enthusiastically Dan Dare's struggles with the Mekon, whose modest ambition was domination of the universe. This even exceeded the aim of my own imaginary conquests. I was not a fan of *The Children's Newspaper*, but readily concede that it was more intellectually demanding than some of today's adult fare.

The eleven-plus exam, confusingly taken usually by ten-year-olds, had been brought in by the 1944 Education Act, one of the most important contributions made by my frequently ambivalent Tory hero Rab Butler, about whom I will say more later. The exam was built on pre-war studies which suggested that the break between primary and secondary education should come with the onset of adolescence at the age of eleven or twelve. It was intended to direct pupils in their onward education to the sort of school that most suited their abilities. State secondary education was divided into three streams: grammar for the most intellectually able, and secondary modern or technical for the majority of pupils. True to British form, the provision of technical education was very limited. We always admired what the Germans had done to develop technical education since the nineteenth century; recognized its economic benefits for that country; and set our sights on replicating this in Britain. But we never really managed to achieve it. Perhaps our heart was not really in it. Certainly our public, tax-funded investment in the parts of the tripartite system that catered for the majority of pupils – indeed that were supposed to suit best their needs – failed to materialize in the required quantities.

A Cabinet memorandum by the intelligent Conservative Cabinet minister David Eccles, in April 1955, succinctly discussed the problem faced by the government at a time when the post-war bulge in the school age population was increasing pressure for the provision of more school places. Eccles pointed out that under the 1944 Act the selection of the sort of school to which children should go after the age of eleven – 20 per cent to grammar schools, 5 per cent to technical, and 75 per cent to secondary moderns – was determined by an exam. This would decide the state education that suited the ability and aptitude of individual pupils. 'It was hoped,' he wrote, 'that the modern school would attain "parity of esteem" with the grammar schools', and that as a result 'the disappointment and jealousy felt by parents when their children failed to qualify for a grammar school would disappear. But this has not yet happened, and the result appears to be growing.' Eccles concluded his admirably clear-cut, brief paper, by noting that 'the feelings aroused by the 11+ exam, both justified and unjustified, force a move either towards selection for nobody or towards selection for everybody. Selection for nobody means comprehensive schools with grammar schools abolished and parents' choice practically ruled out. The Socialists support this policy on the principle of fair shares for all. Selection for everybody means developing in each secondary school some special attraction and giving parents the widest possible choice. I hope that my colleagues will think that selection for everybody is the right policy.' Of course they did; but the words were not accompanied by actions or money. So they failed to provide then or later 'parity of esteem' to the part of the tripartite system that educated eight out of ten pupils. Parents and voters drew the obvious conclusion.

The result was that by the time of Conservative governments in the 1970s and 1980s, ministers (including Margaret Thatcher) were closing down grammar schools and approving new comprehensives – non-selectives – as fast or faster than Labour ministers. They probably had little choice. If there was no 'parity of esteem', parents were being asked to support a system in which their children were likely to be provided with a second-best education on the grounds that this was appropriate for them. Second-rate schools for second-rate children was not much of a slogan or aspiration. Nevertheless, the result was the destruction or total identity change of some great schools, grammar and direct grant (the type of selective school to which I went, in which a quarter of the places were directly funded by government with the rest paid for by fees). There had been nothing quite like it in England as an act of institutional destruction since Henry VIII's and Thomas Cromwell's dissolution of the monasteries in the sixteenth century.

It is true that the grammar and direct grant schools privileged the middle classes, whose ability nowadays to buy more expensive housing in areas with better state schools almost equally privileges them under today's largely comprehensive system. It is also true that selection at eleven was far too rigid – this way goats, that way sheep – with little traffic of pupils from one part of the system to another whatever their subsequent development. A goat at ten remained a goat until sixteen or eighteen, and perhaps for longer. But grammar schools in less well-off areas did provide a way out of cycles of deprivation for clever children; it has subsequently been more difficult to discern any similar exit or ladder. Comparisons conducted by the OECD between teenagers' attainment levels in numeracy and literacy in developed countries (and some emerging countries in Asia) give a dreadful picture of the outcome of the educational revolution in Britain in the final quarter of the last century, despite eclectic and sometimes frantic efforts to reverse the downward drift. The introduction of a national curriculum, the abolition of the local education authority and teacher union monopoly of control over education, the empowerment of parents and local communities, numeracy hours here and literacy hours there: nothing yet seems to have worked very well, though perhaps we need more time to escape from an era in which alleged social equity appeared to trump issues like educational quality and competitiveness, discipline and traditional teaching methods. An age which allowed too many to fail and to be seen to fail – when, to borrow from David Eccles, 'parity of esteem' withered away – has turned into an era when, since no one is allowed to fail, the prospects of success have been cut back for everyone. I do not believe that the sort of working-class aspiration reflected in autodidactic diligence in nineteenth- and twentieth-century Britain has completely died out.

I was lucky. I did not suffer from the pre-exam nerves which clearly affected some ten-year-olds, and probably touched parents just as much. For a start, I had sat so many mock exams in mathematics, language and reasoning that I took the real exam in my stride.

45

Having passed that, I went one Saturday morning to sit the entrance and scholarship exam at the local independent, Catholic direct grant school, St Benedict's, Ealing. If I did well enough in the exam I would qualify for a local authority bursary from Ealing Council and indirectly the government. I think there was also a small top-up by the school itself, a Benedictine foundation run by its monastic community. My parents were thrilled when I got a scholarship and therefore a free place. They had resolved, they told me later, to pay for me if I passed the selection exam even if I did not do well enough to get a bursary. This would not have been easy for them to afford, but they both believed in education opening to possibilities of wider horizons and larger opportunities.

Before starting at St Benedict's, we had to go to Peter Jones in Sloane Square to get me fitted out: elasticated indoor shoes with my number (119) in tacks on the soles, a herring-bone suit, green cap and blazer, rugby shirts in the colours of my house, Gervase, named after the English Benedictine missionary priest who was hanged, drawn and quartered at Tyburn in the early seventeenth century. I was to learn much more about the martyrs of the Reformation in later years – inevitably more about the Catholics than the Protestants. We often sang a hymn by Frederick Faber, a Balliol graduate who like the Blessed John Henry Newman abandoned the Holy Orders of the Church of England to become a Catholic priest in the middle of the nineteenth century. Father Faber's famous hymn is less jolly than his portraits make him appear. The tune thunders along to support some pretty sombre words:

> Faith of our fathers! living still,
> in spite of dungeon, fire and sword,
> Oh how our hearts beat high with joy
> Whene'er we hear that glorious word!
> Faith of our fathers, holy faith!
> We will be true to thee till death.

The Middle School, which I entered at St Benedict's, was housed in a large Edwardian villa and a couple of prefabs in residential Ealing with no sign of the 'dungeons dark' in which Faber suggested in another verse that Catholic boys might one day (if they were lucky) be chained. My first encounters with the other potential martyrs among my classmates brought out the diffidence in my character; these days I identify to some extent with the anti-hero of one of my grand-children's books, *The Wimpy Kid*. At first, I was terrified of commit-ting some unfathomable schoolboy solecism. I was then, and still am, more shy and nervous than most people would believe.

I soon discovered that my fellow pupils had surnames and initials but no forenames. It was rather like the members of the England cricket team who refer to one another by surnames to which they invariably append the letter 'Y' – Broady, Stokesy, Rooty and so on. I can still remember the initials of the other boys – there was Quinnen P. J. (a friend whom I later, much later, called Peter), and Bradford P. W., the first boy I talked to. He was in Powell House, whose rugby shirts were red, like the blood of another English Benedictine martyr, whose name the house carried. Powell was one of those martyrs who, like St Thomas More, faced death with a nonchalant joke, in his case calling for a last glass of sherry. We were not taught history from a wholly blinkered Catholic viewpoint, though it was not really until university that I learned much about the Protestant martyrs who, like their Catholic brothers in Christ, had also died bravely for their Christian faith. With a now-retired Lord Lieutenant of Oxfordshire, I later raised the money for a stone plaque in the University Church at Oxford commemorating all the martyrs, Catholic and Protestant, who were tried there before being burned on pyres in Broad Street. Conscience, I think, is ecumenical.

From the very beginning I learned a lot of Latin and Greek – at the expense of much science – and was taught history by the first in a suc-cession of teachers who made it lively and often contentious. In my early years, Mr Wilding gave us the whole of English history in the school year from September to the following July and then repeated the story in a different but no less memorable way beginning the next September – AD 43 to 1939, and no stopping. It was history which, like the frescoes in the Westminster Parliament, moved Whiggishly from one story of great men, victorious battles and the ascent of lib-erty to another. I do not really understand how later generations cope with the slight knowledge which they seem to have of the way stations of our national journey. It is probably useful to know about the history of medical instruments or the wickedness of twentieth-century dictators. Yet it is surely a pity to know a lot about Stalin and Hitler and almost nothing (or perhaps absolutely nothing) about Disraeli and Lloyd George. Alarmed and doubtless blimpish, I once discovered that most of a secondary school history class to which I was talking as an education minister thought that Henry VI came after George IV. It spoke well for their numeracy I suppose. There was a lot to be said for the David Wildings of the teaching profession.

Later on at school, I was taught history by three very different men – a monk called George Brown, a charming Cambridge cricketer, Steve Walker, and a Christian Socialist, Paul Olsen. Father Brown had a certain Friar Tuck look to him, jolly, red-faced and kind. As passionate a Middlesex cricket supporter as Clement Attlee, he managed to import sporting metaphors into the discussion of most historical topics: King John had his stumps flattened by the barons at Runnymede; and memorably Henry II was bowled a googly by Thomas a Becket. (The metaphor came back to me years later when I first visited the site of his murder in Canterbury Cathedral: some googly.) Steve Walker was another cricket lover and used to wear the sort of blazer for matches which put striped deck chairs to shame. He liked your essays to have a bit of literary flourish to them; this was the time when I learned words like 'nugatory' and 'vicissitude'. Paul Olsen was a serious fellow whose sheets of notes showed how hard he worked. But his main impact on me was to remind me of my real shoe size when I got too big for my boots. I think in my own defence that this was partly because of his encouragement of my slightly accidental but successful choice of university and college.

This happened because of a peculiarity of timetabling. My best subject at school was thought to be English not History. This was above all because of an exhilarating teacher called Ken Connelly, whom we nicknamed Jack for reasons I cannot now recollect. I am not sure he really liked schoolmastering. He had lost a leg in the war, after which he had been taught English at Cambridge by F. R. Leavis. He could be bruisingly sarcastic; charitably we used to assume that the stump of his amputated limb caused him occasional pain and in turn triggered acerbic put-downs. The sound of his approach, his squeaking prosthetic leg sending signals down the corridors of his imminent arrival, silenced the rowdiest class. I remember, aged about thirteen, having to go back to a room which my own class had recently vacated to pick up a homework book. By this time the room was occupied by another class, which Mr Connelly was teaching. I knocked nervously, entered and asked, 'Please, sir, can I pick up one of my books?' 'I'm sure you can,' he replied. 'But the answer to the question you should have asked, "May I pick up my book?", is definitely "No".' I left shaking.

But I was also left shaking in due course by the excitement he brought to teaching us about the authors he loved and about the language in which we wrote about them. He introduced us to John Donne, Christopher Isherwood, Graham Greene, George Orwell and the poets of both great wars. We puzzled over T. S. Eliot with him and learned to love the magnificent dramatic rhythms and sounds of Shakespeare. Aged sixteen, I lay in bed one night declaiming over and over again the coruscating speech of Coriolanus.

> Cut me to pieces, Volsces,
> Men and lads, stain all your edges on me.
> Boys!
> False Hound!
> If you have writ your annals true, 'tis there
> That like an eagle in a dove-cote
> I fluttered your Volscians in Corioli,
> Alone I did it.
> Boy!

Oh to be able to utter that 'Boy!'

Words, words, words, in the most beautiful, subtle and supple English language. Connelly taught us to love words, and the way in which simply putting them together in different ways created different effects. Think of P. G. Wodehouse, he would say, whose best jokes are jokes of language. 'I could say that, if not actually gruntled, he was far from being disgruntled.' Or 'Her pupils were at once her salvation and her despair. They gave her the means of supporting life, but they made life hardly worth supporting.' I suppose that is what he came to feel – that life as a teacher was pretty insupportable. So he went off to write civil service memos, punchier than the usual ones I would think. He left me with what have become some of my lifetime passions.

The calendar, however, meant that he missed out on determining the next stage of my education. In those days the entrance exams for most Cambridge colleges were held in January, the exams for Oxford the month before. You could sit both. Paul Olsen, not really thinking I knew enough history to make the cut, suggested that when I was sixteen I should try for Oxford first in order to give me some experience of the whole Oxbridge entrance process, the cold halls and the hot competition. He advised me to try his own old college, Balliol, where I suspect his post-war socialism had been fired up when he was an undergraduate there by the great Marxist historian Christopher Hill. So I applied to read history at Balliol, went up for the exams full of my English revision (lots of memorized lines of poetry) for the exam at Peterhouse, Cambridge, which I planned to sit in January. To general amazement I was offered a Domus Exhibition at Oxford; with perhaps a dash of indolence I decided there and then to cash in my chips and take what was on the table. Ken Connelly did not seem to mind, and Paul Olsen reckoned that Balliol would knock some of the shine off me.

In the last few years some sad and depressing stories about paedophilia at St Benedict's have hit the front pages of newspapers. There were suggestions that it must have been a grim Dotheboys hell-hole in my day. Far from it. We were beaten from time to time. That happened at most schools, and it was generally regarded by teenage boys as one of life's rites of passage. Otherwise I was in clover, never bored, well taught, not remotely bolshie and surrounded by friends, some of whom I still see. Sport mattered, and it helped that I was good at cricket and rugby, captaining the school at the former and getting my colours at both. All those years with my father on the beach and throwing a squash ball at the garage door paid off. I also learned from the Benedictines a sort of restrained moderation about the way we should behave even in religious observance. A monk who taught us French, Father Casimir, who had lost some of his toes to frostbite as a naval chaplain in the Arctic convoys in the war, used to denounce excessive displays of piety: 'rosary clanking', he used to call them. I am not sure that he would have liked to know it, but he was as loveable as he was fierce in insisting that we all acquire a pretty comprehensive knowledge of French irregular verbs. He would begin most classes by throwing a blackboard cleaner or book of grammar rather indiscriminately at his expectant class. We learned to duck, and also that 'demander' took both 'à' and 'de'.

There is only one thing that I should add, shamefaced, about my afternoons on the games field. I became prey to an insane superstition. I would have laughed off the obvious ones that are so often contradictory. Is it 'warm hands, cold heart' or 'cold hands, warm heart'? I had no problem stepping on cracks in the pavement. But for some reason I became obsessed with the magical properties of the number 3 and its multiples. Whoever taught us that the digits of any number multiplied by 3 always add up ultimately to another number divisible by 3 should have been shot: 27, 1,008, 3,942, etc. I have no idea what name this function bears in maths; mathematicians will doubtless snigger. But, for reasons deep in my psyche, the impact was profound. I uttered instructions or urged the team on with phrases of 3, 6 or 9 words. Thus, 'Come on, boys', but not 'Come on, you boys'. The number 4 being close to 3 was almost as unlucky as the number 8 because of that digit's proximity to the heroic 9. (I was later to learn that 4 is also regarded as unlucky by the Cantonese because it is homophonous to the word 'death' in their language. The number 8 on the other hand – how complicated – is lucky in China because it sounds like 'prospers'.) As captain of cricket, I naturally bowled myself for 3 overs not 4, 9 overs not 8. The penalty for a failure in superstitious numeracy was naturally sporting calamity, a dropped pass or catch. This lunacy leaked into my behaviour at other times and it still does. Driving along in the car, minding my own business, I realize suddenly even today that I have not really been daydreaming at all but aggregating the digits on car number plates until I get to a number which can pass the 'divisible by 3' test. I suppose this certifiable lunacy is harmless enough, even for a Cabinet minister, and that psychologists would think of some reason for it, like the number of times I have recited the Nicene Creed with its 'three in One' deity and the third day resurrection. At least I walk under ladders and do not try to count exactly how many words I write on each page to ensure the triumph of three. For your information, the last sentence contained twenty-seven words – 2 plus 7 equals 9 divided by 3 equals 3. Phew!

At the age of eighteen (another lucky number) I set off for what had long been regarded, with no shortage of immodesty on the part of its beneficiaries, as the great launch pad for success in public life. Geoffrey Madan, the collector and creator of aphorisms, who himself went to Balliol before the First World War with Ronnie Knox and Harold Macmillan, noted what he and his college contemporaries took to be the remorseless and inevitable ascent of their kind. 'At the top of every tree,' he wrote, 'you will find an arboreal slum of Balliol men.' Another Balliol writer, Hilaire Belloc, wrote a poem on the same subject which, happily, is not as well known outside the college as his *Cautionary Tales for Children*. We all know about Matilda, who told lies and was burned to death, and Lord Lundy, who was sent out to govern New South Wales. But Balliol produced a regiment of Lord Lundys in the nineteenth and twentieth centuries who went out to run the British Empire. Belloc's emotional poem 'To the Balliol Men Still in Africa' praised them all, noting the role that the pupils and disciples of Balliol's most famous Master, Benjamin Jowett, had played in standing up for their country's honour thousands of miles from Balliol Hall and Cumnor Hill. Here was a college, Belloc thought, that:

> [. . .] armours a man
> With the eyes of a boy and the heart of a ranger,
> And a laughing way in the teeth of the world
> And a holy hunger and thirst for danger.

He concluded with words that used, I am sure, to echo around Balliol Hall at college feasts and gaudies:

> Balliol made me, Balliol fed me,
> Whatever I had she gave me again:
> And the best of Balliol loved and led me,
> God be with you, Balliol men.

Though dedicated to those in Africa, like the curious, mostly German Lord Milner and his 'kinder-garten' of officials containing so many Oxford men in his government of the Transvaal and Orange

River Colony, it was perhaps even more appropriate if one considers the college's role in India. From 1853 to 1947, 350 Balliol graduates went out to India to serve what Professor Judith Brown called 'the Balliol Raj'. One of them, whose life and death was not celebrated by Belloc, was eaten by a tiger. A college which numbered about 300 in the 1920s and 1930s was, as Professor Brown also noted, 'a kindergarten for national and public life'.

So did that explain me, thirsting for danger, another colonial Governor to add to the long list, like Lord Maclehose, my predecessor but two in Hong Kong? In a way I suppose it did, though by the 1960s there was quite a lot of cynicism about any sort of institutional aristocracy, let alone about imperial obligations and ambitions. But one thing for sure is that I was taught by a galaxy of brilliant and eccentric historians, all of them both clever and kind. I just missed Richard Southern, who was one of those who examined me but had gone to a Chair at All Souls before I arrived at Balliol. He was one of the greatest historians of medieval Europe, and rather typically donated a large prize that he won for being regarded as such to St Hilda's, a poor college, to establish a fellowship in medieval studies. He helped to rescue medieval history from its former preoccupation with constitutional development and wrote several books, three of which influenced me especially at the time: the seminal *The Making of the Middle Ages: Western Views of Islam*, which bears re-reading today, and a biography of St Anselm, a saint whose life fuelled his own sense of a faith seeking understanding. He was a committed member of the Church of England and a great teacher.

In his place, Balliol elected another very fine medieval scholar, Maurice Keen, a quiet and charming angler from Anglo-Irish stock who wrote a book almost as important as Southern's *Making of the Middle Ages*, called *Chivalry*. He exhibited the knightly attributes in his own life. He gave me my first intellectually scorching experience of tutorials, the Oxford system of one on one, or one on two, teaching. Maurice had a set of rooms near Balliol's back gate full of books, sagging furniture and ashtrays. He stammered a little, smoked filthy little cheroots and as he wandered about his room listening to undergraduate essays would occasionally stop to dip a finger in a pot of Oxford thick-cut marmalade, which he would suck ruminatively in between puffing away. I began reading an essay on Charlemagne with a magnificent schoolboy generalization. 'Charlemagne,' I said, 'can truly be regarded as the founder of modern Europe.' I heard Maurice stuttering away behind me, 'I b-b-beg your pardon?' Flatulent clichés should be among the victims of a good education. Maurice helped to inure me against the sort of Euro-waffle which I later had to encounter in Brussels, even while I argued that you did not have to indulge in this vacuous stuff to make a good case for the continued existence of the European Union. To this day, when I hear people talking about the need for 'a vision', I think of Maurice.

Maurice Keen's first year teaching as a Fellow of Balliol coincided with that of Richard Cobb, whose eccentricity was even remarked on by his obituarist in *Le Monde* – 'l'étonnant Cobb', the paper called him. Richard and Maurice encouraged one another's anarchic spirit, especially – and this was pretty frequent – when tanked up with 'the lovely stuff'. Singing Irish Republican songs under the bedroom window of the Master, an Ulster constitutional historian whom no one would have regarded as keen on larks (particularly after an early bedtime), was a typical end to one of their cheerful evenings. Arriving one day for a tutorial in mid-morning I found Richard sitting under his desk nursing a hangover. Cobb was a great historian of the French Revolution but wrote about all things French in a way that became literature. He was fascinated by 'la vie en marge', writing about prostitutes, thieves, drunks, the poor. He recognized that his own principal weakness as a historian was a lack of sympathy for anyone seeking power for whatever cause. Naturally, he hated Robespierre. I am not sure that he would have been happy to teach anyone who did not share his dislike of this self-righteous, Uriah-Heepish Puritan. But how many other monsters could have matched the Frenchman's wickedly sanctimonious remark: 'To punish the oppressors of humanity is clemency; to forgive them is cruelty.' He was always on the lookout for Robespierre reincarnations. In addition to his books and essays, Cobb was a hugely productive letter writer displaying a total indifference to political correctness, a rather absurd snobbery (he loved teaching toffs and receiving academic gongs), and a reckless pursuit of fairly harmless academic vendettas. One of his great school friends had killed his mother; Richard wrote a very funny book about this sad business and, to his credit, remained a friend of the matricide. When the man was released from prison, Richard invited him to dinner at the college and introduced him to fellow diners at High Table as someone with a particular interest in penal policy. A friend of mine going to see him on his deathbed in Abingdon Hospital found him asleep, and walking around his bed waiting for him to wake up glimpsed the nurse's instructions written on the clipboard attached to the bottom rail. 'This patient,' it said, 'will not take his fluids.' It was the only time in his life that this can have been true of Richard.

Cobb himself was fascinated by the idea of identity and its complexities, partly because of his own work as a historian and partly because, though English, he spoke and wrote perfect French and fitted into any French social setting like cassis into Bourgogne Aligoté. Among Richard's villains were those sociologists who tried to define identity clearly with statistical tables and computer printouts. For him I suspect that the accused peasant poisoner Marie Besnard, about whom he wrote an essay, was a parable. In a series of murder trials in the 1950s and 1960s she escaped conviction despite the evidence of lawyers, criminologists and scientists as she demonstrated that the experts had muddled up the evidence, putting one person's gall bladder with someone else's kidney. Above all, an eye had departed its real cadaver for a foreign skeleton. I always thought that for Cobb that eye looked unblinking and sceptical at all those who thought that identity could be easily explained and defined. Cobb taught me to distrust sweeping generalizations, particularly those that exclude the passions, and peccadilloes, of humanity.

My other two tutors were less eccentric in behaviour. John Prest taught modern history, and wrote fine biographies of nineteenth-century politicians. He was a courtly man with apple cheeks and beautiful manners. On one occasion when I overslept and missed the beginning of a tutorial, he arrived with my fellow tutee, entered my bedroom with a polite knock and woke me with the words, 'Good morning, Mr Patten. Mr Massey and I have come to read you an essay on the Great Reform Bill. You may have heard of it.'

What of the historian who had so inspired Paul Olsen to push me towards Balliol? Christopher Hill was described by a fellow Marxist historian as 'the dean and paragon of English historians'. He was certainly, with Eric Hobsbawm, one of the two most influential British Marxist historians of the last seventy years. He transformed studies of English seventeenth-century history, and in particular that of our own Revolution. A member of the Communist Party until the 1950s, he was of course – like Hobsbawm – a subject of interest to MI5; the spook-hunters might have spent their time better in Cambridge than Oxford. Quiet-voiced and personally kind as he was, it was difficult to imagine him having anything to do with the barbarities of a regime which he defended until after Stalin's death. Today I suppose that we all underestimate the moral and intellectual impact of the 1930s at home and abroad on so many clever young men and women. The indefensible things that they witnessed pushed them into defending things that were equally indefensible, and whose true nature they tried not to see. At the very least they were gullible. Hill had two lasting impacts on my personal life. He had been my moral tutor at college, taking a particular interest in my academic development, though the eagle-eyed will have observed that being taught by a great Marxist did not turn me into a raving leftie. But when it came to my later vetting for a civil service post in the Cabinet Office, the men in raincoats who came to interview me were clearly deeply suspicious of whatever effect Hill might have had on me. As a result, the process of my positive vetting dragged on for some time.

Second, Hill (actually his wife, Bridget) left one really substantial and much more important mark on me: without them I might never have met my own wife and best friend. Hill had a party every term for Balliol's historians – beer, cider, hunks of bread and lumps of cheddar. (These were the days before Bulgarian Malbec.) To make for a jollier atmosphere, Hill used to ask Bridget to invite some girls from the college, St Hilda's, where she was Bursar. Bridget in her turn asked Christopher's niece, Pene, now a retired professor of history but then an undergraduate at St Hilda's, to rustle up some female company. One of Pene's friends, Lavender, was the woman I later married, after a few twists and turns. Like a character in a Hollywood musical ('a look across a crowded room', and all that), once I had met Lavender I never thought I would marry anyone else, never. I courted Lavender pretty assiduously. She had told me that she did not get much post. In those days, there were three postal deliveries around the colleges every day. I sent an invitation to tea in three parts, so that only the third post completed the message. This seemed to amuse her and to do the trick. But, as she has pointed out to me from time to time, I have not subsequently written to her three times a day. The most glamorous date in our time at Oxford was a ball at Magdalen at which a sullen 'Rolling Stones' band was the star attraction. They had been hauled back from their first tour of the USA because of a prior contractual commitment, agreed before their first hit made them famous. Later on, I almost lost Lavender for good; too timid to ask her to marry me (and only twenty-one). I went off on a scholarship to America and she fell for someone else. Fortunately, I got a second chance to make up for my folly, and here we are still, together for forty-six years.

Oxford in the early 1960s was on the cusp of previously unthinkable change. Young women went to 'women only' colleges. They could not even be members of the Oxford Union, the university debating society and one of its more prestigious clubs. They could only enter men's colleges – or, more particularly, men's rooms – during the afternoon, the assumption presumably being that intercourse was somehow physically impossible between lunch and supper. Colleges locked their gates at 10.30 p.m. or shortly after, with sanctions against late return. Most colleges turned a blind eye to the hazardous routes which allowed undergraduates to climb in after hours, running risks of serious injury – spiked limbs or broken bones – while simultaneously preparing them for any future Colditz escapades. (Cambridge went further, turning night climbing into a sport; a book about this was written pseudonymously by a certain 'Whipplesnaith'.) Politics at Balliol were routinely left wing – Vietnam, nuclear weapons, South African apartheid. Peace and happiness were largely sought through tobacco and alcohol; I remember one term when I took to drinking stout and cider, a poor man's Black Velvet, which looked like the oil residue you discover when dropping the sump on an old car. As we all know from Philip Larkin, sexual intercourse (though rather discreetly) and widespread drug use lay just over the horizon. I once shared a very soggy joint with a friend who went on to become a very senior judge. Until then I had honestly thought that a joint was what arrived at 1 p.m. on Sundays with Yorkshire pudding or mint sauce.

I disliked the whole experience, mostly because I seemed to get nothing pleasant out of sucking on someone else's spittle-soaked stub. Perhaps it was just another Woodbine, not marijuana at all, but how would I have known? Perhaps, like President Clinton, I simply did not inhale. Anyway, I have never repeated the experience. So while I missed the perils, if such they were, of California's favourite crop, there was one fellow undergraduate for whom cannabis made a spectacular career: Howard Marks, the most celebrated of all my contemporaries and the most dashing and charming Welshman I have ever met. Howard was apparently introduced to the weed by Denys Irving, my next-door neighbour in college, a beautiful, wild spirit, whose denim-clad figure and rock'n'roll music had greeted me when I arrived at Balliol in my sports jacket and cavalry twills, rather alarming my parents who had driven me to Oxford. Alas, Denys was to die not long after leaving Balliol in a hang-gliding accident. Marks wrote very entertainingly about his own life as an international drug dealer. There have been umpteen films about him and cutting rooms full of press interviews. He was courteous, brave and often kind, but the courts inevitably judged him.

The Liberal Prime Minister Herbert Asquith – while, so far as we know, not a cannabis habitué, but like me a man who enjoyed a tipple – once described Balliol men (he was one himself) as possessing 'the tranquil consciousness of an effortless superiority'. Well, the college was never going to be renowned for the quality of its architecture, though the age of the college – the oldest in the university – was something about which we could and did brag. It felt as though we were celebrating half- or full centenaries with great regularity. Lord Peter Wimsey, a fictitious Balliol man, would presumably have matched Asquith's description perfectly if he had governed a few colonies in between discovering who had murdered Professor Plum in the library and Colonel Mustard in the downstairs loo. I love Balliol but do not think that the 'effortless superiority' tag is very helpful; nor was it was very accurate. True, even in the last decades of the twentieth century, Balliol produced a lot of senior politicians, judges, lawyers, journalists and civil servants: Ted Heath, Roy Jenkins, Tom Bingham, Hugo Young, Murray Maclehose at the head of a long list. True, also, that the rise of a few alumni has appeared relatively effortless. In cases like that of Dennis Healey this was simply because he was so very clever; in others, like Roy Jenkins, it was partly because he took considerable pains to make things look so easy. On the whole, however, I do not believe that it helps much to pretend that success comes without breaking into a sweat. The overt, rather arrogant intellectual posing at Balliol which existed as late as the 1940s and 1950s, when some Balliol undergraduates cheered Balliol's opponents on the river and the rugby field for fear that the college might get a sporting reputation, and when no one at the college could believe that Ian Gilmour could possibly be intelligent or interesting because he had been at Eton and in the Guards, had disappeared by my day. Now that Balliol is co-educational, the posing is unlikely to reappear since it always owed a great deal to testosterone swagger.

I had two contemporaries whose superiority might have seemed effortless, though they both worked hard and were extremely modest about their success. One was Neil McCormick, president of the Union and a brilliant lawyer, who later became Professor of Public Law at Edinburgh University, a Member of the European Parliament, and a close and influential adviser to Alex Salmond. Had he not been a Scottish Nationalist from the cradle, I am sure he would have become in due course a senior Labour Cabinet minister, as good a debater as Robin Cook and cleverer than Gordon Brown. The only thing to hold against him was the fact that he played the bagpipes. Neil, who died far too young, was the nationalist (in my own country) whom I have most liked and admired; his nationalism was extrovert, generous and untinged by any xenophobia. The other very superior mind belonged to Edward Mortimer, a friend for life, a brilliant examinee and a beautiful and cogent writer. His book *Faith and Power: The Politics of Islam* was a tour de force and remains for me the most valuable book I have read on this now troubled and hugely contemporary or even just important subject. After All Souls and journalism, Edward went to work for Kofi Annan at the United Nations. Whenever I have been on the other side of an argument from Edward, I have paused to take stock of my position.

Some of my peers went into politics. When I was Secretary of State for the Environment, my shadows in the House of Commons were Labour's Bryan Gould, a Balliol New Zealander, and the Liberal Alan Beith (also Balliol), reputed to have quizzed the college chaplain once on the small size of the congregations in the chapel. The chaplain replied that he had never regarded Balliol Chapel as being one of God's stamping grounds. While at Oxford I was not myself remotely political. I edited a satirical magazine, *Mesopotamia*, wrote and acted in revues, played rugby and cricket for the college, and lagged about in an occasionally industrious way. While we had some excellent sportsmen of our own age – a future international Irish forward in our college rugby team – our principal encounter with sporting stars depended on the late arrival at the college or the return to it of great sportsmen who had done their National Service, or been badly injured, thus delaying their arrival at university. Two of them in my first year were the Indian cricket captain, the Nawab of Pataudi (whose daughter, also a Balliol graduate, was many years later to star with my youngest daughter in a Bollywood film), and the former English fly-half, Richard Sharp. Sharp was the most elegant rugby player I have seen, slipping through defences like a blond wraith. Decades afterwards I saw an elderly silver-haired man at a Varsity match who introduced himself to me as the man who had preceded me as the Balliol fly-half. Such are fame and modesty. I did not play rugby with him – in the year that our paths crossed he was nursing a jaw broken by the Springbok wing-forwards – but we did play in the same college cricket team for which he kept wicket immaculately. Before our first game, he asked me what I bowled. I replied, 'I'm thought to be pretty fast.' He stood back for the first two or three deliveries; as I walked back to bowl the next one, I saw him closing up to the stumps. I bowled as fast as I could from an even longer run than usual. The batsman missed the ball and Richard stumped him. It was one of my greatest humiliations and it took me most of the summer to live down.

My closest friends were not remotely interested in politics either, beyond a broad disaffection from anything that looked like the conventional establishment opinion. Of the four men with whom I spent most time, one became a successful film producer, another a solicitor and high court judge, the third (surprisingly) an entrepreneur and the last a teacher in Mexico. None of us was superior and none of us was particularly effortless, though we did do just enough work to keep our tutors at bay. The only sportsman of the four was the judge-to-be, who kept goal for the Balliol soccer team. His charm was as huge as his laugh. The entrepreneur, Arnold Cragg, was another son of the cloth; his father was the Church of England's foremost expert on Islam. Arnold has a house near ours in France. We meet most summers resuming conversations that have been going on for almost half a century, almost serious but not for long, each of us slightly surprised by what the other has done with his life.

The revues that I mentioned consumed a good deal of time – writing them, learning parts, performing. The greatest fun came from our annual fortnight's summer tour with the Balliol Players. We performed our own heavily rewritten versions of Aristophanes' Attic comedies, our scripts bearing only the most vestigial of relationships to the original plays. We added music so that things would go with a bigger swing. The Players performed at public schools, house parties, the Inns of Court and so on. The scripts teetered on the edge of vulgarity, occasionally tumbling over into it, weighed down by double-entendres which from time to time got us banned from future appearances at some schools like Shrewsbury. The boys, needless to say, preferred our version of Aristophanes to his. I suspect that political correctness might well these days have erased large parts of our scripts. But they were certainly funny, or at least so we thought.

So did Balliol make me? In some ways 'yes', partly because of the opportunity I got to go to America after my final exams. Above all it made me because of the historians who taught me to think for myself and the friends I met. Balliol made me less conventional and more open-minded than I would otherwise have been. I became more curious, more able to argue without being quarrelsome, more able to marshal a case, more prepared to dare. By the time I graduated I was less – well, a bit less – of a wimp. I grew up with the fingerprints of my teachers and friends all over the process. But what had really made me was the fact that I got to Balliol in the first place. I was a pretty classic example of the scholarship boy, for whom Rab Butler's 1944 Education Act had provided a way of combining hard work, the influence of good parents, inherited wits and some luck in order to clamber on to the first rungs of Britain's meritocracy.

I did not arrive at this ladder into the establishment because of my birth, nor because of my social connections, although it is obvious that the contacts I began to make at Oxford helped to secure my

The cover of the Balliol Players dinner, signed by some who became lifelong friends.

onward and upward passage. Without undue vanity I also assume that those who gave me a helping hand along the way thought reasonably well of the jobs I had done at various stages of what became my career. As a nation we tend to be pretty obsessed with class, meritocracy and the existence of an establishment, which is said to run everything. The part of this trinity which should most concern us is class, not because it should be or is at the heart of a continuing struggle. 'The whole question,' Lenin said in 1921, 'is – who will overtake whom.' Trotsky and Stalin used the shortened 'Who? Whom?' formula. This 1920s preoccupation with class should no longer be an obsession in the twenty-first century. In Britain, the greatest Labour leader, Clement Attlee, attempted to end the class war, not to win it. The challenge today is that, despite seventy or more years of welfare democracy, inequality is too high in financial terms (though with more employment among lower income groups it may have recently fallen a little) and it has not diminished as much as it should have done in education. This is in part because the class warriors have often chosen the wrong targets. In education, why have setting, marking and discipline been in their gunsights, alongside selection and of course grammar schools? Why have they consistently behaved as though the principal beneficiaries of public services should be those who provide them, not those who need them? Why have they acted and spoken as though attributes and aspirations like thrift, prudence, family responsibility and ownership are middle-class qualities not classless ones? They help create the very conditions in which sluttishness and yobbishness tend to be associated exclusively and wrongly with those from working-class backgrounds: yet there are sluts and yobs in every walk of life and from every class. The most important issue domestically facing contemporary Britain is not aggressive class politics, but the policies that have allowed so many to fall behind educationally and financially while others thrive. That is the result of bad policies, not class politics. Moreover, the most serious bias in policy making tilts advantage by age not class. The elderly are favoured at the expense of younger families and individuals.

There is, however, one reservation that I would add to those arguments. We do have an establishment in Britain – that is, a group of people who very often know one another, have been to the same universities and sometimes schools, have often worked in the same professions, who run much of the country and many of its institutions. There is similarly an establishment which runs the media. Those who are renowned simply for their celebrity (and are therefore likely to be unknown to me) arrive at the top of whatever it is they do to acquire their fame by a more random process. But the way people arrive in the top flights (or lower flights for that matter) is far more flexible than in, say, France, where the majority of jobs everywhere are secured by those who graduated from the Ecole Nationale d'Administration or the Ecole des Mines, with their fiercesome examination culture, or in the United States, where the system combines the motors of our own establishment creation with prodigious and often dynastic money making. The British system is not, as was argued in a book of best-selling absurdity by Owen Jones – an Oxford graduate – an intellectual conspiracy hatched and sustained by disciples of the free-market prophet Friedrich von Hayek. Men and women on the social democratic left, for example, embraced some of the disciplines of market economics because authoritarian socialism did not work and because it had the grave disadvantage in a democracy of being hugely unpopular because it was unsuccessful as well as bossy. On the political flipside, men and women of the right accepted the importance of the welfare state and occasional government intervention because these things were required for a successful and harmonious society. Where there was a consensus it was based more on sense than ideology, and of course like every other human enterprise it sometimes made dreadful mistakes. They were not, however, the sort of mistakes that undermined pluralism and created gulags.

Our own establishment has been based for fifty years or more principally on merit. That is not a pure and undefiled thing. Sometimes parentage, wealth and connections have helped; luck plays a part; so too willingness to take on the jobs offered that are sometimes well rewarded, sometimes lead to the award of a bauble or two, and sometimes bring with them nothing much more than the end of a private life and the derision of the media. It is also fair to say that there is little mercy when the merit that was assumed to exist in the recipient of an establishment position proves illusory. On the whole, however, the people who do the establishment's jobs are in my experience qualified to do them by ability. (We can all count the exceptions that prove this rule). The trouble is that the number of them who wish to run this or that for the rest of us and are capable of doing so is steadily diminishing. 'Jump into the pool with us,' we shout, trying to disguise the growing number of sharks' fins and the spreading pools of blood visible in the water.

So on the whole I think it is brain and effort that win the day. There are a lot of Oxbridge graduates at the top of every profession, including Owen Jones, because they had to be clever to get to those universities in the first place. When Beethoven was asked whether the 'van' in his name suggested that he was a landowner, he denied it with the brusque retort that he was a brain owner. Brain owners are far more likely to be running things today than in the middle years of the last century. It is striking how the spying scandals of the wartime and post-war years were incubated and protected from discovery by silver spoon old-boy networks. No more. Would a drunk and oafish spy like Guy Burgess today survive his outrageous behaviour simply because he had a cupboard full of old Etonian ties? Would Philby escape undetected for so long because his father was a senior member of the Indian Civil Service? Yet there is a different challenge for today's establishment. Meritocracy can be a pretty unattractive tyranny of the able, whatever its intentions, looking down on those whose merits are less visible or marketable. There is also an awkward truth about meritocracy in a society which is not growing or changing economically: for meritocracy to do what it says on the tin, some must go down the ladder as others climb it. This is not likely to be a message well received by middle-class parents. But if by meritocracy we mean above all advancement by ability then that is plainly better than other ways of ordering society today. Above all, to remain what it says it is, a meritocracy has to remain open; it must not become blind or indifferent to the importance of continuing to refresh itself by ensuring that talent can emerge from outside its own ranks and those of its families. The great American sociologist Daniel Bell argued for 'a well-tempered meritocracy'. This point has been very well argued too by the contemporary historian Lord Hennessy, who believes that the members of the establishment should remember where they came from, how much support from the public sector they required to achieve their present eminence and why they should work to increase the number of well-repaired ladders enabling others behind them to climb. They should recognize that too few women are able to make this ascent, and do more to put this right. And they must always show equality of esteem and respect for those who do not choose to climb to the top of the ladder or fail in the attempt. The social mobility problem in Britain is not how many members of the establishment went to a small number of our best universities, but how we can give more young men and women the opportunity to gain places at these universities without lowering the qualifications for admission. There is nothing wrong with elite educational institutions – indeed we should build more of them – provided access is open to the best, regardless of their background, and provided as well that these institutions bang the drum for social inclusion through the raising not lowering of standards.

4

'The Last Best Hope of Earth'

And not by eastern windows only,
    When daylight comes, comes in the light;
In front the sun climbs slow, how slowly!
    But, westward, look, the land is bright.

Arthur Hugh Clough,
'Say Not the Struggle Naught Availeth'

'The glamour of it all! New York! America!'

Charlie Chaplin

I never, of course, fluttered any Volscians in their dovecotes. But playing cricket I did occasionally have a good opening spell as a fast
bowler – there was for instance that morning on Balliol's cricket pitch
when I skittled the Gentlemen of Oxfordshire. A business friend of
Dad's came with us to that slap-up lunch at the Bear afterwards. I
was just a few weeks from my final exams and departure from the
dreaming spires. 'So,' the genial pal said, 'now you've made it. The
world's your oyster.'

But what exactly had I 'made'? My parents were so proud of what
their son had done at school that they had no real ideas of what
should or could come next; and the son for his part was too comfortable coasting and too timid to do anything daring. I had actually got
my unanticipated minor scholarship to Balliol at the age of sixteen,
and could have gone off for a gap year to learn French at a lycée in
Dijon or to study girls on a beach in Thailand. But no one ever really
suggested this or pressed me to do it, so I wasted a real chance to
broaden my horizons and stayed at school for another year, adding

rather unnecessarily to my A Level count, captaining the cricket team and the school, writing rather mannered essays, and traversing the foothills of young fogeydom with a Stuyvesant between the ends of my fingers. Now I had no excuses. I had to take a plunge. The apprenticeship was over. Life did not end at twenty-one; as Dad's friend Roy said, it began.

But began as what? I had no idea. I could make a pretty good fist of analysing the barons' motives at Runnymede or the downfall of Madame Roland and the Girondins, though I was not so hot on Disraeli and Gladstone and the Eastern Question. I could write passably funny sketches, songs and revues, and did quite a good camp impersonation of Queen Victoria. I was capable of charm and of making a speech. For what sort of career – ouch, the very thought of having to embark on a career – would that cut me out? I had made little effort to apply for jobs. I was turned down by two international advertising agencies, in one case discovering that they did not share my sense of humour. In their psychometric test, when replying to a Tom-fool question about what sort of animal or bird I might like to be, I responded by writing 'a seagull'. I answered the rest of the questions as though I was indeed a seagull. 'What do you most like doing?' 'Swooping low over the waves catching fish', etc. Plainly, I thought this funnier than the advertising agency did. Perhaps as a result of this experience I have never myself taken any interest whatsoever in these tests, relying on the whole on interviews, CVs and references. I have never tried to discover whether the job applicant might have preferred to be a mongoose. I had also applied for a graduate traineeship for the BBC for the year after my graduation. In the meantime, I would comfort myself with the fact that at Balliol I had won their equivalent of the lottery, a Coolidge Atlantic Crossing Fellowship. This was to prove the oyster, though I was not to know then exactly what sort of pearl lay inside.

These Coolidge fellowships were the first example of many I have now encountered of the astonishing generosity and imagination of much American philanthropy. Bill Coolidge, then in his sixties, was a Charter member of the Boston-Brahmins – rich by birth and then by shrewd investment. He had been at Harvard, then Balliol, and was a keen member of the Episcopalian Church. Bill was a bachelor and these institutions became the principal members of his family; each of them received shed-loads of his generosity. In the case of Balliol, the benefaction mainly took the form of the scholarships awarded to several members of the college each year for general all-round good chappery. Bill paid for you to travel by liner to New York, stay with him at his country estate in Massachusetts, drink quantities of his first growth claret, get kitted out at the Harvard Co-op – blazer, chinos, Oxford button-down shirts, brown penny loafers – and then set out with a Hertz credit card, 1,000 dollars renewable, and a list of Bill's friends and Balliol alumni around the United States who were prepared to put you up and show you around their city or state for a few days. We travelled in pairs; I went with Edward Mortimer to cover the United States anti-clockwise from Boston. Like Balliol, this trip was the making of me. Good fortune once again took me under its wing.

We travelled to New York in late June 1965, on the SS *France*, and learned for the first time how easily a patina of Oxonian self-confidence and the accent that went with it opened doors, in this case those to the liner's first-class bars and lounges. The trouble was that, despite the free frozen Daiquiris that my vowels earned me, the atmosphere up in First was far too formal: all white tuxedos worn by young men with licks of dark hair over their foreheads who looked as though they might be training for roles as Ripley gigolos in pursuit of American grand duchesses. I suspected that they did not tie their own black dickies. One evening of this was enough to persuade us that we were better off with the proletariat, who seemed to be having a rather better time without the tuxedos. Several passengers from First plainly felt the same, drifting past the stewards and across the class barriers to enjoy the cruise with the 'sans culottes'.

Two of our sailing companions conformed so much to type that their photos should have been stuck straight away in an album of our American safari. One was straight off the pages of Scott Fitzgerald or the *New Yorker*: his underwear probably came from Brooks Brothers; his Oxford cotton button-down shirts (just like the ones we were soon to purchase) and blue blazer certainly did. He was a great patriot and about our age. I remember his outrage that President Johnson's daughter chewed gum in class and that both his favourite Bowery

restaurant and his favourite Fifth Avenue clothes outfitter were closing down. I imagined he would become a banker in Wall Street in the
days before the barrow boys took it over. But I learned a couple of
years later that Bill was splattered over a Vietnamese paddy field like
so many others. I do not think that any other country produces an
exactly similar type: decent, likeable, beautifully mannered, a bit
reticent, old-fashioned, all too easy to caricature. Rather too many of
these young men, along with many more working-class American
boys, have died in the last century for what have often been primarily
other peoples' causes. The passenger who was for us an archetypal
American was John – the American in (or, strictly, from) Paris. He
exuded all the sophistication of a young man who had spent a year in
Montmartre living beyond the Place des Abbesses. John was returning to America to scandalize his friends with a trunk load of de Sade
and Henry Miller, naturally including the sexually explicit *Plexus*,
Nexus and *Sexus*, the last of which I had once sneaked a look at on
the shelves of a young woman reading Philosophy at St Anne's College while she was out of the room making a pot of Earl Grey. John
was in his mid-twenties, and had a rather world-weary manner that
was clearly a great turn-on for women. He appeared to have seen and
experienced most of what life had to offer, especially the racy and
louche. I could never manage this look myself, the hint of danger that
so many women love. Not everyone on board was as much fun as Bill
and John. One morning I had breakfast with a Swede who worked in
Welwyn Garden City, which he praised for its night life.

Many of the initial surprising impressions of a 21-year-old in
America have been borne out by scores of later visits (I suppose the
tally could have reached a hundred by now). For a start, while one of
course knows that Americans speak English, they sometimes speak
other languages too. Driving through Texas for instance on our journey in 1965 we encountered communities where German and Spanish
were languages of choice. Spanish is used increasingly as immigration
from Central and Latin America adds to the US population. An
increasing number of American politicians now feel it necessary to
know at least some Spanish. The use of German reflects the number
of German immigrants in the nineteenth and early twentieth centuries. The First World War reduced public enthusiasm for speaking the

German language. Despite the majority use of English, the visitor from Britain has to remind her- or himself continuously that America is a foreign country. In Athens, Ohio, I felt a greater sense of being foreign than in Athens, Greece. America was globalization on one continent, long before we became obsessed with the concept on every continent. How can the USA be both so global and so insular, an American identity made up of so many smaller parts? I sat one morning recently on Madison Avenue in the window of a deli near St Patrick's Cathedral and watched the office workers trudging past. How would they identify themselves first and foremost: Viet-namese Americans, New Yorkers, White Anglo-Saxon Protestants, Afro-Americans, Chinese Americans, maybe Black New Yorker Catholic Americans? Or perhaps they just thought that they were what it said in their passports – US citizens. Except, probably six out of ten would not have a passport, a lower figure than a few years back but still a lot higher than the figures for comparable countries, for example Canada's four out of ten or the UK's between two and three. Yet as the American seal says, borrowing from Cicero or St Augus-tine, 'E Pluribus Unum'. Despite mostly coming from abroad in their recent ancestry, many Americans are surprisingly uninterested in what happens beyond America's shores. Julian Barnes once noted that if you want your country to disappear before your eyes just visit the United States and open a newspaper. Though many Americans speak (up to a point) their diaspora languages, they do not appear to be very good or particularly interested linguists. I suppose that, like my own fellow citizens, they are spoilt. As the world speaks English, why speak Italian, French or Japanese?

This paradox of being a kaleidoscope of national, racial, linguistic and religious identities, and being (still, for the moment) the world's biggest economy and its political and security leader, while at the same time being pretty dubious about having too much to do with abroad, is a main reason why America is not, never was and never will be an empire like Rome. This forms part of America's ineffable charm and attraction. It is an emporium but generally not an imper-ium. It can be missionary; fight in far-flung deserts and swamps; sell to the world; try to teach the world as Athens taught Greece. But it does not really become enthusiastic about speaking the local dialect, mastering other people's customs, or coping with diarrhoea, as the British did in their day. America would have needed scores of universities educating imperial administrators to change this, and plane-loads of American Lord Milners would have been thoroughly bad for the world. Far better the America we have had than the America that some think might have served us better, more worldly-wise and know-all. American naivety is a quality from which we have often benefited.

Perhaps America has always been a little uncomfortable with the world because it has its work cut out feeling comfortable with all the different parts of itself. As Edward and I discovered in the summer of 1965 in our Hertz-rented Dodge Dart, it is so damned big. We drove quite a bit of it on those wonderful roads built under President Eisenhower's National Defense Highway Act, a huge Republican public works programme. We flew over large tracts of the continent in between our stopping-off points – high over the Little Big Horn from Chicago to Billings, Montana – at which point we realized how far away Boston, New York, and Washington were. There is an old Chinese saying: 'The sky is big and the emperor is far away.' The same is true of America. No wonder so many American politicians like the Democratic Speaker Tip O'Neill opined that all politics is local. It surely was in Billings or Salt Lake City, our next stop. Only the other day, a very clever young American D.Phil. student at Oxford, now a member of the State Department, confessed to me that he had never been to Washington.

The foreignness of America is manifested in its food and in its sport. I recall my first encounter with a prawn cocktail and a T-bone steak at an eatery in Ohio. The prawns, large and tasteless, were deluged in pink gunge and served in frosted glass the size of a flower vase. The steak would have fed a small village in the developing world. At the other extreme you find the celebration of all natural ingredients, accompanied, or rather drizzled, by pretentious descriptions. The famous Alice Walters restaurant in Berkeley, Chez Panisse, announces the distinction between a Tom Thumb and an Iceberg lettuce as though it really mattered. Human shapes more than anywhere else I have been reflect class. The poor are often large on fast food, the rich trim on all those green salads, vitamin tablets and gym subscriptions. American protein consumption caused a diplomatic row when the second President Bush noted (correctly) that the cost of meat was increasing around the world partly because economic development in Asia meant that more Indians and Chinese were eating it. Indian politicians were apoplectic, noting that the consumption by their fellow citizens was chop size compared to the haunches eaten by Americans. American waiters, terribly over-tipped in posh restaurants, are more patronizing and unctuous even than in Paris. After I ordered skate in a New York restaurant the waiter opined, 'What a very European choice.' I did not make myself any more popular by asking to his confusion what this meant.

America's most iconic sports – baseball and American football – are hardly played elsewhere, though basketball is played in countries which can find enough giants to excel at the sport. Some soccer has been infiltrated into the American psyche, giving its name to a particular sort of middle-class mother and being played exceptionally well by American women themselves. I was first taken to a baseball game by a professional American diplomat, Ray Seitz, one of the smartest public servants I have known, who eventually became the US ambassador in London. It is one of those deceptive games where clearly a great deal more is happening than the amateur eye can detect. It is also a game, like cricket, which provides boundless fascination for those interested in the statistics of sporting warfare. I was once treated to a lecture on baseball by the great Socratic Harvard philosopher Michael Sandel which jumped enthusiastically from one decimal point to another. None of it made as great an impression on me as Sandel's assertion that the common, socially binding experience of attending a game (queuing for the lavatory, eating cheese-burgers, getting drenched in the rain) had been lost with the introduction of special seating and boxes for sponsors and the rich.

I have not enjoyed my experience of watching American football as much as baseball. It is a game in which long, static periods are interrupted by sudden flurries of athleticism; as it were, board meetings punctuated by well-organized violence. This game of football is extremely popular at universities and is indeed one of the ways in which alumni are bound into their alma maters. Going to speak at the University of Oklahoma, where a Balliol contemporary and former Governor and senator, David Boren, was president, I was shown the university football stadium, which had a crowd capacity of almost 90,000. The funding of football at American universities is huge, and not without controversy. There is a great deal of criticism of the treatment of large kids from poor, often black backgrounds, who often contract serious injuries while playing football and end up with a free but not very useful or extensive education. But my favourite American football university, Notre Dame in Indiana, is not like that. Football is important there: the team – known as 'the fighting Irish' – has a great reputation, and a mural of the resurrection of Jesus, arms upraised, which overlooks the stadium, is known as 'Touchdown Jesus'. But you do not get the impression that everything else at the university takes second place to football. Notre Dame successfully asserts its academic personality as both a centre of scholarship and as a genuinely Christian (indeed Catholic) foundation with more than a generation of commitment to the improvement of civil rights in the United States.

Even the greatest empires fall, often, as Herodotus argued (when writing about the Lydians, the Babylonians, the Egyptians and the Persians), because they grow soft. Countries with tried and tested constitutional arrangements can be undermined from within, by personal ambition for instance. Cicero died in part for making this argument in Rome. They can also be weakened by a failure to understand their complex, beautifully constructed political symmetry, a point understood by Bagehot in the middle of the nineteenth century as Britain floundered to adapt its own unwritten constitution to changing needs: 'all our pomp of yesterday ... is ... one with Nineveh and Tyre', as Kipling put it so elegiacally. American experience itself shows how successful political establishments and economic settlements can be weakened by ideology, by simple, sharp-edged ideas that appear to explain everything. One of President Reagan's favourite jokes, going back to the days when he was paid as a motivational speaker by General Electric, and polished when he supported Barry Goldwater's presidential campaign in 1964, captured the dogma perfectly. 'The scariest words in America,' he used to say to loud laughter and applause, are 'I'm from the government and I'm here to help you.' This crowd-pleasing right-wingery, so reactionary as to be beyond conservatism, was pulled into an extremely influential and beautifully delivered speech entitled 'A Time for Choosing'. It was delivered just before Goldwater went down in flames in his contest against Lyndon Johnson. A principal reason for Goldwater's defeat was his apparent advocacy of the use of nuclear weapons to end the Vietnam War. Reagan's scintillating speech dealt with war and peace in rich, 1930s anti-appeasement language. Moses and Jesus Christ were called on to support the Goldwater military doctrine. The main part of the speech went on to assemble all the artillery of anti-state rhetoric that was to become the Bible for the right wing of the Republican Party for the next fifty years. It was one of the most influential speeches ever given by an American politician. It helped to catapult the originally New Deal Democrat into the governorship of California as a Republican and not long after into the presidency, defeating Jimmy Carter, one of America's greatest ex-presidents.

For a political hack like me, the Reagan speech later became a masterclass in drafting simple and effective rhetoric and delivering it, like the great performer Reagan was. I thoroughly disagreed with it, but it was beautifully crafted. Reagan was pitch perfect, infusing traditional, very conservative themes with the Messianic libertarian, market economics of the Russian-American writer Ayn Rand. The speech contrasted not right and left, but up and down: up – freedom; down – totalitarianism. There seemed to be no mezzanine floor. According to Reagan, America was confronted by an assault on liberty. Government was set on trying to solve misery, as if such a thing was humanly possible. Many of those whom it was claimed were going to bed in America hungry every night were feeling peckish because they were on diets. Departments in Washington were the nearest things on earth to examples of eternal life. At home the US faced the advance of socialism; abroad, subservient as it was to the United Nations General Assembly, it could face a millennium of darkness unless it pulled its socks up. Reagan's speech is not for the squeamish.

What is interesting is how different that sort of brilliant reactionary tosh was from the way Reagan behaved in office. Johnson had probably pushed domestic spending programmes too far and was certainly wrong to try to fight the Vietnam War and increase social spending at the same time, without calling for any sacrifice from tax-payers. But the slash-and-burn rhetoric about the size and spending of the state was light years from Reagan's actual deeds. His great strengths as a politician were geniality, the clever choice of colleagues like George Shultz, and his ability to radiate self-confidence and hope: hope, that sublime four-letter word. This was certainly not accompanied by a blitzkrieg on the state and the spending needed to maintain its institutions. Reagan was a big spender – one of the biggest – in the last few years, supported by Congress. The annual growth of federal spending was 8.7 per cent in Reagan's first term, 4.9 per cent in his second. Federal spending as a proportion of national income was higher than under his predecessor, Jimmy Carter, and the federal budget deficit rose from $997 billion to $2.85 trillion. These levels of deficit spending and especially debt were not surprisingly regarded by Reagan (at least rhetorically) as the 'greatest disappointment' of his presidency. They helped to fuel a long period of unbalanced economic expansion but also to solidify the associa-tion of Reagan with happy days. The man from the government really did seem to have come along to help. Reagan went on whistling cheer-fully as he ambled past the cemetery of his ideology. It was left to President Clinton to bring spending growth to less than 4 per cent and produce budget surprises. Obama's spending growth figures are lower still – not surprising, perhaps, given the financial crisis which began shortly before he was elected.

Why dwell on Reagan and his philosophy – Hayek out of Disneyland – when writing about the 1960s? Because whatever Republican presidents may have done in practice – and both Bushes were big spenders too – they were tossed politically like corks on the waves of anti-government, deregulatory, anti-tax rhetoric, as were their Democrat opponents. The deficits on the whole went up; the regulatory restraints came down. Too many Americans came to believe that the land of the free had defined itself and earned its glory days through individualism alone, through rejecting a role for the state in America's life. They were evangelized to believe that any gov-ernment action was a step towards socialist tyranny. This argument has been a damaging historical fraud. It has nothing to do with real conservatism, but everything to do with the defence of plutocracy, a refusal to accept the costs of citizenship, and populism: in other words, with the steadily growing extremism of the Republican Party as its historic patrician core has been hollowed out. The intuitive traditional understanding of balance in the Republican Party – balance between the state and citizens, between taxing and spending, between international engagement and the national interest – was over time replaced in large part by the fanciful faith of the Tea Party and the very special interests of plutocrats and lobbyists.

The America that we travelled in 1965 was enjoying (with one huge exception) the fruits of the conservatism of President Eisenhower's 1950s, the long Age of Ike, which baked in the successful economic and social advances of the New Deal. Eisenhower, a great organizing general and a fine president, had read enough history and was a wise enough man to know that the 'city on a hill' had not been built just by individual sweat and prayer. It owed much to community solidarity and state action directed by effective politicians. George Washington's chief aide and Secretary of the Treasury, Alexander Hamilton, led the way. A believer in strong central government, he promoted industry, commerce and banking. A century later, (Republican) President Teddy Roosevelt took on the robber barons of American minerals, commodities, railroads and banking. He regulated monopolies and used anti-trust legislation to break them up. Fast-forward to the ending of the Depression with (Democrat) President Franklin Roosevelt's New Deal with an active government intervening in the economy to promote growth, jobs and the construction of a modern infrastructure. Eisenhower did not regard this as an assault on freedom. A wise conservative, he recognized, like Deng Xiaoping almost thirty years later, that pragmatism which delivered the goods trumped ideology that filled the seminar halls. So the 1950s brought huge housing and highway programmes, the financing of great universities, the support of new technologies through the defence budget – the core technologies of the digital economy, semi-conductors, computing, jet aviation. Federal spending under Eisenhower as a proportion of national wealth was double the figure it had been under Roosevelt. These were the best times for the white middle class of the American dream. And the middle class thrived as income equality advanced. The financial sector represented

3.7 per cent of the economy; today that stands at 8.5 per cent. Then a US chief executive was paid thirty times the average pay in his company; today that figure is well above 300.

It is particularly interesting to see what happened to income equality in those days. The internationally accepted measure for determining this is called the Gini coefficient. Everyone accepts its credibility to such an extent that some like the Chinese try to cheat on the figures, worried about what they tell the world about the real nature of socialism with Chinese characteristics. Named after an Italian statistician with fascist sympathies, the Gini coefficient operates on the basis that if one person in a country had all the resources and no one else possessed anything, the index would be 1. If on the other hand, the country's resources were spread evenly between everyone the index would be 0. The index in America dropped between 1947 and 1974, after which it began to climb. When Edward Mortimer and I were in the United States, it was falling to its lowest ever level, touching the bottom figure of 0.386 in 1968. By 2013, the index had climbed to 0.476, the highest figure for any prosperous democracy. These figures, which seem so prosaic, measure pretty accurately variations of inequality. We can consider later the consequences of income inequality in the United States, but for the present I simply want to make the point that for most people – certainly for white citizens – America was a fairer society in the 1950s and 1960s than it is today. Fairer and probably more content: Americans were living 'the Dream'. Today, George Carlin has argued that the reason why it is called 'the American Dream' is because you have to be asleep to believe it.

In 1965 we went from one community of wide-awake Americans to another; 'the Dream' looked like life in one of the television comedies that emanated from Hollywood. 'Suburbanophilia' celebrated happy families living in comfortable homes full of the latest gadgets – televisions, washing machines and air conditioning – surrounded by manicured lawns and white paling fences, and with front porches onto which paper boys cycling past would toss the morning's edition of the *Buffalo Bugle*. One morning I saw this happen! The family in *I Love Lucy* admittedly lived in an apartment, but we all know what they represented, happy families and happy days. Gradually the love affair with this middle-class suburban life was challenged by novelists and moviemakers. The oppression of suburban wives, even the prospect of invasion by alien body snatchers, cast shadows over the idyll. What we saw on our tour of the country was its apogee. Suburbs, shopping malls, spired clapboard churches – these were comfortable neighbourhoods joined physically by a great highway system and spiritually by the intensity of America's sense of community.

This America was the product of a combination of 'can do' entrepreneurial energy and pragmatic government intervention. Unlike Jeremy Bentham, Eisenhower and those who worked with him did not have a prior assumption that government intervention was generally 'needless and pernicious'. As the President once wrote to his brother Edgar, 'to attain any success it is quite clear that the Federal Government cannot avoid or escape responsibilities which the mass of people firmly believe should be undertaken by it'. The Federal Housing Agency helped build the homes; the Highway Trust Fund met most of the cost of constructing the Interstate Highway System. In the background a tightly regulated banking system provided the cash to finance commerce and home ownership. What was good for Wall Street really was good for Main Street – because Wall Street was hemmed in by restrictions to make it boring and safe, and avoid the bubbles, panics and crashes that had periodically shattered lives and business and set back the economy.

What happened? In the 1980s (though it started earlier) Hayekian Austrian economics captured the commanding heights of public debate, often supported by rich men's money and financial service lobbyists. Rules introduced to make bank deposits safe, to control stock markets tightly, and to keep investment banking and commercial banking separate were scrapped. The repeal of the Glass–Steagall Act (passed in the 1930s to separate commercial and investment banking) in 1999 enabled banks to take on ever greater risks with ever less oversight. This was the biggest of all the changes in the thousands of cuts in regulations that led to gunslinger banking and the crash of 2007–8. There had been no crash like it since the Second World War: a reason perhaps for taking very small helpings of ideological spinach. Moreover, all this deregulatory frenzy was accompanied by growing inequality in the United States. As the incomes of middle America were squeezed, families and individuals made up for the fact that they had less disposable income by borrowing on a vast scale, encouraged by banks and others through a range of arcane but dodgy instruments, especially tied to house purchase. Household debt increased from $680 billion in 1974 to $14 trillion in 2008, including a doubling between 2001 and 2008. By that date, householders possessed on average thirteen credit cards. Alongside this steep increase, federal debt soared as well, to over $10 trillion by the year's end. Americans were spending far more than they earned, and the country as a whole was doing the same, becoming the world's biggest debtor, the global borrower of last resort. It is difficult to command the world's respect when you are so dependent on borrowing what other countries are earning in order to pay for what you are spending. It undermined America's global leadership. But the banks were happy; bankers were prodigiously well-paid; and the larger banks provided the high command for the Washington establishment. Democratic government had perhaps become in reality the cash nexus to which Thomas Carlyle argued capitalism had reduced all social relationships.

If a large section of American society seemed happier in the 1960s than it is today, that sense of middle-class well-being did not extend to families with a black skin. In the diary I kept of our visit I note today that I sometimes referred to African-Americans as negroes, not then regarded as anything but a conventional and polite description. In his great speech 'I have a dream' in 1963, Martin Luther King used the word several times. But as the 1960s and 1970s wore on, the Civil Rights Movement came to prefer other descriptions of black identity. African-American was one of them, though a journalist friend of mine, himself the descendant of slaves, refuses to use this term about himself, having spent several years as chief correspondent for his paper in Africa during some of the worst atrocities on that continent in both Rwanda and Somalia: he wants to be regarded as an American, not an African-American. Even the most sensitive souls these days, meaning no offence, can find themselves in hot water when they appear to put a foot wrong on this issue. A white English actor advancing an argument well disposed to actors who did not share his colour, referred to 'coloured people' when he should apparently have said 'people of colour'. He beat, poor man, an embarrassed retreat. No one should want to give offence describing other, too often oppressed or disadvantaged, racial groups, indeed one should lean over backwards to avoid it. But this can, I suspect, be an area in which some hunt out offence where none was ever intended in an excessively prickly assertion of identity. I hope that my three mixed-race grandchildren, smart, feisty, beautiful kids, will grow up in a society where sensitivities about these issues have been marginalized by equity of respect and opportunity. Where I admire the work of the British organization Black Boys Can, I observe that the boys are indeed black, but the problem is that (to take the grammatical distinction mentioned earlier) at the moment while they can, they may not because too often their background condemns them to an inferior secondary education.

In 1960s America, we witnessed terrible evidence that the American dream did not encompass the black, African-American community. Martin Luther King's dream that out of a 'mountain of despair' it should be possible to hew a 'stone of hope', with the call for freedom ringing from the top of every mountain and hilltop from Stone Mountain of Georgia to the hills and molehills of Mississippi, was very far from fulfilment. The valleys were not yet exalted, nor the hills and mountains laid low.

We saw this in two places in particular: Los Angeles and Alabama. We arrived in Los Angeles in late August and went first to the charmingly tasteless Forest Lawn Memorial Park, which boasted not only a replica of the Wee Kirk o' the Heather where Annie Laurie waited and prayed through that long and turgid Scottish ballad, but also what was apparently the biggest reproduction of Leonardo da Vinci's painting of the Last Supper in America and presumably in the world. It was curious to be in a cemetery in which over a quarter of a million were buried where, nevertheless, the very idea of death had, as in much of America's culture, passed, moved on, departed, gone to a better place. We went from there to a place that was definitely not better, the suburb of Watts. Riots had broken out the week before we arrived in southern California, following the arrest of an African-American motorist. Six days of looting and arson followed. We went into the suburbs of mostly detached run-down bungalows, described by some Angelinos as 'a decent slum', the day after most of the

National Guard were withdrawn. This area, Watts, still bore all the marks of violence – walls pock-marked by bullets, burning over-turned cars, smashed shop windows. There were knots of young black men, frequently drunk, on the street corners. We had seen worse signs of urban deprivation in Chicago, but there was no doubt that it was a pretty grim and impoverished area, where already high levels of unemployment were made worse by a steady influx from the poorer, rural South.

It was far worse in Alabama, where Jim Crow, racial segregation, was sovereign. In 1957, Vice-President Nixon had been invited by the Prime Minister, Kwame Nkrumah, to Ghana's independence celebra-tions. At an official reception it is said that the Vice-President went over to speak to a group of black guests. 'It must be great,' he said, 'to be citizens of a country where you can now vote in freedom for your own government.' 'I don't know what that must be like,' one of them replied. 'We are from Alabama.' The Civil Rights Movement was still fighting in 1965 to get voting rights for African-Americans as well as equal treatment to that of their white fellow citizens across the board. In Washington, with a mixture of legislative aplomb and political bullying, President Johnson was himself battling reactionary forces in the Senate and the House of Representatives on those ques-tions. This was to be his greatest triumph. But we turned up in an Alabama city as guests of a courtly newspaper editor while the battle was still joined. We had flown in from New Orleans and collected our rental car at the airport, not noticing that it had Pennsylvania number plates. (We probably wouldn't have realized the significance anyway.) Stopping in the car a day or so later at a bar, the place fell ominously silent as we walked up to the counter, Beatle haircuts and English accents. Fortunately, our host was with us and followed us in. 'Don't worry, boys,' he said loudly. 'They are English. They're not from the north. They are just like us.' Not long before this, civil rights campaigners from the north had been shot down, and there had been a number of students from universities in Pennsylvania among them, campaigning for black rights. We were lucky our host was with us.

We spent two or three days with him. A widower, I think, he was looked after by black servants and driven by one of them to the office. He explained the protocol of this. He could not sit beside his black driver, a woman, in the front of the car; if he was driving, the servant had to sit in the back. If there were three people in the car, including one white female and two blacks, the latter would sit in the front rather than having black and white thighs in any sort of clothed proximity. He was a gentle, well-read, likeable man, ran what was for the times and the community a pretty moderate newspaper, and had no truck with the Ku Klux Klan or violent prejudices. But he was not going to challenge the old culture of Confederacy politics: change might need to come, but it could not be hurried. Maybe all men were created equal – and should be able to go to the same schools, clamber on to the same buses, eat in the same restaurants, sleep in the same motels as one another. But it would take time to bring this about. Dignity could be acquired in a dignified way, step by step. He wanted 'the rough places to be made plain, and the crooked places made straight', but perhaps not just yet. He was a good and decent man, a kind man, and it was easier to think that you knew what he should be doing than to be in his position yourself. When you're able to move on, it is plain sailing to be more courageous than those who have to stay behind, anchored in their own cultures and communities. Self-righteousness is a curse of the judgemental liberal.

So the great stain on America's honour in the 1960s was race. Could I have imagined then that just over forty years later a black man would be President? I was in Hong Kong on the night that news of Barack Obama's victory came through in November 2008. So too was Colin Powell – we were both making speeches there. He came up to my hotel room to have a drink afterwards and watch the results. He was pretty emotional, as far as generals allow themselves to be. It was not difficult to sympathize: 'Free at last.' Except that Obama had to cope throughout his presidency with a slick of racism in the water behind his ship of state. Racism was not dead and buried, as we were to see in the run-up to, and in the course of, Donald Trump's electoral triumph.

I worked closely with Colin Powell when I was a European Commissioner; I had already had a couple of years working with his predecessor, Madeleine Albright, the Secretary of State in the Clinton administration, especially on the Balkans after the Kosovo War. We rarely had any differences of opinion with her. She was smart, firm in her views and charming; she was particularly kind to me, Europe's Commissioner for External Affairs, very aware that I was suddenly playing in a league of big hitters. I remember she loved jewellery, particularly big brooches. I told her about a little shop in Brussels which sold classic costume jewellery (where I bought Lavender a few pieces) and she used to visit the shop every time she came to Brussels. I would then enjoy seeing her wearing her spectacular purchases. Like others in American administrations, she was sometimes both frustrated and puzzled that the European Union found it so difficult to adopt quickly, and stick to, common positions.

The relationship with Colin Powell, Madeleine's successor in the Bush team, was more difficult. This was not because of him. He was one of the most decent and intelligent people I have ever met. The three people I have met who most exuded grace and natural authority were all African or of African heritage – Nelson Mandela, Kofi Annan and Colin Powell. The problem for Powell was that he was serving an administration which was doing some pretty crazy things. He never birked the task of defending the Bush administration, though I sometimes felt that there was a hint in his body language of what he really thought. It undoubtedly undermined his ability to speak up for sense that the Blair government was such a gung-ho supporter of some of the wilder Bush–Cheney schemes, above all in Iraq. I always assumed that there was something about being a soldier which made Powell go along with his commander-in-chief, even when he disagreed with the policy. On one occasion, when I was in Washington, a columnist on the local paper, the *Post*, wrote an article saying that European policy in the Middle East was anti-Semitic. I wrote a strong, angry rebuttal, which the paper published. Two days later I was being driven through Madrid to a meeting with the Spanish Prime Minister, José María Aznar. My mobile phone rang. It was the US State Department. The operator said, 'I have the Secretary of State for you.' He came immediately on the line. 'Great piece in the *Post* today,' he said. I would have had no difficulty following this general over the top.

From Alabama and then Texas, Edward and I headed north for New York and at about this time Edward decided that he should go back to Oxford to sit the All Souls Prize Fellowship Exam. He had already got a congratulatory first-class degree, like getting a homerun at baseball or a century before lunch at cricket in a Test match at Lord's. To win in addition the All Souls Fellowship (which he did in due course) would be like doing both back to back. Edward's wholly understandable decision left me with a quandary: should I cut short my time in the United States and return home with him or should I stay on alone and find something else to do? I consulted Bill Coolidge and his formidable personal assistant, Mary, who handled the nuts and bolts of the scholarship programme, also acting as a kind but forceful aunt to its beneficiaries. Bill immediately suggested that I should go and see a friend of his in New York, who was fund-raising for the newly announced Republican candidate for the mayoralty, John Lindsay, and see if there was an opening for me on his campaign staff. There was. So I joined the team, working out of the Roosevelt Hotel on Madison Avenue and East 45th, and was offered a room in a mostly unoccupied apartment on 5th Avenue and 69th. This was another example of rather casually winning one of life's lotteries, and it not only changed my life, but sent it off in the direction that has carried me all the way to writing this book.

John Lindsay was a tall, good-looking Yale graduate and lawyer who had been elected for the so-called silk-stocking district of Man-hattan (the Upper East Side) as a very moderate, independent-minded Republican congressman. He was sufficiently moderate to attract the support of New York's small Liberal Party and the scathing hostility of the equally small but noisy Conservative Party. His main opponent was a machine Democrat called Abraham Beame, and as ever in New York it was the Democrats' race to lose. The motto of Lindsay's campaign was taken from a local journalist: 'He is fresh and everyone else is tired.' More imaginatively, Times Square had an advertisement in lights stating, as Mary Poppins might have said, that Lindsay was 'supercalifragilisticexpialidocious'.

Lindsay had assembled a team of sparky young men and women who went on to all sorts of glittering careers from politics to direct-ing the Metropolitan Museum. I worked for a clever and charming graduate of Yale and Balliol, a lawyer from Texas called Sherwin Goldman. We prepared much of the briefing for Lindsay's debates. Sherwin provided my first education in politics and a rolling seminar on New York. Civilized and well-read, he took me around town: jazz clubs, best restaurants, American Ballet Theatre, the Frick. I had a daily tutorial in politics, and evening and weekend seminars during a glorious East Coast autumn on New York's contribution to civilization. Sherwin went on to become a successful impresario, helped run the New York City Opera and the Glimmerglass Opera Festival, gave my youngest daughter a backstage job at the City Opera before she went up to Cambridge, and – a happy finale – married his male partner once the law caught up with love. He has been a lifelong friend and would be surprised to know how great an effect he has had on my life. To my surprise, young and inexperienced as I was, I was taken seriously, greatly enjoyed what I was doing and found that I was good at it. I had found politics, or, rather, politics had found me.

John Lindsay was a wonderful campaigner, never fearful of plunging into a crowd, however hostile it might be. He won the election and then, with a transport strike on his first day in office, had two torrid terms in Gracie Mansion. New York at the time was well-nigh ungovernable, drowning in debt and regularly capsized by awful unions. One of the best things that Lindsay was able to do was to keep the lid on the racial tensions which boiled over into riots in other cities in the late 1960s and early 1970s, a consequence in part of white, middle-class flight from city centres and growing deprivation, drug-dealing and crime there. This success was partly a result of Lindsay's own personality and courage in dealing with incipient racial hostility. Lindsay graced politics but was probably better at getting elected than at governing. His journey across the political landscape eventually carried him all the way into the Democratic Party.

He had begun his career in a Republican Party which still provided a home for conservatives with moderate views and a justified suspicion of ideology. Until the election of Bobby Kennedy as a New York senator in January 1965, there had been two Republican senators there, Keating and Javits, both of them internationalist moderates. The state's Governor was Nelson Rockefeller. I rather doubt whether any of them could get chosen these days as a Republican candidate. Again and again over the following years traditional Republicans were stalked by right-wing zealots and cut down. As the party's base became narrower, and the number of its party supporters diminished, the power of a fairly small band of militant activists became all the greater. This is a familiar pattern in democratic politics. Parties that lose mass support become prey to extremists. They become ripe for a wholesale takeover. That was eventually what happened to the Republican Party: taken over by a master of the process, with too few sensible leaders and members around shouting 'caveat emptor'.

During that summer of 1965, and working with American politicians in later years, there was no doubt which country in the world was top dog. Hubert Védrine, President Mitterand's adviser and later French foreign minister, used to talk about American *hyper-puissance*. It rested on a combination of economic strength, demography, public support and the will of successive leaders and the establishment that they commanded.

American economic power has been formidable. The USA, with 4–5 per cent of the world's population, has accounted for between 20 and over 30 per cent of the world's economic output for over 130 years. Partly because of their large populations, other countries have begun to catch up to the overall size of the American economy, but in terms of wealth per head they are still well behind. China – whose economy may now be bigger than America's by some measures – has one fifth of America's wealth per head. Moreover, the rise of other countries is to a considerable extent because they have benefited from the economic structures that the United States more than any other country began to put in place over sixty years ago, and because America has been such an open market for them. China's exports to America grew by 1,600 per cent in one fifteen-year period at the height of that country's breakneck growth spurt either side of the millennium. When I first visited the United States, its economy was about 36–7 per cent of the world's. Today that figure stands at about 22 per cent. That is mainly an indication of how well the rest of the world has done, not – pace President Trump – how badly America has performed. So if you are placing a bet on who is going to stay Number One, it must make sense to follow Damon Runyon's rule. 'The race is not always to the swift,' he wrote, 'nor the battle to the strong – but that's the way to bet.' Big economies, with great wealth per head of population, take some beating.

The United States, of course, made a huge contribution to the defeat of Nazi Germany and Japan in the Second World War; many Americans died in Europe and Asia, and America's naval might and industrial muscle were especially significant factors in eventual victory. In comparison with America, which only endured a direct attack on its territory in Hawaii, others took a heavier toll in human casualties and economic destruction. Ninety times as many people from the Soviet Union died – 27 million – as from the USA during the Second World War, and almost no one died in the USA from military action. Theodore von Laue, the brilliant German-American historian, whose Nobel Prize-winning physicist father was a hiking companion of Albert Einstein, sketched the political scene in 1945 in his book *The World Revolution of Westernization*: 'At the end of the war, the United States was the only belligerent physically untouched by battle, its prosperity and system of government enhanced and its power in the world unprecedented. Whatever the country's post-war stance, it had earned its pre-eminence in the world thanks not only to its civic virtues – much advertised at the time – but also to the privileged historic conditioning and geographical advantage that had made possible its immense cultural resources (including its virtues).'

The key to America's post-war leadership was responsible magnanimity, exemplified by the Marshall Plan. Naturally, this leadership was accompanied occasionally by almost as much hypocrisy and as many double standards as the Victorians had displayed. Democracy in other countries was never as popular in Washington when it produced left-wing governments. Sanctimoniousness travels far and wide without a passport. Equally, America's role on the world stage was accompanied by criticism both from those who thought that America should do or give more, and by those who believed that it should do less. Sometimes both criticisms were deployed simultaneously. The left was very partial to this behaviour, so too in particular the French, who often seemed to be arguing in the same paragraph that the Americans should both be providing more assistance and not providing it at all. Why was America's cheque not much larger, and why did Washington demean beneficiaries by offering it? Yet, overall, America behaved like no victor before or since. It set itself the task of building a better global order whose rules should apply to the victor

. My handsome parents on their honeymoon in 1938.

. 1930s style: Dad (third from the right in the back row), the drummer in the smartly dressed hil Richardson Band.

3. My sister Angela, with her younger brother and the brick inglenook fireplace, symbol of Greenford's aspiring middle class.

4. The holidays of an English childhood on a Devon beach with my parents.

5. Greenford Broadway in the 1950s – we turned right at the Red Lion pub for church and school.

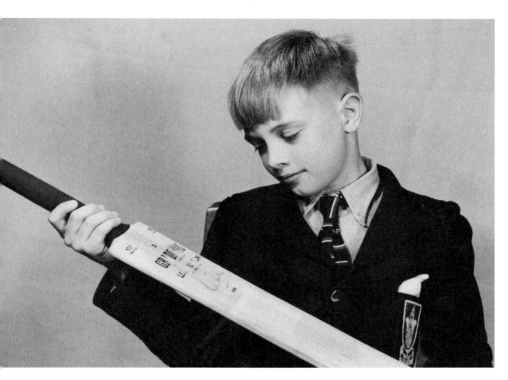

Gazing lovingly at my cricket bat, which scored many imaginary centuries.

Plastered in Brylcream, I lead the May procession at Our Lady of the Visitation, Greenford.

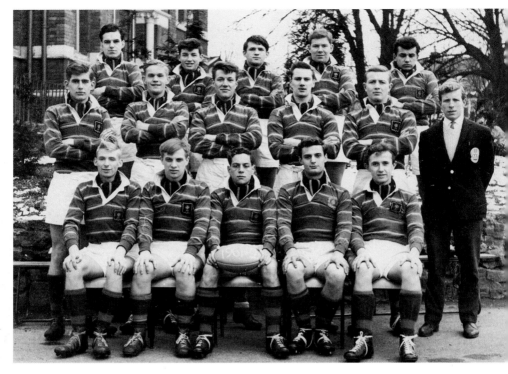

8. The keen young rugby player at the right hand of the ball-carrying skipper.

9. The school prefects of St Benedict's, Ealing. I am on the left at the back, sporting a new Brillo-style crew-cut. Father Brown, left of centre, memorably described Thomas a Becket as bowling Henry II a googly.

10. Matriculating in 1962. Balliol College, political nursery.

11. *L'étonnant* Richard Cobb, who almost always took his fluids.

12. The chivalrous Maurice Keen. 'I b-b-beg your pardon?'

13. The young MP and family (from the left, Lavender, Laura, Kate and Alice). Vote for us!

14. The 'Blue Chip' dining club of MPs – a happy mix of toffs and scholarship boys. Clockwise from the left: Robert Cranborne, Richard Needham, Jocelyn Cadbury, Chris Patten, John Patten, William Waldegrave, Alex Pollock, Nicholas Lyell, Peter Fraser, Robert Atkins, Tristan Garel-Jones and Michael Ancram.

15. Ted Heath in 1975 – despite the sticker, forty-one years later we didn't. His passion for Europe was the best of him.

16. Rab Butler, the Mount Fuji of the Tory Party. I carried a photograph of him from office to office.

17. Peter Carrington, the best natural leader I ever worked for.

18. Waving from a window in Conservative Central Office with John and Norma Major on the night of 9 April 1992. We had just won the election and I had just lost my seat.

19. With the Prime Minister and well-wishers in Downing Street the next day. The Conservatives had won more votes than any other party in British political history.

as well as the vanquished. (The major exception to this was America's refusal to participate in the international court system.)

It was generous in shaping its strategy and in supporting it with dollars. After the First World War, despite Woodrow Wilson's fourteen points to make the world better and safer (the American democratic response to Lenin), America had gone home, not wanting to be entangled again in Europe's civil wars. The result was another European civil war. In 1945, President Truman and his colleagues recognized that it would be dangerous to do the same again. America's security was closely tied to Europe's, especially with the communist Soviet Union on the rampage. The worry, however, was that, if the USA retained a military presence in Europe without the Europeans sorting out their historic arguments, young Americans might once again find themselves fighting and dying to stop Europeans killing one another. There was an implicit bargain. America would work with its Western European Allies to open the NATO umbrella, whose purpose (according to its first British Secretary-General, Lord Ismay) was 'To keep the Americans in, the Russians out, and the Germans down.' In return, Europe would put behind it the decades of xenophobic nationalism that had led to two world wars. The original architects of what was to become the European Union were much better received in post-war Washington than London, as they hatched the plans for a historic reconciliation between France and Germany, with these countries lashed together at the heart of a European structure which belatedly Britain asked to join in 1961, the year before I went to Oxford. General de Gaulle vetoed Britain's bid for a second and seemingly decisive time two years after my trip to the USA.

America's policy in Europe in the second half of the twentieth century was the greatest success story for its post-war geo-strategy – Western European countries helped the USA put in place global institutions and agreements like the United Nations, the Bretton Woods organizations and the WTO. In return, America gave great financial support through Marshall Aid for the rebuilding of Europe from the rubble of war. This assistance helped Europe not only to re-establish its industrial base and rebuild its cities, but to sustain alongside them the entitlement programmes that were at the heart of welfare democracy. The success of America's strategy in Europe came eventually with the collapse of the Soviet Union and its Central and Eastern European empire. The Soviet Union fell, with its armaments still intact, because it simply did not work as a model which gave its citizens a decent life, nor as a way of government which attracted others – if they had much of a choice in the matter – to try to replicate it.

Outside Europe, American policy was less effective. True, the case for capitalism, the rule of law and democracy slowly won converts around the world, and the global economic rules that others came to accept spread prosperity especially in East Asia. But, too often, Europe's Cold War was allowed to turn into a series of hot wars or dangerous stand-offs in other continents, premised on the assumption that communism was everywhere on the march and therefore had to be everywhere resisted. Sometimes, America's allegedly wise and special friends in Britain egged America on to act foolishly, for example in overthrowing Mossadeq in Iran in 1953 by persuading Washington that he was turning into a Russian communist stooge. Britain's real grouse was that he was threatening to increase the domestic Iranian take from UK oil interests. At least Americans did not believe that London was right to regard Abdul Nasser as a threat to global freedom in 1956 when President Eisenhower pulled the plug on the British–French–Israeli invasion of Egypt. In the Middle East, however, as time went by, American policy was hijacked by Israel (both because of the folly of most Arab states and because of the ever-powerful diaspora politics of Washington). One of the smaller proxy wars during the Cold War flared into a big and dangerous confrontation in Vietnam. This was in its early stages when Edward and I were crisscrossing America. The tragedy of Vietnam was that communism was eventually defeated there, and elsewhere, not by American arms but by globalization and capitalism. It was a point understood to his credit by President Nixon, whose aim, pursued in a sometimes indefensible way, was to get out of the conflict and concentrate on bigger and more important issues, like the US relationship with China. Nixon was destroyed not by Vietnam but by the fact that the United States placed the rule of law over political power. This commitment to pluralism, accountability and due process has been one of the reasons for America's global ascendancy for seventy or more years, helped by its military dominance which during the coldest days of the

Cold War ensured a grim peace, with both Washington and Moscow understanding that a false move could trigger nuclear Armageddon.

There are three pre-eminent reasons for America's status as the principal world power for so long. First, the American system has by and large worked, delivering the economic benefits both for its own people and for others. Second, America has been able to deploy soft power as well as hard; it could get other countries to go along more or less with what it wanted them to do without the use of force. Third, America has been the only country that matters everywhere, to some extent because it is prepared to do so. This has required it to be serious and usually consistent everywhere too. America has not on the whole taken other countries by surprise.

Americans have also usually chosen presidents who, perhaps in part because of their pre-eminence, are capable of gathering other global players into their tent. The two presidents with whom I had the closest dealings were rather different in this respect. President Clinton was a natural consensus builder, a reflection of the engaging personality of a man who loved to be loved, by men, women (of course) and I am sure cats and dogs too. George Bush Junior was a genial soul, and much sharper intellectually than the outside world usually reckoned. A friend of mine thinks that at school he would have been a natural towel-flicker in the changing room, rather small, a teaser, difficult to dislike, but probably not someone you would seek to emulate.

Clinton pursued a pretty conventional policy overseas, probably more aware of the economic consequences of international politics than his serious and wiser predecessor, George Bush Senior, reluctant to be dragged into international conflict, yet not so sophisticated in his use of America's global authority as the senior Bush had been. In action he was the most impressive politician I have ever seen. This was partly because of his high intellectual ability and the easy way in which he could conceptualize from anecdotes. He was extraordinarily articulate and entirely at home with the peaks and troughs of policy wonkery. But, above all, unlike many politicians, he clearly liked people; it is extraordinary how many politicians in my experience do not seem to like people – their voters – very much: a bit like doctors not being able to stand the sight of blood. Clinton could make the most cynical of hardened 'pros', the most resistant to political ham, go weak at the knees as he turned on the blowtorch of his charm. I recall one occasion at my first meeting of the UN General Assembly. On the first day, there is a rather grim lunch. The Secretary-General and the US President address the assembled heads of government, foreign ministers and UN hot shots. I was sitting at a table, about two rows back from the route the President took in and out of the room, with a group of foreign ministers from West Africa, the Gulf and Eastern Europe who had not been enthralling company over lunch. I had only recently published my report on policing in Northern Ireland, which the Americans had greatly liked. Spotting me as he was shepherded out of the room by bodyguards with bits of plastic in their ears, Clinton pushed through them and a crowd of other notables to give me a hug, tell me what a 'helluva' fellow I was, quite the greatest peacemaker since doves had first flown from the Ark. I modestly twinkled. For five minutes, maybe more, I would have followed him anywhere. What a wonderful operator! 'You've just got to love him,' someone said to me afterwards, and indeed you did.

A schoolmaster's report, at least an old-fashioned one, would surely have raised questions not about his ability, achievements or intelligence, but about his character. Sexual behaviour that might be frowned on in the very young rightly brings heavier censure when the older and more mature do the same things. The undoubtedly great George C. Marshall, general and diplomat, one of the major figures in the twentieth century, is said to have turned down the first ever seven-figure advance for his memoirs, on the simple grounds that he did not want a million dollars. It is hard not to conclude that one reason for the unpopularity of the Clinton and Blair camps today is that no one thinks that the ex-president and ex-premier would have given a similar answer. Both Bill Clinton and Tony Blair exude a sense of needless but greedy entitlement which is pretty unattractive.

Like Clinton, George Bush, the forty-third President, could also lay on the charm. At the beginning of a meeting in Ireland, just after the outbreak of the Iraq War (which I had criticized publicly), he gave me a big Texan handshake and said, 'Dad told me to say "Hi".' The idea that Dad had ever said anything of the sort seemed to me exceptionally unlikely. He was rather kindly trying to put me at my ease. I could never really understand how he had escaped the sensible policy embrace of his father and his father's advisers like Brent Scowcroft, and thrown in his lot with the crudest of neo-cons and their Lord of the Night, Dick Cheney. He just did not seem like them at all. Maybe he reacted to the fact that his father, for all his foreign-policy sophistication, had lost his attempt to secure re-election. Maybe, being perhaps rather lazy (though he played less golf than President Obama), he found it too demanding to see the greys of the world rather than the blacks and whites. Whatever the reason, he always appeared to me to be a whole heap nicer in person than his administration, which drained American soft power to the bottom of the tank.

I am sure that one of Bill Coolidge's hopes, never expressed and kept close to his chest, was that those who benefited from his scholarships would return from the USA not only with greater knowledge of his country but also with the beginnings of an affection for it. That sentiment has for me grown over the years, though it is fair to say that it is directed towards the America that I know. It has been a country that has by and large led the world by example, usually but not always on the right side of the biggest global issues, always stronger because it got involved in solving international problems, though sometimes it was confused about whether it had to intervene whenever others simply looked the other way. America has been open to other countries, usually accepting the same rules as them, and as a result it has been a huge force on every continent. In practice America has been 'First', precisely because it has ensured that others have a piece of the action, a place in the game economically and politically. This is the approach apparently challenged by President Trump, though major flip-flops over Syria and Russia suggest that he may be amenable to more conventional advice. In the election campaign he convinced enough of those who have done badly in the last few years that their misfortunes could be blamed on America's international leadership and responsibilities.

How much do I know about these voters? While we visited back in the 1960s parts of what is now known as rustbelt America – the older industrial areas – and city slums, I have not over the years gone back to the neighbourhoods that prosperity seems to have partially passed by. My America has been the coasts, and their cities, the great universities (though you do have to travel through the rustbelt to get to one of them, Notre Dame in Indiana), Chicago, museums, the *New York*

Review of Books, Chinese and Italian restaurants and embassies and conference rooms in Washington. I do not think that this America has been blown away by the recent presidential election. Nor is it other than absurd to regard America overall as a failed country. But those of us who have been marked by America for life are going to have to fight hard for this positive view of a great country and the good it has done and can do in the world in the years ahead.

The surprise for me was that I not only fell in love with much of what I saw in America and above all with Americans themselves on this first visit. Above all, I fell in love with politics and its hazardous charms as a political career. So after that Lindsay campaign, still in penny loafers and chinos, in late November 1965 I sailed home from New York and 'the land of the free', on an elderly Cunard liner which rocked and rolled through strong seas. I was returning to surprise everyone who knew me in England, injected by a political virus which shaped the identity of a not very sophisticated, even slightly clueless, 21-year-old. On the rough passage home, I seemed to be one of the few passengers who could keep down my gin and tonics. I was going home to my mum and dad in Greenford. I was off on the search for a career. But neither I nor my parents would previously have predicted where I would find it.

5
'Wet'

'Oh, Eeyore, you are wet,' said Piglet, feeling him. Eeyore shook himself, and asked somebody to explain to Piglet what happened when you had been inside a river for quite a long time.

A. A. Milne, *The House at Pooh Corner*

'If we want things to stay as they are, things will have to change.'
Giuseppe Tomasi di Lampedusa, *The Leopard*

Most people are not defined primarily, or even partly, by their political affiliation. Other things take precedence: race, nationality, religion, language, looks, bank balance, job or profession, and so on. But political success, or lack of it, can give you a certain celebrity, or it may simply mean that you are remembered for some generally acceptable or obnoxious or peculiar set of views. I invariably chat to taxi drivers, who are usually good company with views that are less predictable than is often imagined. I have been driven by a Buddhist communist, who apologized for not being in saffron, and by a man who looked as though he had once been a boxer and had strongly libertarian views on issues of gender self-identification. I have also been driven by a large number of cabbies who venerated the memory of Margaret Thatcher, and would like to have had 'that Ken Livingstone' in the back of the cab to tell him what they thought of his mayoral record in London. These days Uber and cycle lanes tend to be the principal subjects of these conversations, hardly surprising since together they are helping to bring London to a standstill.

The other day a driver put me on the spot. Half recognizing me, he asked, 'Didn't you used to be that Conservative?' What was he getting at exactly? Did he want to isolate what the nature of my formal Conservative vocation had been: that Conservative minister or MP? Did he question whether I was still a Conservative? Did the 'that' suggest a particular sort of Conservative – an odd ball, a quisling, a dubious bounder, potentially (worst of all) a friend of David Mellor or Boris Johnson? What was it all about? The question was of course bound to elicit a positive response, in the present as well as in the past tense. I was a Conservative and still am.

I have to say that an even more basic question would have been and indeed was asked by my Oxford friends when, on returning from New York, I wrote to and was offered a job by the Conservative Research Department, in the run-up to the 1966 General Election. Having got more than a taste for politics in America, I thought that it might be rather fun to work on a campaign in Britain. Then, I hoped, I could go on after a few months to a post as a general graduate trainee at the BBC. In the event, I so enjoyed the politics that I gave the BBC a thumbs-down when they offered me a job, which they clearly regarded as lèse majesté and my friends as an act of complete insanity.

But why, my friends asked, the Conservative Party? The truth is that when pushed I have always known two things about myself politically. First, I am not a Liberal (though I am certainly liberal) and, second, I am not Labour. Nor am I or ever will be a right-wing Conservative. I strongly endorse the proposition that in politics your opponents are in other parties, while your enemies are usually in your own. Though I am a pretty calm fellow, some of my alleged colleagues on the right have sometimes made me throb with rage. I have always thought myself a moderate Conservative about the things that matter most in politics. Margaret Thatcher, though she was kind to me, regularly employed my pen and promoted me in government, would certainly have thought of me as a card-carrying 'wet', to use the rather odd public school lingo used to describe almost any political view to the moderate left of her own. Tamurlane would definitely not have been regarded as wet but I am not sure about Genghis Khan. For the time being I will skirt around the fact that Margaret herself could show signs of rising damp from time to time.

My first political act occurred at school. Aged about fifteen, I joined a group of friends to heckle a rather polite Labour Party candidate in the 1959 General Election at an open-air meeting in Ealing. We were in the safe Conservative part of the borough and (with no idea of how fogeyish we must have seemed) shouted questions about Labour policy on grammar and independent schools at the candidate, standing on his soap-box on the green just outside the gates of the very good local grammar school. I hope we did not actually shout, like so many *Beyond the Fringe* parodists, 'What about the public schools?' though I cannot give a cast-iron assurance on this point. That was the entirety of my teenage political experience. There was not much insurrectionary fervour at my school. But one boy in my class used to wear a CND badge, and went each year on part of the Aldermaston March with his parents, shouting, 'Ban the Bomb.' This was much less selfishly oafish than 'Save the public schools.' He became a chartered accountant. The cause of nuclear disarmament deserved more serious political and moral attention than it usually received. As a constituency MP in later years, I didn't duck challenges to debate the issue with people like Bruce Kent.

Revolution came no closer than this to my youthful days of cricket and rugby, Salinger and Isherwood, and inhaling tipped cigarettes behind the gym. But, just in case the revolution roared down the Central Line from Holborn to Ealing Broadway, I was in the school Combined Cadet Corps, an under-officer no less, with an Irish beret called a caubeen sporting a green hackle befitting my rank. I would not have been much good in the event of hostilities. I am the worst shot I know, embarrassingly bad, and would not have hit the barn let alone its door. When my sporting friends ask me whether I shoot, I have to respond, 'Not to kill.'

After all this, no surprise then that I have always viewed with a sense of wonder those politicians who seemed to emerge fully formed from their chrysalis as soon as they got to university, who moved seamlessly from school to debating clubs and dodgy political society elections. How remarkable to be that sure of oneself at eighteen or even much younger. Maybe I was a bit callow. I suppose that both the main political parties have been fortunate that so many clever young women and men sprang so early and so surely from the traps and stayed the course. Both Labour and Conservative leaderships have been replete with the best that Oxbridge in particular can offer, politicians who served their apprenticeships during their years at university, dreaming and scheming. The trouble is that some of them go on behaving like that when politics should no longer be regarded as a jolly game. At Oxford, I went to one Union debate which I quite enjoyed; Richard Crossman made a funny speech on a motion of 'no confidence' in the government. But it was not really my scene. All around me ambition was almost bursting a blood vessel. Anyway, while I felt sort of Conservative, largely because I distrusted systems and certainties, I was not wholly and adamantly sure about it yet. On some issues I have never had any doubts – capital punishment and gay rights, for example. But I was not prepared to sign up to the whole canon, left or right. Indeed it is a secret shame that I have carried guiltily throughout my life that I do not have views on everything.

So what after university swung me moderately to the right? Trying to rationalize it a few years later, I concluded that there were three principal reasons for my decision which crept up on me on slippered feet rather than arriving with the clarity and suddenness of a bolt of lightning. First of all, studying history at Balliol I knew that the one thing which made me uneasy was a grand theory or over-arching generalization. You may recall my unwise early observations on Charlemagne. I found the Whig view of history – Britain's inexorable rise to ever greater liberal triumphs – as unconvincing as Marxist efforts to fit everything into the straitjacket of class conflict. I liked history as sweeping narrative, at its best a real literary endeavour, but also admired the patient investigation of the lives of sugar barons, police informers or provincial French prostitutes. When offered a confident judgement about what had happened 500 years ago, or yesterday for that matter, I usually wanted to hunt out a 'but' or a cautionary qualification.

Second, this wholesome scepticism disposed me to take seriously any political philosophy grounded in a hostility to the easy explanations offered by all-encompassing analyses of the world and its problems, explanations which in turn gave birth to exact plans about how to put everything right. The only thing as bad as a prescriptive plan was its mirror image: a plan to rebut plans. This point was succinctly made by the often beautifully obscure Michael Oakeshott, the greatest of modern Conservative political philosophers. His critique of Hayek makes this point very directly. 'A plan to resist all planning,' Oakeshott wrote, 'may be better than its opposite, but it belongs to the same style of politics.' This approach seemed to me to correspond to real life: managing one's way around one predicament after another, never finding a 'Promised Land', eventually coming to terms with the fact that all political careers – especially those which begin with the assumption of the imminent sighting of sunlit uplands – are bound to end, as Enoch Powell observed, in failure. So, if you spend your years struggling through life's swirling waters, you are bound like Eeyore to come out wet, unless, that is, you allow dogma to crowd out inconvenient facts and to colour reality. 'Wet' is usually the climate of the real world in politics.

Third, I formed a pretty early dislike of the Prime Minister, Harold Wilson, after the 1964 Labour Party election victory. A clever man, he managed to pull together an appeal embracing professionalism, modern classlessness and science-based economic advance that left Conservatives for a time looking like Wodehousian fuddy-duddies. It did not ring true for me, from the very beginning. Part of the political story of the 1960s and 1970s was about Wilson losing the moorings to his own carefully burnished public identity. From the pipe-smoking, no-nonsense, astute political manager and performer, he was portrayed (not least by some party colleagues) as turning into a brandy-swigging, paranoid conspiracy theorist, rather too many of whose friends sailed perilously close to the wind – or sometimes ploughed straight into it. To be fair to Wilson there did turn out to be conspiracies against him and he was certainly slandered by a nasty cabal of intelligence service members and their hangers-on. But from the outset I did not believe that, on the essentials, he would marry socialism to science and plan Britain to an economic miracle. The 'planning' was initially in the hands of the frequently inebriated but shrewd George Brown. It said most of what many people felt often unfairly about Harold Wilson that there was no great sense of outrage when a newspaper editor asserted that George Brown drunk was better than Harold Wilson sober. Attempts at Mr Wilson's historic rehabilitation have made some progress. He tried to balance the needs of party management with saving the economy from decline. Most important, he kept Britain out of the Vietnam War. (Mr Blair could have learned from his experience when he signed up for Mr Bush's war of choice in Iraq.) However, what seemed to be the more sensible aims of the Wilson government were taken from Harold Macmillan's play-book: membership of the European Common Market and an attempt to house-train the unions by giving them a share of the keys to the economy's front door with a place in modestly corporatist institutions like the National Economic Development Office, set up in 1962.

So, in any contest for my affections, Macmillan beat Wilson hands down. This victory for the old Edwardian encouraged me to apply the test once suggested by A. J. Balfour and look at history before deciding which party to join. I would begin my tramp through the pantheon of Conservative heroes with Edmund Burke. The Conservative Party can probably be dated from the time that, hating what he saw happening in France, Burke crossed the floor of the House of Commons with the Portland Whigs to join the younger Pitt in the task of assisting the country to 'weather the storm' unleashed by the revolution of 1789. Burke wrote of the theorists of the Revolution, 'In the groves of their academy, at the end of every vista, you see nothing but the gallows.' Since then there has been a continuous and definable Conservative tradition and party. There were three strands of thought that characterized Burke's opposition to the French Revolution, and they have subsequently run through the whole history of the party. First, there was opposition to utopianism and political blueprints, hand in hand with scepticism about an excessively rationalist approach to life. Secondly, there was patriotism, and the defence of Crown, country and the national interest. Society was, in other words, a living collection of relationships bound together by traditions, affection and mutual dependency, not only a partnership between those who are living but a contract between those who are living, those who are dead, and those who are to be born. Carelessly uproot one value or institution and the consequences spread out with who knows what results. Thirdly, there was defence of property, of order and of an organic view of society.

After Burke comes Robert Peel, arguably the statesman who

created the modern Conservative Party, splitting it over free trade, setting out a generous programme of change in the Tamworth Manifesto (Conservatives should 'reform to survive'), founding modern policing and emancipating Catholics. Peel is the last Prime Minister who was not photographed. He was opposed by the right – or rather by both the right-wing Conservative factions described by Douglas Hurd in his fine biography of Peel. There was the nostalgic right, lamenting the passage of good times, and the sour right, prejudiced against foreigners, immigrants, Catholics, Jews and Muslims. Peel, whose U-turns were as spectacular as they were right, repealed the Corn Laws (which maintained the price of corn, and so bread), in part in response to the Irish potato blight and famine. This split the Conservative Party he had created and sent it into Opposition for twenty years. It was rescued from the political margins partly by Disraeli, who knew how to appeal to working men as well as to his Queen Emperor. Though himself an exotic creature, he understood that gravity rather than levity was the attribute required of those who sought to govern a country wreathed in fog and with a large middle class. I pass by, with only a small nod of reverence, his truly awful novels, which are much mentioned in speeches by Conservatives who have wisely never tried to read them. I much admire Stanley Baldwin also, a great political artist, who was able to manage party arguments rather than turning them into knock-down ideological tussles. A man of generous sentiments, he was able to appeal across party boundaries from the centre left to the centre right partly because he was prepared to give serious attention to other points of view. He believed that Conservatives should 'avoid all extremes'. England mattered much more to him than the Conservative Party. He had a real feel for the country – for its history, its landscape, its institutions and its language, which he used beautifully. Look up, for instance, the speech he made at the Scott Polar Research Institute in Cambridge in memory of the great explorer and hero, and his particular tribute there to the gallant failures of British history. Baldwin was a hero of one of my own paladins, though perhaps that description is too assertive for a man so ambivalent and even diffident about his own personal ambitions.

I carried with me from office to office in my political years a photograph of Rab Butler, a man whom I only knew slightly but admired hugely. He always comes high on the list of those who never quite became Prime Minister, but should have got the job. He was a member of the House of Commons for thirty-six years and a minister for over twenty-six of them. His ministerial career rested on the same tripos which he described as the base of his whole life – India, education and Conservatism. Rab held all the great offices of state, was a notably good Chancellor of the Exchequer in the early 1950s, piloted the great Education Act of 1944 which bore his name, and played the pivotal role in the intellectual renaissance of Conservatism after the war through his office at the Conservative Research Department, where I had gone to work at the beginning of 1966. 'I may never have known much about ferrets or flower arranging,' he once said, 'but one thing I did know was how to govern the people of this country.' No one knew better. As even Enoch Powell acknowledged, he was a master of the art of political administration. He managed to find the right balance between expediency and Conservative principles, a very British mix of practicality and precept. 'Untouched by morality and idealism,' he argued, 'economics is an arid pursuit, just as politics is an unprofitable one.' He attacked those who called for old-style Montagu Norman austerity economics, reckless of the consequences. For them, public spending was like an enemy regiment, to be gunned down at every opportunity. 'Those who talked about creating pools of unemployment should be thrown into them and made to swim.' This moral dimension to politics and economics was closely related to his lack of ideological zealotry. While there was always a philosophical framework to his decision making, he would not push his own philosophy to other peoples' breaking point, partly because of his intense attachment to the notion of community. No political philosophy should be 'an incitement to envy, malice or uncharitableness'. A natural task for the politician was to bind people together, not split them apart, recognizing that in any real community justice was insufficient without charity. All this is what helped make him such a consummate man of public affairs.

I once heard a former French aide of President Mitterand, while apologizing for his allegedly poor English, claiming that his description of his old boss often having contradictory feelings about things

did not mean that he was ambiguous. 'No,' he protested, 'not ambiguous, ambivalent.' I felt the same about Rab Butler, and I mean it as
a compliment. Of course, he was sometimes deliberately ambiguous;
deliberate ambiguity was at the heart of many of his best jokes. I
liked the telegram of apology he sent crying off sick from a Tory
grandee's retirement dinner. 'There is no one,' he wrote, 'whose farewell dinner I would rather have attended.' I mean something more
profound than this sort of barbed joke. While he was cutting flowers
for the wife of an assistant in his beautiful garden in Essex one late
summer afternoon, the aide asked him what was the most important
lesson he had learned in politics. 'That's easy,' he replied. 'It's more
important to be generous than efficient.' He knew perfectly well, of
course, that you often need to be efficient in order to be generous. But
I got the drift. Value comes before price in politics as in life, always.

Rab was a great patriot; while he loved the Highlands of Scotland,
especially the Isle of Mull, you cannot write about him without noting his deep feeling of Englishness: not surprisingly, he loved books,
gardens and dogs. His sense of his own identity infused and reflected
his philosophy, and set him apart – the same is true of other British
conservatives – from much modern American conservativism, with
its ideological fervour about small government, low taxes and less
regulation, its culture wars against changes in the law on sexual
behaviour, and the rigid interpretation of the eighteenth-century US
constitution as it would have been understood when it was adopted.
These American conservatives favour compulsory school prayer, are
frequently against teaching Darwinian evolution, are rock solid in
opposing any change in America's gun laws, and usually believe
strongly in American exceptionalism – an attitude which brings with
it a hostility to international institutions and laws. Economic issues
have been given a greater neo-liberal (as it is now called) tilt among
American conservatives in recent years by writers like William Buck-
ley. It is of course possible to be of a conservative disposition in
America without signing up to this whole gallimaufry, but even so
the differences with the collection of political, moral and economic
positions usually espoused by British conservatives is very marked. I
have sometimes found myself across the Atlantic expressing the
pretty mainstream views of a moderate Conservative politician to the

evident surprise of American conservative audiences. I spoke two or three times at an extraordinary mid-summer camp for well-off conservative businessmen, politicians, journalists and academics in northern California. Called Bohemia Grove, it offered comfortable log cabin hospitality to a diverse group who gathered for music, lectures, seminars, a comfortable experience of tamed nature and dry martinis. I lectured there, a slightly exotic European. The audience was told that I was a Conservative, but some of them clearly thought I was a raving socialist because I evidently did not believe that government was the enemy.

Like other Conservatives, I have always felt that at our best we do not need books to explain our philosophy, although I confess that I once wrote one, *The Tory Case*. I sought there to argue above all that Conservatism by its very nature defied every description, giving us neither precise and immutable rules of political or social conduct nor revelations about the truth that might explain the world in which we live. 'As for certain truth,' Xenophanes wrote, 'no man has known it . . . all is but a woven web of guesses.' So Conservatism is not dogmatic. It suggests a way of looking at the world, not an exact way of running it. But the fact that Conservatism is not an ideology does not mean that it is nothing much at all, resting on little more than a majestic pragmatism. While it is a pretty good starting idea for a political party to try to keep the government of the country afloat, Conservatives in Britain have survived longer than in most other parts of the political world because they have always managed to engage with the real world better than their opponents, at least until recently, and have usually reflected the best (though very occasionally the worst) of our national community – above all practicality, moderation, tolerance and generosity.

For many American conservatives and for European, including British, socialists the relationship between the state and the individual creates problems. Where exactly should the border be? It creates similar anxieties as well for some British conservatives. Should we worry quite so much about whether the state has got too big for its own boots? The temptation to seek some antithesis between the individual and the state should be resisted. It is wrong, for instance in reaction to socialism, to expound a creed based solely on the individual, on the view that society (which despite Margaret Thatcher's momentary denial, does exist, as she knew perfectly well – comprising families, churches, voluntary associations, trade unions, firms and so on) only has one role: to provide a legal framework within which individual opportunity can flourish without becoming self-destructive. Carlyle called this 'anarchy plus the constable'. If that were true, all those other things for which the Conservative Party has stood – patriotism, duty, loyalty – would be meaningless. None of this strikes me as difficult to understand or controversial. If you could pin down what they think about politics, it is, I suspect, what most people who do not regard themselves as political animals would accept as a reflection of their sentiments. Man is not only an individual answerable to himself, 'the master of his fate' and 'the captain of his soul'. He is also a social animal who can attain his full stature only in groups greater than himself, acquiring a broader identity or series of identities in his family, his work, his church, his country or many other groups or organizations of which he may be part. This balance, intuitively perceived rather than articulately expressed by Conservatives during decades, indeed centuries, of changing intellectual fashions, corresponds to one of the fundamental balances in the whole of life. In all civilizations and in all living things, there must be a balance between the forces of creativity and growth on the one hand, and order on the other. Unbalanced, the one leads to chaos, the other to sterility. Likewise, I do not wish to make a once-and-for-all choice between the state and the individual; sometimes I lean one way and sometimes another. This may be called 'trimming', but that is of course what helps to keep a sailing boat from capsizing. Life is not a collection of clear-cut problems to which there are equally clear-cut solutions. The most profound political observation I know is Michael Oakeshott's view that life 'is a predicament not a journey'.

The primary role of the state is to provide order and harmony within which individuals and their social groups can flourish in a stable environment. Without this, civilized behaviour is very difficult. Government itself needs checks on the use of its powers. These should be provided by the diffusion of authority and accountability, the spread of property, and the health of what Burke called 'the little platoons', all operating under the rule of law which applies to rulers as well as ruled. I am suspicious of zeal, respect institutions and historical forces, and favour consensus and co-operation where possible.

These are some of the reasons why I became a Conservative and this is the sort of Conservative I have tried to be. I used to be surprised by the fact that trying to behave according to these precepts in fashioning a response to life's predicaments was regarded as 'wet' by the right wing of my own party. These days nothing much surprises me about them any more, except that time and experience still seem to teach them so little. A thick skin of prejudice, reinforced by reading the tabloids, is proof against the dilemmas of the real world. In addition to being criticized for my political approach, I have often been attacked for the number of things I have done alongside political jobs; apart from their innate interest, I have done them precisely because of the beliefs I have just tried to articulate. What strikes me most forcefully looking back now is how much of my life, maybe too much of my life, was spent with my nose to a political grindstone. For years I really did nothing else.

When I joined the Conservative Research Department just before the 1966 General Election, the director, Brendon Sewell, an amiable man (who, if the expression had then been in vogue, would certainly have been reckoned to think outside the box), seemed to be rather taken by the idea of recruiting someone hotfoot from an American campaign. My first job was to sneak into Labour Party press conferences and then report back to Edward Heath and his senior advisers on what had happened there. This exposed me to the party's nabobs and, for that matter, them to me. It should have come as no surprise that they usually seemed to agree with the Leader. After the Conservative election defeat, I worked for a series of backbench committees and policy groups until 1970. Conservative victory then saw me posted as a politically appointed civil servant to work on the co-ordination of social policy in the Cabinet Office. Similar efforts are still being made to co-ordinate the approach to many of the same problems almost fifty years on. Having done that for two years, I was offered the chance to work as the political assistant to the chairman and deputy chairman of the Conservative Party (Lord Carrington and Jim Prior), in which job I was on the inside track of the painful weeks of indecision about whether and if so when to call the 1974 election, when the country was held to ransom by the miners. Defeat then saw me offered two jobs. Christopher Soames, one of Britain's European Commissioners, asked me to go to Brussels to work for him. Despite a charming interview during which the two of us spent twenty minutes chasing mice around and under the chairs of Claridge's, I opted instead to go back to the Conservative Research Department as its director. I was just thirty and, though the pay was derisory, thought I had landed in paradise. It was a slightly oddball institution which worked rather well – typically Conservative perhaps.

The Research Department had in effect been founded by Neville Chamberlain before the war acting virtually as a private office for him. It was re-established after the war under Rab Butler as a think tank for the then Conservative Opposition, which was attempting to come to terms with welfare democracy. It also played the role of a nursery for talented young politicians, many of them entering from military service, who went on to distinguished political careers, like Iain Macleod, Reggie Maudling and Enoch Powell. Partly because its alumni provided several of the leaders and much of the intellectual firepower of Conservative governments from 1950 onwards, it enjoyed quite a privileged position among the party's institutions. In the 1960s and 1970s it was housed in two pretty but chaotically organized Georgian houses in Westminster. There were about sixty staff, more than half of whom were researchers (mostly men). The supporting staff were young women chosen by successive female ex-army establishment officers from the better sort of secretarial colleges. They were the sort of women ('my girls', the ex-colonels would call them) who would today go to university. They were also invariably pretty and usually good at covering up for their bosses, some of whom took a rather Alexandrian view of working hours. There were always one or two people in stockinged feet and several dogs and cats around the place; in my early years a pretty pungent smell of wet hound cut across the atmosphere of pipe and cigarette tobacco.

When I was director, the team was a nice balance of age, eccentricity and, I am led to believe, sexual preference. (I am not sure what it says about me, probably nothing, that I do not usually notice people's sexual orientations. I have never anyway regarded what people do in private as any of my business.) Most of the staff were clever and the majority of the young ones ambitious for a political career. We recruited mainly from those who had just left university. Some went on to their own celebrity, like Matthew Parris, Michael Portillo and Michael Dobbs; others made their careers on the touchlines of Westminster politics, like Adam Ridley, Nick True, Dermot Gleeson, Stephen Sherbourne and Patrick Rock. A later vintage, when I was party chairman, included David Cameron, George Osborne and Edward Llewellyn, who worked for me for about ten years in a variety of posts from Hong Kong to Brussels before becoming Cameron's chief of staff. Edward is very able, very discreet and very nice; he is one of those people who has made my life happier and more successful than it would have been without him. Entirely on merit (of course) he was posted as ambassador to France after David Cameron's resignation from the prime ministership. He is an excellent example of how a politically appointed chief of staff should behave in government. Good political advisers operate below the radar; when they fail to do so the outcome is invariably a train wreck.

The Research Department was a unique flowering of amiably and lightly managed talent. A management consultancy would not have allowed it to survive for five minutes, yet it mostly worked rather well. There were some older, worldly-wise sages like James Douglas, a great expert on psephology and the husband of Mary, the social anthropologist, some of whose academic interest would have rubbed off usefully on anyone trying to understand what made the place tick. She had after all tried to answer the question of whether dogs laugh, so nothing was beyond her. There were a few coasting eccentrics and some very knowledgeable people who could not bear the thought of moving on to anywhere more orthodox. One wise old colleague knew every twist and turn in the Conservative Party's arm wrestling over grammar schools; another acted as a sort of intellectual firewall around Margaret Thatcher and whatever was her current policy preoccupation; another knew everything, indeed more than anyone might want to know, about the brick industry, in which there always seemed to be an actual or incipient crisis. There were a very few driven ideologues and sharp-elbowed political climbers. Private incomes were not unknown, nor was bullshitting. Drink and sex took a small toll of talent. Overall, it was a great little naval destroyer and managed to hold its own – or rather more than that when from 1975 to 1979 Keith Joseph was allowed to establish a more ideological think tank, the Centre for Policy Studies, which searched for the agonized soul of Conservatism and occasionally came back from the quest with something clenched between its teeth. The CPS, however, suffered from being so weighed down by dogma as to be a bit light on the sort of ideas required to win elections in Britain. Most important, the Research Department contained some people who could write conspicuously well, so that policy documents, speeches and manifestos tended to finish up in our hands. It was a very happy place if, as I say, a little batty. Half a dozen novels by Anthony Powell or Simon Raven could have bloomed there.

From the Research Department, it was pretty inevitable that a career in Parliament would call. So it did, without my ever really seeming to make a decision that this was what I wanted to do. I followed the approved route. First of all, I fought a strong Labour seat in Lambeth. It covered the area where John Major grew up, though Conservatives like him were thin on the ground. There was a large West Indian community and too many high-rise blocks of flats where the lifts did not work. At the count on polling day, the elderly Labour MP (actually he was not much older than I am now), Marcus Lipton, took me to one side. 'Don't worry about losing,' he said accurately and without difficulty predicting what would happen that night. 'Conservative Central Office send a lot of fine young men down here to fight me. They all lose and then go on to get chosen for nice constituencies with big, green fields and even bigger majorities.'

This was only partly true, certainly in my case. In the mid-1970s when I started looking for a seat with a good Conservative majority and a nice slice of country or suburb I fell by the wayside again and again. I was usually thought to be favourite; I am not sure that this helped. As an intellectual from the party HQ, I was suspect from the word go. Moreover, I might be clever enough to be made a minister and taken away from the constituency wine and cheese parties. (I was also thought to be slightly unkempt, a point picked up by Bryan Organ, who painted my portrait for Oxford University. 'I think you're naturally scruffy,' he said, on first inspecting the new Chancellor.) I lost out among others to two subsequent friends, John Major in Huntingdon and Richard Needham in Chippenham. I was firm favourite (again) for South Dorset. Then Bath brought forward its selection meeting ahead of Dorset and I was chosen there rather than another older Balliol man, Peter Brooke. Disappointed, he travelled home to London and was shortly afterwards chosen to fight the very safe City of London in a by-election. Bath was not safe; in fact it was very marginal. The majority depended on the balance between the Labour and Liberal votes. Giving advice to anyone today embarking on a political career, I would strongly counsel in favour of targeting safe seats. Marginal constituencies are inevitably even harder work and threaten the perilous prospect of losing your seat and your career at just the wrong time, often for reasons that bear little relationship to how hard and well you have worked at holding on.

My constituency was a beautiful city and my local Conservative supporters were friendly, diligent and kind. During the period when I was a Cabinet minister, I was asked by a neighbouring constituency with a large Conservative majority and a retiring MP to switch to them. I could not imagine how I could be disloyal to my team in Bath. This was regarded by one or two friends as a very unprofessional decision on my part. But, even though my local Conservative council, without ever consulting me, had appealed successfully against a change in the constituency boundary which would have benefited the Conservative Party (I cannot remember their reasoning, if there was any), I could not imagine how I would explain to my supporters that I was quitting and carpet-bagging elsewhere. There was, for example, one real 'salt of the earth' woman who ran the Conservative committee in a difficult, mostly Labour, ward. How would I possibly tell Joyce Godwin that I was off? She would have defended me loyally but it would have hurt her. Joyce never knew it but she was always my litmus test for the acceptability of a policy or political behaviour. (She was not a fan of the poll tax later, but then who was?)

I worked hard in the constituency, harder when I was a minister than before. But the higher I went, the more local Liberals said that I was deserting the city for my Westminster ambitions. In my experience, and that of most of my political friends, there was invariably a disjuncture between the squeaky-clean image of Liberals and the way they fought elections. In my last Bath election, they targeted my party agent, who was 'outed' by the Sunday tabloids as an office holder in a regional gay organization. They need not have bothered. My ministerial responsibilities for the poll tax (I was moved to the Environment Department the year it was introduced) was like being handed the ten biblical plagues; moreover, it was coupled with a new local business rate, fairer than its predecessor but higher in a city like Bath, where the local economy had thrived. The Liberals could have sunk me on these issues without dragging my poor agent into the campaign.

My feeling about Bath fell short of dewy-eyed love. I found regular surgeries burdensome but worthwhile. Sometimes you could sort out a problem and improve a constituent's life. I was lucky to have a great House of Commons PA, now a Church of England vicar, called Freda Evans. She worked tirelessly to help those who came to my surgeries (with her charming spaniel, Sammy, at her feet day and night) and as a priest she looks after her parishioners in a run-down part of Birmingham with equal kindness. Yet so often I had to explain to a constituent that, for example, he or she was getting all the help that the state deemed proper and that there was no more that I could do to help. I am sure that in a marginal seat you have to say 'No' a lot more frequently than in a safer one. I liked getting involved with local churches, the university, the arts festival, civil society organizations. There were, however, a number of rather unattractive and mildly snobbish middle-class voters who wanted a Conservative Party strong enough to protect them from Labour taxes but could only imagine actually voting Conservative with their noses firmly held. They were a bit pleased with themselves, as if simply living in a neat Georgian house in that beautiful city and belonging to the Wine Society set them apart from the rest of humanity. When I lost Bath my sentiments at parting company were thus not those of unalloyed gloom. There were lots of exceptions: people like the single parent for whom I struggled for years to get proper recognition of the needs of her dyslexic child, a boy who went on in the year I lost my seat to win a place at university. I got particular satisfaction when I was able to deal with people's housing problems. In Bath we had had a very tricky issue involving the maintenance of houses from a period when the quality of the concrete was suspect. There were enough cases like that for me to feel that the whole constituency relationship had been worthwhile, though sometimes it was touch and go as to whether I could satisfy all the demands made on me. Heaven knows what it must be like today with the internet and emails.

The reward for constituency effort was Westminster, a seat in the self-styled Mother of Parliaments. In retrospect – I am not sure that I realized this properly at the time – the life is only really possible, fruitful and enjoyable if you have a great partner. All my closest political friends – William Waldegrave, John Major, Tristan Garel-Jones, Richard Needham and John Patten – have terrific wives who have sustained them through gloom, public failure, tabloid assault, boredom and a horribly demanding working regime. Of course, there are other occupations where success (or survival) must be as demanding. But I reckon that there are particular combinations of circumstance which make a political life a killer. Compared to average earnings it is well paid – and much better today than was once the case. But I cannot think of any of my political friends who could not have made more, far more, in another job, and probably without similar stress. When I became a Member of Parliament, the salary was £9,450. Today, it is £74,000 and all the allowances for offices, housing and pensions have increased substantially. The system got into disrepute because instead of taking higher salaries, there was a 'wink-wink' connivance at allowing these allowances to drift upwards with insufficiently rigorous oversight. So Parliament endured a torrent of journalistic outrage at MPs inflating their expenses. It was inexcusable but expressions about pots and kettles did come to mind.

What of the other strains? How, first of all, if you are married or have a partner and family do you organize your family life in a way that balances it, Westminster and the constituency? We decided that we had not got married in order to live apart as many MPs and their wives do. Over the years I have been quite surprised not by the number of MPs' marriages that fall to pieces but the number that survive. But having two homes – in our case a central London flat and a cottage just outside the constituency – put a lot of pressure on my family. I would usually go down to the constituency by train on Friday mornings in a first-class carriage. Lavender would follow in the car full of yelling children, dog and the weekend's provisions just in time for the rush hour, and in the winter the dark woods and narrow lanes of west Wiltshire. Who do you think got the better part of this deal? We shared the rush hour journey home on Sunday evening in our second-hand estate car. I bought my first new car (a Vauxhall) when I joined the Cabinet. After all this shunting about how do you explain to your partner the ridiculous disparity between perceived success and failure. You are either too much in the spotlight or not in it enough. You do not have to go into politics. No one is forcing you. So don't ask for sympathy or tears. Today, though this may just be an elderly man's view, I have the impression that fewer really good people think that the political game is worth the candle.

So my friends – all of us have remained married to our partners – were lucky, and I have been too. I cannot imagine my life without Lavender; indeed the thought of her dying before me (the bloodless word is pre-decease) fills me with horror. I have no idea how I would deal with electricity failures, or leaks, or the car or pretty much anything technical, or bills, or tax returns. But far, far more important is the great void there would be in my life. Since we met and fell in love at university – she is still today as pretty, cool and feisty as she was then – I have never thought that I could spend my life with anyone else. Lavender lost her father, an Olympic athlete, before she was born (he was killed – we recently discovered – by 'friendly fire' in Normandy), and her mother in a car crash when she was sixteen. Maybe this has helped to make her such a good mother – best friend to her daughters as well as one they clearly think is, like their father, occasionally a bit dotty. Like the Old Testament Ruth, she went where I went and lodged where I lodged, not without questions but always without reproach. She also sacrificed her career as a barrister for me (though when we returned from Hong Kong she successfully retrained and practised as a family mediator). Today, I sometimes look at couples in restaurants, dining together and never exchanging a word beyond 'Put your phone away.' Life is not like that for me. So we get older together, enjoying most of the same things, like sport, travel, books and dogs and of course arguing about them; forgetting these days many of the same things; helping each other to remember names of friends, books and flowers; suffering just a little from similar aches and pains. I regularly count my blessings but perhaps do not celebrate them sufficiently often, or with sufficient noise.

Arriving at Westminster was not as big a deal for me as for most new MPs. As a member of the Conservative Research Department I had been in and out of Parliament, not least in the days before there was much in the way of security. I knew my way around the great neo-Gothic building with its frescoes recounting what we imagined our history to have been – the rise of a great sea-faring nation from one triumph of liberal accountability to another. Everywhere were the statues of the parliamentary giants who had preceded us. They had presumably found themselves as nervous as we were when confronting a chamber when in political trouble, full of colleagues whose notion of collegiality would often be overwhelmed by the prospect of an enjoyable brouhaha. It was the chamber that excited me; I never felt a sort of clubman's affection for the place as a whole. At least I did not encounter such a sentiment until one occasion after I had lost my seat, when I was dining with friends who were still MPs, and said 'goodnight' to them as they dashed off at ten minutes to ten to vote. For a few moments I really did feel bereft.

All that voting, in those days at all times of the night, meant that you had to hang around the building for hours. It was not in fact quite as bad for me because we had a flat 'on the bell', which would literally ring just inside our front door to summon me to do my democratic duty. I could just get back to the division lobbies within the ten minutes allowed for a vote. As it was a bit of a scramble, like the rest I spent too much time drifting around the library and the bars. Once I was a minister I had a reasonable cubby hole of an office to which I could disappear and get on with my official boxes full of briefs, committee papers and letters. The bars were a menace for some. We used to have the opportunity of an annual health check by St Thomas's Hospital on the understanding that the anonymized results could be used as part of a comparative epidemiological study. I once asked the doctor who was organizing the work how Westminster compared with St Thomas's. He said that there was higher alcohol consumption in Parliament but less sexual activity than at the hospital.

The Chamber was, and perhaps still is, the real centre of everything. I only raise a doubt about its centrality because clearly fewer people today attend debates. Speaking in a full house could be a terrifying experience. One verbal slip – a pause, say, in the wrong place – and you could be lost in a storm of laughing and bellowing, particularly late at night when the House was inevitably more rowdy, wine having been taken (as Ian Gow MP would have said). As a backbencher it was scary being called to speak after one of the crowd-pullers like Tony Benn or Enoch Powell. Unless you said something arresting, perhaps funny, right at the start, your speech would be given to the backs of MPs departing from the Chamber for tea, whisky or work. The speakers who made the greatest impression were those who (as on a public platform elsewhere) were speaking, or appeared to be speaking, without a text. (David Cameron managed this in a remarkable tour de force when he was running for the Conservative leadership and speaking at the party conference.) There is of course today a question of appearance and reality. So many public figures (think of American presidents) use glass plates onto which their text is reflected, so that their audience have the impression that they are spontaneously thinking of what they say in front of you. In fact they are reading the carefully drafted speech which is reflected onto the glass tablets that the TV cameras do not pick up. I used them once or twice and hated the experience. I went slower and slower and so the page turner somewhere under the lectern went slower and slower too, so these speeches degenerated into funereal processions of words and phrases. At that rate I could have turned the Gettysburg address into an oration of Castro-like length. The reason why a textless speech is so much more interesting is that the audience know that you are only certain in a general sort of way what is going to come out. The speech can respond to the mood and inter-jections of the audience, who know that the speaker is on a verbal high wire. It also helps to have something original to say, an interest-ing take on a familiar issue. The best speaker on these criteria among my young peers was Matthew Parris, who later became such a wise and funny commentator on others' parliamentary performances. Overall, the best speaker in the Commons when I was there was the old-fashioned radical Michael Foot, whose swoops and pauses and mixture of the demotic and the literary made him funny, cutting and effective in every sense except one: many of his ideas on economic and social policy came straight out of the Ark. At the end of the day, as bishops say, it does matter to have something sensible to say as well as to say it well. But, for debating style, he is the person I would most like to have resembled.

The main problem about Westminster, and indeed our whole system of government, is that we have forgotten why and how the system used to work so well and appear incapable of reforming it in order to restore its relevance and vitality. Parliament itself is far too large. There are too many MPs and too many ministers. There are far too many members of the second chamber, the House of Lords, which has only a rather hazy idea of what its purpose should be. For decades people have been predicting that Brazil would be the next emerging economy to become a superstar, but it never seems to progress beyond this 'about-to-be' status. Equally, reform of the House of Lords has been predicted for years. It will go on being predicted. The main reason for reforming it would be to make it more credible as a functioning part of our democracy. But why should the principal democratic chamber, the House of Commons, devote its energies to creating a real rival? So the reform of the House of Lords will remain a subject for debating societies. For the time being we should at least do something about its Topsy-like growth, partly a consequence of muddling up appointments to it with the honours system. Modest state funding of political parties, and tougher limits on private benefactions, would also remove some of the rich entrepreneurs who have been sprung into this part of our legislature, primarily because they have dropped a few cheques into the collection tins of the political parties.

Reducing the size of the Commons and of the number of government ministers should be accompanied by far more devolution of power to local government. This has started to happen but should go much further. We are still a horribly over-centralized democracy. When I was Environment Secretary a large proportion of the decisions I had to take should have been the preserve of local councillors. I was usually running on four or five hours' sleep: boxes until after midnight; up again for more work at 5 or 6 a.m. Much of what I was doing should have been done far from Whitehall. Our flat in Victoria was in a block just behind the home of the Archbishop of Westminster, Basil Hume. I mentioned to him one day that when I got up in the early morning and pulled the curtains before getting down to work I frequently saw him walking up and down behind his house with his breviary saying his office. 'Yes,' he said. 'And I see you. I think you should put on your dressing gown before pulling the curtain.'

With fewer MPs should also come the further empowerment of Select Committees, not least giving them greater responsibility in the drafting of legislation. The establishment of the Select Committee structure was begun by my first parliamentary boss, Norman St John Stevas, for whom I acted as a parliamentary dogsbody, the lowest rung on the ladder of Westminster. Some Select Committees have done very well, for example the one on Treasury affairs intelligently chaired recently by Andrew Tyrie, a fiercely independent Conservative MP. You have naturally to make allowances for the opportunities for some MPs to show off their poopery in Select Committees in front of the cameras. When I was Chairman of the BBC Trust I had to deal with one MP who managed to embrace an astonishingly varied collection of primitive views with no evident embarrassment at how ridiculous he was. Naturally, the more he behaved like a right-wing buffoon, the more press attention he got. You also find that some MPs have difficulty, when they have an important witness in front of them, distinguishing between forceful questioning and being simply rude.

I was fortunate in my parliamentary friends and in spending as much time as I did as a minister. My closest colleagues were all members of an informal dining group which in a rather random way somehow came together soon after the 1979 election; we tried to look after one another as we scrambled onto the political escalator. The Whips dubbed us 'the Blue Chips', which gave a slight impression of a group of weak-chinned and self-satisfied chaps who thought themselves born to rule. There were indeed four proper toffs – two sons of marquesses, and two of earls (one of them Irish, so perhaps he counts as four-fifths toff) – but the rest of us were a pretty mixed bunch: middle-class scholarship boys on the whole. Nor were we all on the left of the party. We represented most of the available Conservative points of view, except the nasty right wing. Robert Cranborne spoke for centuries of deep-blue Cecils. Jocelyn Cadbury, who tragically shot himself while in a deep depression, was the best sort of social worker MP. John Watson was a Yorkshire businessman with a radical streak. The friend I had known the longest was my namesake, John Patten, known in the family as 'no relation'. He had been an Oxford don when I was running the Research Department, and convened like-minded academics to help us with policy work. The cleverest among us were John Major and William Waldegrave. William would always be one of the cleverest in any gathering, a widely read classicist who taught himself enough about science policy and industry to hold his own and more on both subjects. He and his family have been very close friends. William is cursed by a strain of modesty, verging on melancholy, which has prevented him from recognizing for much of the time just how good he is. I will talk about John Major later. The other two very close friends were Richard Needham and Tristan Garel-Jones. Richard became a terrific minister, under-promoted because one of the reasons that he got so much done was precisely because he was not safe. He has made me laugh more than anyone else in my life. Tristan (who hosted our dinners at his home) has caused me much more pain and grief than almost anyone since he has spent his whole lifetime smoking himself to death. If he dies before me I shall be devastated, since there has not been a day when I have imagined coping without him at the other end of the phone. He has a reputation for scheming, mostly because he has allowed others sedulously to spread this largely fictitious description. He is usually all too happy broadcasting exactly what he is doing, which is not always predictable but invariably smart.

There were other MPs, from a slightly older generation, whom I greatly admired, like George Young and John Cope. Young and Cope were examples of the sort of MPs who help to make our whole political system work, as they continued to do later in the House of Lords. They did conscientiously and competently whatever jobs they were asked to undertake, without any indication of great personal ambition. They were the best sort of amiable, selfless, decent public servants, and always excellent company.

My own first ministerial job was in Northern Ireland, about which I have written in a separate chapter because that experience bears very directly on my views of politics and identity. After two years in Belfast as a Parliamentary Secretary, I was promoted in 1985 to be a Minister of State in the Department of Education and Science. I was deputy there to Keith Joseph for a miserable year, not because of him but because of the near impossibility of getting anything to change in the dour world of education policy. Education should involve a partnership between parents representing the interests of their children, the government on behalf of the national interest, the teachers' unions with a professional commitment to delivering as good an education to pupils as possible, and the local education authorities organizing the various parts of the system in their communities. But by the 1970s and 1980s, two of the partners had been pretty well eliminated as serious players. The government's ability to do anything at all was so constrained that the quality of officials to administer a policy void had badly declined, despite the presence of a very good Permanent Secretary (head of the department) who was there because Margaret Thatcher wanted him out of the Treasury (she didn't like his middle-of-the-road economic views). Parents were naturally regarded as far too personally involved in the outcome of education of their children to be, well, personally involved: their role, it was thought, should be confined to whatever happened outside school. That left the teachers' unions and local government. The teachers' unions had allowed their commitment to professionalism to be eroded by the worst sorts of public sector defence of special interests. When Keith Joseph went to address one of the union's conferences he was greeted by its senior officers wearing rubber gloves and surgical masks and aprons as though he was an AIDS patient. The local authorities employed much expertise but were too inclined to reduce everything to a fight over cash, and they were usually locked in a duopolistic embrace with the unions. Breaking this hold on education has taken years, and it was not something Keith Joseph – an intellectual rather than a toughie – could do in a short time despite his passionate commitment to raising educational quality.

Our department was housed in a scruffy building next to Waterloo Station. It was rather like two other offices in which I had to spend many years – the Conservative Central Office, in Smith Square, and the Department of the Environment, in nearby Marsham Street. When you went in – even when you approached the entrance to these buildings – you could feel your spirits retreating for cover. One of the few advantages of working in the Environment Office was that from the inside you were one of the lucky few in London who could not see its full brutalist horror. My own office in the Waterloo building was, rather curiously, separated from Keith's by a sliding door. I had not seen one of these since our home in Hillside Road, Greenford. With my back to the door, I would suddenly be aware of Keith (if I had missed his ever so discreet knock) looming over me, clearing his throat. He was a good and kind man, but not, to put it mildly, a political natural, and too easily influenced by mad or bad ideologues. Few people can have been so disappointed at their inability to change the nation's soul. At Education, we would spend days arguing with him backwards and forwards before, invariably and contrary to his philosophy, he plumped for the most centralizing option. He was pleased with me when I once made a speech which caused a stir at a headteachers' conference suggesting that if we were to avoid presiding over the creation of a yob society, we should put in place some elements of a national curriculum.

I lasted at Education for a year before being transferred sideways – actually it felt like a huge promotion– to the Overseas Development Administration. I was the only minister there, typically the feudal subject of the Foreign Secretary, who was too busy to bother much at all about us. Britain had one of the best overseas-development programmes in the world, smaller than it had been and much smaller than today. But it was a classy operation, much admired globally, and with a team of first-class officials whose hearts were in their jobs. Travelling the world (sorry, again, Lavender) dealing with the various problems of impoverishment, principally in Asia and Africa, was an extraordinary education in geopolitics and, frankly, geography. I was happy non-stop, with two great private secretaries, first, Martin Dinham, who later came to Hong Kong with me (in a very competitive field, the best person who ever worked for me), and then Myles Wickstead, who went on to be ambassador to Ethiopia and head of the secretariat of Tony Blair's Africa Commission.

While my friends at home wrestled with intractable economic issues, tortured themselves trying to comprehend and reform social security, invented the poll tax and so on, I flew around running some pretty effective aid programmes and in the course of that work achieving some of development's basic aims, like preventing babies dying prematurely. I hardly ever had to engage in domestic political arguments, rarely went to meetings with the Treasury or with Cabinet committees, and got most of my flavour of British politics from my constituency and my surgeries, three Fridays out of four.

When I came down to earth it was with a mighty bang. Following a larger than expected Green Party vote in the 1989 European Parliament elections, it was thought sensible to replace the clever but not very user-friendly Environment Secretary, Nicholas Ridley, with someone who would stand a good chance of not scaring the horses, or more to the point the voters. The fickle finger of fate pointed at me. So I got promoted to a seat in the Cabinet to run the biggest government department, with seven junior ministers, to draft and promote the first ever Environment White Paper by a government, but also to implement the poll tax, of which news had reached me literally on the bush telephone. The day after my promotion to the Cabinet, there was an Opposition debate in the Commons about it. I had first to learn the rudiments of local-government financing, before – up all night – getting my head around the scheme invented by several of my cleverer colleagues. I gave the worst speech I ever made in the Commons, including the shaming line (drafted by my otherwise astute political adviser, Patrick Rock) 'the community charge' (Tory for the poll tax) 'puts the community in charge'. But I do not grumble about Patrick, a hugely gifted political operator; it is only because of him that I have ever made it into books of quotations, with real humdingers like 'gobsmacked' and 'double whammy'. The story of the poll tax has been written about so much already, and since I intend to write a little more about it in relation to Margaret Thatcher's leadership, I will at this point lock it away for a while. It was the worst thing about running a huge department, whose Permanent Secretary was a great cockney auto-didact, Terry Heiser, as good at the task as anyone I saw doing that or any similar job. Terry had left school in his mid-teens and joined the civil service, where he worked his way to the top. He helped me, in the margins of poll tax damage control, to produce a pretty good White Paper on the environment, *This Common Inheritance*, which was naturally a disappointment to environmentalists, who wanted to see every green target hit first-time round. Our main environmental achievement was to install in the department a serious economist, David Pearce, who made sustainability a central feature of subsequent government policy. David died horribly young, but was a key figure in making environmental economics respectable in Whitehall.

I was at the Environment Department from 1989 to the fall of Margaret Thatcher in 1990. The new Prime Minister, John Major, invited me to become the chairman of the Conservative Party to plan and run the next election campaign. I was made Chancellor of the Duchy of Lancaster, which gave me a few largely ceremonial duties relating to the Royal Family, but otherwise I worked mainly out of the Conservative HQ in Smith Square. In a sense my Westminster career had come full circle. The rest of my political life was spent away from London, in Hong Kong, Northern Ireland and Brussels.

My years spent between the Commons and a variety of government departments from Stormont in Belfast to Waterloo to Victoria Street and Pimlico had left me with some strong views about how well we are governed in Britain. The answer is, not as well as we think. Over the whole post-war period we have been better governed than some other countries, for example Italy. We have avoided calamity, sometimes narrowly. We dissolved our empire, no small thing. We have become more prosperous, though we are a diminished country in terms of our relative economic and political clout. I hope I am right that we are fairer than we were, and also much more tolerant of diversity. But the EU referendum campaign and its aftermath produced some worrying signs of intolerance. Some problems seem beyond our government's ability to resolve them – low productivity, welfare reform, a health service weighed down by the requirements of longevity and social care, an over-centralized system of government, a penal system that imprisons too many and has turned into a revolving door for crime, growing inter-generational unfairness. It should not be impossible to make more headway in unpicking these problems. But the question of how good our government really is is raised above all by some egregious policy failures in the last few years, for example the poll tax, the second Iraq War and the Brexit referendum. These were not indications of a well-led country, and in the case of the Iraq War the Chilcot Inquiry showed how widely the blame for lamentable failures should be apportioned: the political, diplomatic, civil service, intelligence and military establishments all helped to write this horror story. Any fundamental change in our system of government is overwhelmed by an implacable complacency about how good we are at managing our country. There are three main causes of our troubles.

First, policy and the favoured options for resolving our problems emerge from a very narrow funnel. The political parties and those they select dominate policy making, and the choices they propose take little account of the need to build consensus and to take a long-term view. Too much attention is paid to the tabloid press, which becomes more shrill as it becomes less commercially viable. What makes this party dominance even more absurd is that the membership of the parties (with one recent exception) has been in free fall. This is particularly true of the Conservative Party. When I first got involved in politics there were about 1.5 million party members; when I was chairman there were about 450,000; today there are fewer than 150,000. Before long you will be able to fit them all into Wembley Stadium. There are far fewer members of political parties in Britain than in most other European countries. As a proportion of the national electorate, party membership in the UK in the first decade of the century was lower than in any European country other than Poland and Latvia. The Democratic Party in Italy had more members (about 500,000) than all UK parties combined, until the recent rise in Labour members. While political party membership falls, membership of other voluntary organizations rises. The Royal Society for the Protection of Birds has over one million members; The National Trust has more than 4 million; there are over 40,000 members of the Royal National Lifeboat Institute, who support those who risk their lives for those in trouble at sea. The recent increase in Labour Party membership was largely the result of attempts by the left (including the extra-parliamentary left) to keep Jeremy Corbyn in office as leader; a leader widely regarded, not least by many of his parliamentary colleagues, as a literally incredible candidate for residence at 10 Downing Street.

With this recent exception, party membership has got smaller and, in the Conservative Party, older. The party is fortunate in its opponents in England. Yet this largely unrepresentative section of the community is the principal sounding board for policy discussions; it selects MPs; and it plays a large role in choosing the party leader. Paradoxically, the Conservative Party in particular has introduced more democracy into its processes while becoming less representative of our wider electorate. No wonder it chose to be led not long ago by the alas unelectable Michael Howard and Iain Duncan-Smith rather than Kenneth Clarke, one of the best Chancellors of the Exchequer since the war. No wonder too that it led the charge for the EU exit, choosing to dwell in an imagined past rather than make the most of a challenging future. Conservatives are in danger of becoming a narrow party of English nationalists; they seem to have hoovered up many UKIP voters for the time being, which is bound to drag the party to the right. For its part, a main consequence of Labour's recent up-tick in membership is to make its approach to policy even further removed from what most voters regard as an acceptable mix of welfare and the market. These new members are alienated not only from the views (left and right) of the political establishment, but also from the traditional core Labour vote.

I have already mentioned our second problem, over-government at the centre. While this tendency developed, we also foolishly undermined the quality of what had always been one of the best, most effective and creative bureaucracies in the world. Successive governments have run down the policy-making, problem-solving elite of the civil service while contracting out much of the most interesting and important public-service tasks to consultancies. They are more expensive and need to have the details of the problems they are bought in to tackle explained to them by existing civil servants. This undermines civil service morale and recruitment. If you are a clever graduate, why join a government department rather than go to a consultancy at a far higher salary? Civil service mistakes are caricatured and publicized. Repeats of the *Yes, Minister* television programmes feed the idea that civil servants are there to stop ministers doing what they want to do. In my experience good civil servants like decisive ministers who know what they want to do. They implement these decisions enthusiastically, occasionally too enthusiastically. No one ever logs the failure of consultants. I am, however, pleased that recent comedy programmes have shown us some of the worst aspects of the awful growth of ministers' special advisers, or 'spads' as they are charmingly called. Quite why ministers need two, three or four 'spads' to help them act as ministers has always puzzled me. This is one part of our apparatus of governance which needs a Herod-like cull.

Third, political leaders have ceased to be as brave as they might in speaking up for what seems to them to be the public good and the national interest. Worrying that their political authority is too fragile to enable them to do this, they conspire to make it more fragile still. This should be one of the lessons that we take – all of us for example who supported the campaign to keep Britain in the European Union – from the Brexit vote. Nigel Farage was turned into King Kong because he was not actively confronted over every fabrication and half-truth over the years of his rise. The right wing of the Conservative Party was allowed to peddle its illusions and delusions about Britain's future with who knows what consequences.

What are the qualities that a leader requires to be successful? Are there any lessons to be learned from Farage and Trump, even discounting campaign flirtations with dangerously extreme populism? In the next chapter I will consider the three leaders, all very different, for whom I worked directly, and try to understand what can be learned from them about practical political philosophy and about governing in a democracy.

6

Leadership: Heath, Thatcher, Major

If the highest aim of a captain were to preserve his ship, he
would keep it in port forever.

Thomas Aquinas, *Summa Theologica*

The great man of the age is the one who can put into words
the will of his age, tell his age what its will is, and accomplish
it . . . he actualizes his age.

Georg Wilhelm Friedrich Hegel, *Philosophy of Right* (1820)

I worked closely for the first three leaders of the Conservative Party
who were, like me, middle class and, indeed, from towards the
bottom end of that complicated social classification. They all went –
Heath, Thatcher, Major – to state schools. Before Heath no post-war
Conservative leader could possibly describe himself in any sense as
middle class, let alone as a scholarship boy or girl or an example
of social mobility. Harold Macmillan might demur in his thespian
way, occasionally describing himself as though he was 'in trade'.
What he meant was that he was from a family of distinguished
publishers.

This was one of the charming affectations of the Etonian, Grena-
dier husband of the daughter of the 9th Duke of Devonshire. Talking
late with whisky after dinner one night to a small group of Balliol
undergraduates, he told us that when he had been interviewed for the
scholarship exam to the college, the only question he had been asked
was where he had his boots made. We looked around the room at one
another's knockabout shoes and Hush Puppies. Edward Heath's
father was certainly 'in trade'. When my wife was staying with school

friends at their holiday home in Broadstairs in the 1950s and there was any household problem – a blocked lavatory, a window that would not open – the family would contact Ted Heath's father, who ran a successful small building and maintenance firm. He was by all accounts charming, affable and very proud of his clever son. Ted's mother was a maid, presumably of the sort known to dukes' daughters. Heath won a county scholarship from the local grammar school to the same Oxford College that Macmillan had attended long before and where I followed. Margaret Thatcher came from a similar social background. While Heath earned the nickname 'Grocer', presumably because of his successful battle to abolish retail price maintenance, she was a real grocer's daughter, from Grantham in Lincolnshire, an upbringing often used by her to define her identity as a no-nonsense advocate of simple household economics – pennies in, pennies out. Like Heath, she went from a local grammar school to Oxford – Somerville College. John Major came from a very different, rather down-at-heel background, in Brixton with an elderly father who had been a music hall performer before running a declining garden ornaments business. He left school at sixteen and was turned down for his first job as a bus conductor because he was too tall. Through a correspondence course in banking, he eventually found a job in the Standard Chartered Bank. I daresay you could have got long odds from Ladbroke's in Brixton back in the 1960s on him becoming the youngest and one of the longest-serving Conservative Prime Ministers of the twentieth century. These were my three Conservative leaders and not a grandee among them. Not one of them was groomed for leadership in the chapel or on the sports field of one of our great public schools or in the drawing rooms of a country mansion, though Heath did wartime military service, rising to be a regimental adjutant in the Royal Artillery.

What lessons about leadership did I take from working for this trio, and how much do leaders change or shape their time? Views differ on this. Marx, who regarded Napoleon as a 'grotesque' mediocrity provided with a hero's role by the class struggle in France, believed that while men (or women) might make their own history they did not do so in circumstances chosen by themselves. Bismarck, who, had he lived a century earlier, would probably have achieved little, was close to Marx, arguing that great leadership was really about 'listening to the rustle of God's cloak' and 'seizing the hem as He passed across the stage of history'. The size of the stage – think of Lee Kuan Yew in Singapore – affects the scale of what someone can achieve, as do the circumstances which a leader confronts. But whether you believe that women and men can change history, or that they simply navigate its tides, there is a huge appetite for ransacking the lives of the famous to discover how they accomplished what they did and whether there are formulae that others can usefully apply. The counters of bookshops in airport terminals are piled high with books on the subject of leadership which appear to offer a swift passage to the boardroom for all aspiring business-class travellers if only they follow the example of this or that baseball coach or hero of antiquity. Alexander the Great's *Ten Tips for Conquering the World*, or alternatively becoming global vice-president of marketing, are thrust forward at every opportunity.

The military historian John Keegan's book *The Mask of Command: A Study of Generalship* had some sage thoughts on how Alexander himself and other generals built success. Some of what Keegan wrote would resonate with contemporary authors of books on leadership, like the football manager Alex Ferguson and the philanthropist and businessman Michael Moritz, who have together written one of the better books in this genre. Keegan would talk down the importance of the more heroic virtues in a nuclear, democratic age without entirely dismissing the value of some brave and muscular assets.

The two principal pieces of advice I would draw out from, and for, politics are simple: first, to know what you want to do and why you want to do it; and, second, to explain it clearly, preferably in ways that are both understandable and motivating. How many contemporary leaders would have the clarity of mind and expression of the great Duke of Wellington, especially if they had to write out their orders sitting on a horse with shells whistling overhead and exploding all around? Better make it clear that the Coldstream Guards are to go immediately to Hougoumont. In addition, leaders who can weave their aims into a story that connects with people's experiences, hopes and fears (while grabbing on to the hem of God's passing cloak) have a considerable gift; it is close to that ability to speak to and for one's own times about which Hegel wrote. These days this is usually called providing a political narrative. The person in my experience who did this best was Bill Clinton. He would begin his remarks, for instance, with an anecdote about visiting a village in India where electricity had just been installed. He had met there someone who had recently acquired a laptop. He would then muse on the digital divide between countries and people, rich and poor. Concluding, he would offer some smart policy wonkery that could play a part in bridging this division. It was all done humorously, with an easy authority, and it persuaded people.

A leader who had a similar gift was Helmut Kohl, one of the greatest politicians of the second half of the twentieth century. He benefited from the fact that he was consistently underrated (not least by Margaret Thatcher, who could never have comprehended a work ethic which incorporated so much of what she would have regarded as self-indulgence). Kohl once recounted to me a story which for him encapsulated what would happen in Central and Eastern Europe as communist autocracy crumbled like (he said) an old cheese. He had been visited by a senior communist Polish minister just before Pope John Paul II visited his native country. The minister was explaining the security measures taken to prevent euphoria for the Polish Pope dominating the day. He described the number of the police guarding the routes of the papal journey. 'What,' Kohl said to the minister, 'do the policemen do at the end of the day?' 'They go home,' said the minister, 'and have their supper.' 'Who cooks their supper?' asked Kohl. 'Their wives of course,' replied the minister. 'And then I suppose they go to bed with their wives.' 'Yes,' said the minister. 'Are those the same wives who were kneeling in the streets as the Pope passed by earlier in the day?' Kohl had an extraordinary instinct for the spirit of the times. When the possibility of reunification of Germany came, he acted decisively and generously, while others muttered, criticized and tried to play the accountant. Kohl was a great leader, who like some others toppled over when he rather casually assumed that rules were made for others, in his case those regarding party financing.

The best man I ever worked for, and the finest natural leader, was

Peter Carrington. I spent two years as his Political Secretary when he was chairman of the Conservative Party, a job he cordially disliked. Working for him was incomparably the best part of my education, not just about public service, but about how to behave in any position of responsibility. Intelligent, drily witty, self-disciplined, kind, beautifully mannered – all those qualities were still on show years after he had left behind the Foreign Secretaryship and was cantering serenely through his nineties. I recall long and very fast drives in his Jensen through the countryside to some cheerless political meeting (warm white wine, Coronation chicken and a political homily) and his first call when our cavalcade made it home to the accompanying police bodyguards to thank them for their help. He was the best delegator (along with Douglas Hurd) for whom I have worked. They both had the intellectual self-confidence to delegate, were prepared to give the credit (even publicly) when things went right and to take the blame when things went wrong, even when it was not their fault. Consequently, those who worked for them tried very hard to make sure that things did not go off the rails.

Some readers of this book might, I imagine, assume that I would want to be indulgent towards Ted Heath and his memory and record. He was a middle-class scholarship boy from Balliol like me. His journey there for the first time in a Hillman Minx with his loving and proud parents reminds me of my own arrival at the college with my parents, like Heath the first in my family to go to university. There was then his perceived position – though I am not entirely sure that this is accurate when you look at his whole career – on the left of the Conservative Party, where I have always found my own perch.

I must also take account of the fact that he made me the Director of the Conservative Party's Research Department when I was just over thirty. Finally, the great cause of Heath's life – membership of the European Union – has been of greater importance to me than any other political issue; now bedraggled and fallen in the dust, it always exemplified for me the sense of international co-operation which had seemed to be snuffed out in the West for much of the first grim part of the twentieth century. I have always believed that membership of the EU helped to accommodate the fact that one can be a patriotic British citizen while recognizing the opportunities, obligations and challenges we all have as citizens of the world.

All that is true. But I came to think of him as too often selfish, tiresome and even sometimes boorish: a collection of gifts which did not include as many as are usually important to a successful political leader. Chivalry was certainly not his strongest suit. Perhaps I would have liked him more and better if some of the virtues on show for the first sixty years of his life had been on more public display later. The penultimate paragraph in Philip Ziegler's clear-eyed but on the whole complimentary authorized biography of Heath notes that 'he was a great man, but his blemishes, though by far less considerable, were quite as conspicuous as his virtues, and it is too often by his blemishes that he is remembered.'

Any Balliol man is bound to wonder why Heath made it to 10 Downing Street, but not his Balliol contemporaries Denis Healey and Roy Jenkins, both like him presidents of the college Junior Common Room. They had at least as broad a hinterland as the musician and sailor Edward Heath: in Healey's case, languages, literature and music; in Jenkins's, history and a well-earned reputation as a serious biographer. It is fair to say that they also had one advantage denied to Heath. They were both married. Their wives were intelligent, good-looking women with, in due course, considerable careers of their own. This must have helped to keep Healey and Jenkins in touch with the world and, if my own marriage is typical, assured them of the sort of advice about their appearance, behaviour and opinions which they might not have received or been keen to receive from others.

Moreover, Healey and Jenkins had some political gifts that were not in Heath's kitbag. They both spoke very well – Healey with the old bruiser's gift for the joke that kills, Jenkins showing the value of a nicely turned sentence in advancing a cool and rational argument. Healey's rough allure was probably an acquired taste. Certainly it was one I came to appreciate myself – that extraordinary mixture he had of Renaissance and Rabelais. Jenkins, despite a slightly patronizing manner, was capable of charming the birds from the trees, but probably not of attracting a following in a public bar of beer swillers. He once wrote me a letter out of the blue about something I had written which made me go pink with embarrassed vanity as I read it. It was probably a misfortune that he had the dangerous capacity to attract super-loyal disciples. Acolyte entrapment invariably threatens to frustrate the careers of the ambitious.

Ted Heath of course – this is much to his credit – had true friends, but not I think any starry-eyed acolytes. His friends were dog-loyal, often in the face of rather than because of his behaviour and of the way he displayed loyalty to them. Another man would have given Francis Pym the credit he deserved for determinedly pressing the case for allowing a free vote on the initial EU legislation. Another might have stood aside earlier to let Whitelaw or Prior contest the party leadership in 1975. His best and closest friends in politics would, I suspect, have sympathized mightily with what Ziegler wrote at the end of his biography. Hurd, Prior, Whitelaw, Carrington – they all, and others, crawled over broken glass for him. They thought him, rightly, a man of the greatest integrity, with an unshakeable commitment to public service. But I can imagine them now rolling their eyes – small, rather despairing smiles playing across their lips – as they sought to explain away another of Ted's gallery of bloody-minded solecisms. The fact that these men were his friends speaks to his credit; whether the way he treated those closest to him does so is more doubtful.

In comparison with Healey and Jenkins, Heath – with what Douglas Hurd has called his Easter Island face – was all too often solitary, gruff, angular and strangely inarticulate (except perhaps in his later and even ruder years), revelling in his own charmlessness and also perhaps in the surprising extent to which others seemed to revel in it as well. My first encounter with Ted's limited emotional intelligence (to be kind) came when I went with my fellow speech writer, the playwright Ronnie Millar, to Heath's chambers in Albany, Piccadilly, to write a party-political broadcast for the leader to deliver on the radio. We were summoned for 10.30 on a Saturday morning. Heath appeared in a vast kimono-style dressing grown about an hour later, like a character from a Savoy opera. No apology, just a brusque 'Right, care and compassion this morning, I believe', outlining the theme he wanted to address. At about one o'clock his housekeeper came in with a tray bearing a half-bottle of Chablis and a lobster salad. He began wolfing the meal down, eventually looking up over the napkin tucked into his kimono to ask, 'Have you chaps eaten yet?' 'No,' we replied, enthusiasm mounting. 'You must be jolly hungry then,' he replied, munching and sipping on. Was this a joke? If it was, as jokes go I would not have given it a pass. All of us remembered similar behaviour over the years, sometimes accompanied by much shoulder-shaking laughter. All who ever worked for her know that Margaret Thatcher would, in any similar circumstances, have had to be dragged back from the kitchen, where she would have been making sandwiches whether you wanted them or not.

Now it may be that this sort of thing does not matter. We are only talking about food. Perhaps such small kindnesses have no part in leadership. The great man or woman has too much important strategic thinking to do to bother about social niceties with the staff. I simply do not buy this. Looking after those around you, noticing them, seeming to care about them (or actually doing so), treating them as far as possible as equally human if not as equals, is a fundamental aspect of leadership.

What was it then – certainly not much in the way of lovability – that fired Heath (or others for that matter) into orbit, catching for a brief moment the rays of the sun before burning out in the infinite dark? Was it and is it simply luck? Was Ted Heath Prime Minister mainly because he was lucky? Did he subsequently fail simply because he was massively, disproportionately unlucky? How much did his inability to speak for and to the age matter?

Heath's career certainly bears the imprint of good fortune as he rose to the top, and then the luck turned dramatically. He had been a new MP with the 'One Nation' generation of young former soldiers like Iain Macleod and Enoch Powell. He was not as clever as them; he did not dazzle. But he made a career for himself in an arena where dazzling is not required, is even frowned upon: he became a government whip and moved up from one adjutant's post to another, in the days when backbenchers were expected to be loyal and usually were. This was, one should not forget, a long time ago. He rapidly became Chief Whip, adept at counting the bodies and slipping the occasional warning in the ears of the potentially mutinous and an inducement or two in those of the ambitious. By the time of Suez, the most disastrous foreign-policy debacle in Britain until the Iraq War and the Brexit referendum, he was Chief Whip, doing the business for a beleaguered government and like Harold Macmillan avoiding blame for a disaster on which his personal views remained (probably necessarily) impenetrably opaque. There is no question that he had a good invasion and a good retreat, helping to keep the government and the parliamentary party together. Macmillan – 'first in, first out' – not surprisingly gave him afterwards ministerial jobs at the Ministry of Labour and then as Sir Alec Douglas-Home's No. 2 at the Foreign Office.

Ted Heath was fortunate that Douglas-Home rather than Rab Butler succeeded Macmillan. He doubtless knew the way the land was likely to lie when he himself backed the 14th Earl. Had Butler won, the succession to him would likely have run in another direction, through Macleod and the rest of the old Conservative Research Department group. As it was, the Etonian earl – match sticks, shotguns, fishing rods and old-world decency – was followed by Ted, who beat the ubiquitously idle if clever Reggie Maudling, largely because of the perceived skills of the leader of the Labour Party, Harold Wilson. One modern man, who could talk credibly about economics and technology, deserved and was matched by another. It was time for the professional scholarship boys to show what they could do. The answer was the 1960s and 1970s, from which it seems to me just about the best things to emerge were the Open University, Roy Jenkins's reforms at the Home Office, avoiding getting involved in the Vietnam War and joining the European Common Market. Beyond those things, I think that we should pass politely by, looking forward to better days.

Having become leader of the Conservative Party, and lost the 1966 election, Heath was lucky to win in 1970, perhaps because Roy Jenkins was such a responsible Chancellor, something that must have peeved his Prime Minister, Harold Wilson. It is sometimes said that this or that election would have been a good one to lose. As an ex-party chairman (oh not so happy days!) this is an idea with which I wrestle. No election seems at the time a good one to lose. But given what was about to hit Britain, I think you could make an exception for 1970. Machiavelli's 'fortuna' – his idea of luck which you could if bold and skilful turn your way – was about to make way for demons and avenging angels.

The lack of competitiveness of British industry, the all too potent and irresponsible arrogance of the trade unions, the exploding tensions in John Bull's slum, Northern Ireland: all these calamities were about to break over the Heath government's head. At the same time, the world economy was turning sour with commodity prices (particularly for energy) soaring, when our own North Sea oil wells were not yet on stream. Their contribution to our national wealth was yet to be garnered and frittered away by future governments.

So the dark clouds rolled in. I do not believe that any Prime Minister since the war has confronted such a combination of malign events. They wrecked a programme devised for government which focused on reversing Britain's downward drift by rebuilding competitiveness and increasing the efficiency of government. Truth to tell, 'Selsdon man' (as this programme was known because of the hotel where the core document was drafted) was not all that different from 'Finchley woman'. But the second time round it all worked much better – maybe because of Margaret Thatcher's canniness; maybe because she had previous disasters from which to learn; maybe because she was fortunate about North Sea oil revenues and a downward drift in world agriculture prices; maybe because by the 1980s Britain was fed up with the tacky and unsuccessful compromises of the past.

The Heath government's excessively rigid and legalistic approach to union reform – well-intentioned as it was, and a centrepiece of its strategy – came apart in the government's hands. An attempt to get industry to brace up and make its own way was sunk on the Clyde with unemployment there and everywhere else on the rise. Macro-economic policy was dominated by stoking a boom, racking up deficits and trying to control inflation by encouraging pay moderation. Fatally for the presentation of the government's case, and for the shaping of policy itself, Heath's first Chancellor, Iain Macleod, died within five weeks of taking office. In later months and years, Britain seemed forever shut down, locked out, stumbling from one candlelit crisis to another. The Conservative Party shuffled, confused, with the Cabinet Secretary, William Armstrong, at Ted Heath's side, from a market-oriented policy, designed by a regiment of policy groups in Opposition, to dirigisme and corporatism in government. There is a sense in which you can best gauge the depth of gloom and schizophrenia in the Conservative Party at the time by the fact that after losing two elections in quick succession it elected 'that bloody woman' – as Heath and others called her – as leader. By the end of 1974, the party's rank and file – the envelope stuffers, *Daily Telegraph* readers and the unpromotable backbenchers – turned on their officers and gunned them down. Ted Heath's ill-fortune blew him and his close colleagues away.

While it is plainly wrong to suggest that in politics you make your own fortune, the way you handle what comes your way can break you or promote you. At crucial moments, Heath was uncertain about whether to tough things out with the unions or back off and live, just about, to fight another day. In the winter of 1973/4, he could not decide whether to hit the election button quickly and decisively or postpone an electoral reckoning. Maybe it was honourable to try to avoid a divisive election campaign. But, in the event, he chose to go to the country despite what may well have been his own principled reservations. So the election came too late. It should have been earlier or not have been called at all. Hamlet tossed and turned, and the King lived on:

> The time is out of joint; O cursed spite,
> That ever I was born to set it right.

'Who governs Britain?' Conservatives asked in February 1974. 'Clearly not you, mate,' replied voters. But they didn't vote Wilson in decisively either. I do not believe that Heath's indecision was reprehensible, but it proved politically calamitous.

Sometimes of course Heath had been dramatically decisive. Which other contemporary political leaders have moved so swiftly from one philosophical end of the economic and political argument to the other? For example, it looked to many of its supporters that a Conservative Party elected to bury Mr Benn and all his works had dusted him down and installed him at the heart of Whitehall, intervening in the economy incontinently. Whatever the excesses, it was difficult to swallow this reversal.

Fortune only tells us part of the story of a political career. There is also the question of where a man or a woman stands on the big issues of the time and whether he or she makes a difference to the way they play out. On these scores, Edward Heath comes out ahead of many of his contemporaries in politics. He was right about the perils of nationalism in Europe; right about self-determination in the old empire, at least in all but the last of Britain's colonies; and right about racism.

Heath's views on Spain, on the rise of Hitler and on Munich in the 1930s – he had travelled in Germany as a young man and seen Nazism at first hand – were part of the narrative that carried him on to the negotiation of Britain's membership of what was to become the European Union. He saw the terrible harm that nineteenth-century nationalism had done to Europe in his own century. Had he been able to express himself as well as Macmillan did, I guess that his primary declared motivation for Britain's Common Market membership would have lain in the obscenities of European history. Among those from Heath's and Macmillan's Oxford college who fought in the First World War, three men won Victoria Crosses (two posthumously) and two the Iron Cross. For both these Conservative leaders it was appalling that young men were brought together to study the classic works of our civilization and were then trained to kill one another by the countries that had created this civilization. The destructive nationalism of twentieth-century European history impelled Heath into the crusade for reconciliation and integration. Whatever the imperfections of the architecture that was created, at least the second half of the century was a lot happier than the first. Moreover, Britain itself – in the 1960s and 1970s, the sick man of Europe – became thereafter one of the strongest and most competitive European countries, with pretty much 'à la carte' membership of the club. Heath understood how Britain could, over time, transform itself; he understood too the difference between patriotism and nationalism, though it was his and his cause's misfortune that he could not express it very well.

It was Heath's own dogged diplomacy that eventually unlocked the French door to EU membership. He courted President Pompidou assiduously and successfully. When the suit was successfully brought to the altar, it was the French President who best expressed what was happening. 'Through two men who are talking to each other,' President Pompidou said in an after-dinner speech during the 1971 negotiations, 'two peoples are trying to find each other again. To find each other to take part in a great joint endeavour – the construction of a European group of nations determined to reconcile the safeguards of their national identities with the constraints of acting as a community.' Quite so.

As Opposition leader and in government, Heath refused to compromise with Ian Smith over Rhodesia's claim to be an independent racist state, and he was equally uncompromising in resisting racism within his own party and country. Heath rode the storms, which Enoch Powell helped to stir up, and he was right to do so.

In his last years, there was one other issue which raised my doubts and my hackles about Ted Heath. When Britain signed the Joint Declaration with China over Hong Kong in 1984, Heath criticized the British government for not pressing ahead faster with the democratization of the colony. When I went to Hong Kong as Governor in 1992 and tried to ensure that the elections held there were at least free and fair, without introducing greater democracy than the limited amount allowed for in the Joint Declaration and the Basic Law, Heath denounced me and came to Hong Kong each year during my governorship, staying in my official home and criticizing us privately and publicly for what we were trying to do. Why? I think the reason is the mildly discreditable one that the Chinese leaders continued to treat him in his long wilderness years as though he were still premier. Flattery, and perhaps his commercial interest, blinded him to the sins of Leninists in Beijing and to the importance of treating our last colonial subjects honourably. I suspect his attitude also owed something to the fact that Margaret Thatcher supported me. These were not his finest moments.

I have mentioned my surprise at the number of leaders in politics who clearly do not like people very much. It will be evident from what I have said that Edward Heath was one such, by no stretch of the imagination a great 'people person', and he was certainly uncomfortable with the vulgarities of politics and campaigning (which is not necessarily to his discredit). But, whatever he thought of all those imperfect voters, not least the Conservative ones, and their resistance to his dreams and his managerial schemes, he did his best by the British people. He was a patriot, and he gave them his best shot. When that sadly was not enough for them, he retired for almost three decades – such a waste – in a massive sulk, retired not to his tent but to his handsome house looking on to one of Britain's great and most iconic buildings, Salisbury Cathedral. If they were fair-minded and charitable, people surely felt just a little bit sad and sorry for him there. He had become 'grumpy and disappointed of Salisbury'. Perhaps less grumpy after 1990 and the fall of Margaret Thatcher, but never less than disappointed until his death in 2005.

One very obvious difference between Heath and Thatcher, whose emergence as Ted's successor was in part a result of his failures as a leader, was their use of language and their attitude to it. The language of party manifestos was an example of this. Manifestos came with a variety of titles usually close to the theme that tomorrow would be better than yesterday or today. A famous advertisement for *The Times* used to announce, 'There's something interesting in tomorrow's *Times*', which invited the response, 'Damn it, I bought today's.' I was frequently given the job of writing these documents, which were largely treaties between different factions in the party and read, if at all, by very few outside Whitehall and special interest groups. The best one I wrote, in 1979, with Angus Maude, a senior Conservative MP, went without a title, simply announcing that it was the Conservative Manifesto. But, inside, it was rather more informative and certainly managed to avoid the usual clichés, describing the way in which a new government would 'move forward to confront the challenges of change firmly but fairly'.

Ted Heath's manifesto in 1966 went far to summarize his own approach. *Action Not Words*, it announced briskly: so there. This meant: 'We don't want any more of this guff about prosperity on sustainable foundations. What we want is a plan in a few clear sentences and then we'll get on and do it.' *Action Not Words* overlooks the fact that a lot of politics in a democracy is about words – words that motivate, give a sense of direction, mobilize to action to secure an objective that may not at first blush appear to be in the listener's interest. As I have argued, this was not Heath's strong suit, a point picked up in *Private Eye*'s caricature of him as a corporate executive obsessed with the operation of the automatic beaker disposal unit. Even on Europe, where Heath was passionately clear about what he wanted to do, the words rarely moved beyond the tepidly managerial.

Margaret Thatcher loved words. She carried around in her famously capacious handbag all manner of scraps of paper (House of Commons writing paper or Basildon Bond) on which she had jotted down the wisdom of the ages. Occasionally, after scolding her speechwriters for their inability to find a bit of poetic text to elevate an argument, she would produce these bits of paper and read some of them out, occasionally with a slight shake of the head as if admonishing her small audience for the fact that they had not produced anything as resonant as Rudyard Kipling or Milton Friedman. She liked clarity as well as poetry and usually had a direct message, partly the result of her methodical approach to life. (According to her biographer, Charles Moore, she explained to a friend on a walk at Christmas 1942 why she could not believe in angels. 'I have worked out scientifically that in order to fly, an angel would need a six-foot-long breastbone to bear the weight of the wings.') Conservatives, she thought, needed an equally methodical approach to deciding what they stood for: socialists had an ideology, so Conservatives needed one of their own. During the days of the party leadership election, I was visited at the Conservative Research Department, where I was by then director, by Rab Butler, who came to give his episcopal blessing from time to time to the little political cloister which he had helped to create. In the department's Georgian premises in Westminster we had an ancient caged lift which squeaked and hiccupped its ascent to my office bearing Rab and me, Rab in his black overcoat, the collar lightly dusted by dandruff making him a passable impersonation of Mount Fuji. As we rose slowly through the building he asked me, 'Do we have to take this Thatcher business seriously?' To my reply in the affirmative, he responded with a question about what she believed and wanted to do. I began to reel off, as accurately as I could, what I thought she stood for. 'Too much, too much,' he opined. 'Like the motions at a Party Conference.'

It was true, with the rather dangerous addition that everything had to be joined together by an uninterrupted and uninterruptable umbilical cord. If they – the socialists – had an 'ism', we must have one too. Her intellectual mentor, the charming and kind Keith Joseph, was to say about that time that after years in Parliament and in government he had only just discovered the 'ism' that represented Conservative thinking. Like a former but now guilt-laden agnostic, he suddenly discovered God and His testaments, written by Hayek and Friedman. Before taking up any further public office, we Conservatives should all do penance, confess our sins and self-flagellate before the electorate whose interests had previously been betrayed by our benighted apostasy.

Margaret, not being as gentle a soul as Keith, took things a stage further. If you did not accept the whole package – monetarism, cutting back the state, reducing taxes, ending the dependency culture, affirming stridently whatever she believed to be middle-class values – you were worse than a non-believer; you were a heretic, quisling or (in short) wet. Keith never put it in such uncompromising terms. When in 1985 I became his deputy in the Department of Education and Science, he asked me to go round to his home off the King's Road to have tea with him. 'I know,' he said, 'that we have rather different intellectual positions. So I thought I would give you a list of the books that have most influenced me.' He was surprised that I had read some of them – including Hayek's *The Road to Serfdom* and Sam Brittan's *The Treasury under the Tories*. I once asked Keith whether he thought I was a wolf in sheep's clothing or a sheep in wolf's clothing. He quite liked the joke.

A few of Thatcher's more mindless acolytes regarded my own opinions, and presumably the unfathomable fact that Margaret used and promoted me, as a reason for particularly vehement hostility to my unashamed wetness. Perhaps the problem was that I did not seem to mind too much about their personal malevolence though it did puzzle me. I had always thought myself, if not exactly herbivorous, at least reasonably affable. A manifestation of this rancour occurred when I lost my seat in Bath when I was party chairman in 1992. Some of these hardliners were at a party held in the home (I was told) of Alastair McAlpine, the party's treasurer, where the assembled Thatcher groupies apparently cheered my defeat as a Conservative gain. Many of those present were birds of passage through the Conservative Party, going on at a later election to support Jimmy Goldsmith's Referendum Party. Lavender said I should have been flattered by the identity of most of my antagonists. As I said, your opponents are in other parties, your enemies are in your own.

Margaret Thatcher's freedom from doubt helped give her rhetoric a self-confident drive that frequently belied what was really happening. At its outset her government had marched for a dismal year or two to the brass bands of monetarism, a funeral march for much of British industry. Over time she somehow managed to muffle the drums and trumpets, fudging the ideological commitment to this creed in its most dogmatic form. Her government slipped out of the straitjacket it imposed. Algebraic equations and the letter 'M' with a variety of numbers attached elided into a generalized call for honest money, low taxes and fiscal rectitude (a determination to some extent honoured in the breach).

But the party knew what she was on about. For many, what she regarded as the economics that she had learned from her father, Alderman Roberts, behind the grocer's counter, were part of their DNA. Keynes was associated with fiscal irresponsibility, or, worse, socialist depravity. It was never difficult to write a speech for her which a party conference would cheer; this is a sentence which is accurate as it stands but would have failed a lie detector test if it had finished after the words 'for her'. The trouble about these drafting sessions was they were often dominated by a spurious search for an intellectually coherent thesis with its roots in what she argued was Conservative philosophy.

Nevertheless, she did find a language which resonated abroad as well as at home. For example, the Technicolor dramas of her assertion of freedom in politics and economics made her an iconic figure as Russia's empire crumbled away. This was principally a consequence of its own internal contradictions and failures, steady external pressure over four decades, the mistaken Soviet intervention in Afghanistan, and the comparison which acceptance of the Helsinki Final Act allowed the citizens of communist tyrannies to make with pluralist values. But Thatcher's heroic rhetoric and record certainly provided hope and inspiration to many in Central and Eastern Europe.

At home, her tone and her rhetoric defied the notion that in the 1980s running Britain was an exercise in managing decline. Her success in making Britain governable again was an enormous achievement, for which the majority of Britons, including Tony Blair, should be hugely grateful. It is the main reason, and no slight one, for asserting her claim on some great qualities as a leader. It is more difficult to regard Thatcher's record as providing a template of Conservative government. She did not define the identity of Conservatism. Thatcherism – not a fully worked-out doctrine, but in effect simply the aggregate of what she did – was not always very Conservative, and in the end she came close not only to wrecking the Conservative Party but also, in the longer term, to corroding the middle-class values whose preservation was the objective of her furious activities.

As I argued earlier, Conservatives should run a mile at the suggestion that they have an ideology aimed at changing the culture of the nation. Yet this construct was nailed in 1979 to a prospectus of Friedmanite monetarism for which there was very little empirical evidence, and even less evidence after the early 1980s. Could you really control and even define the quantity of money in the economy? Was the demand for money stable and the speed of its circulation almost constant? Was a market economy self-regulating, so that a government should not bother itself with trying to manage demand for goods and services, but focus on its finances and the reduction of the Public Sector Borrowing Requirement? This was a faith-based project which, when combined with the impact of the global increase in the price of oil, applied a tourniquet to the prospects for industry in Britain. Interest rates and the pound rose; costs were increased because of oil and wage increases; demand fell at home and abroad. Profits fell; output fell; unemployment soared. Government policy cut a swathe through manufacturing industry; between a quarter and a fifth of manufacturing industry was wiped out. It was what Peter Walker (he is the presumed author of the remark) called 'the economics of the mad house'.

The senior Conservatives who put these criticisms of monetarism most forcefully were Ian Gilmour and Jim Prior. Ian was a fine journalist and, that historically endangered species, an intellectual in British politics. There was a maddening gap between his aggressive and razor-sharp debating style around a dinner table and his rather drooping manner of public speaking; he was a tall man, but always seemed to be trying to hide behind the lectern. Every conversation with him was a delight, a really tough and witty give and take. I enjoyed his company as much as that of any older politician I have known. I think Margaret rather cared for him too, admiring his brain and his old-world charm. But eventually she obviously felt that she could no longer keep such a dissident member of the crew on board the ship. Being slipped over the side was rather a relief to him. Jim Prior was the other formidable critic of the economic policies of 1979–81, watching with bewilderment as clever people destroyed industries whose needs they could not apparently comprehend. Michael Foot made a brilliant speech about this in the Commons, comparing their surprise as large chunks of British industry disappeared before their eyes with his favourite comic magician who used to borrow a watch from a member of the audience, cover it with a cloth, smash it with a hammer, and then – the pieces in his hand – apologize to the owner for having forgotten the rest of the trick.

Fortunately, at about the same time that 'the wets' like Gilmour and Christopher Soames were expelled from the garden because of their (fairly muted) opposition to this ideological folly, the government relaxed its fiscal policy and set off a mini-boom in July 1982, abolishing hire purchase restrictions, dismantling other controls, and expanding consumer and business credits. Recovery began once the government slipped off its monetarist shackles. The Falklands War and a credit boom in 1983 helped to secure the government's re-election. Maybe the freezing-cold bath in which industry had been immersed meant that the survivors of the shock emerged fitter and more efficient. Certainly they were helped by tax cuts, the relaxation of controls, reform of the unions and the changed climate about enterprise – though the firms that were sold off to the public had to operate within tight regulatory constraints. But it is easier with hindsight to see a real break between the policies of 1979–81 and what followed, rather than regard the first period as paving the way for later success, marked by the scarcely surprising popularity of a credit-consumption boom. In the ten years after Margaret's first election, consumption rose by nearly seven points as a percentage of GDP while manufacturing investment fell. Nevertheless, inflation was sharply reduced and productivity rose, though it still lagged behind our competitors. While many benefited from the consumption boom and tax cuts, this did not include the poor. Moreover, even despite the huge benefit of North Sea oil, revenues from which accounted for about one tenth of the Chancellor's budget by the mid-1980s, praise of Victorian values seemed to preclude the replacement of a large part of the infrastructure that the Victorians had bequeathed.

A reasonable verdict might be that the most transformative thing that the Thatcher government did on the economic front was to redress the balance between the unions, other economic actors and the national democratic interest. But this was no small thing. The unions and an unreformed public sector had defeated Harold Wilson and Edward Heath. Jim Callaghan had simply tried to manage the slide downhill with a rueful suggestion that there was nothing much anyone could do about it. But there was, and she did it, cannily and bravely riding her luck, doing a bit at a time, falling back when she was not going to win, digging in when she absolutely had to win. Was she fortunate, making the most of her luck from time to time? Of course she was. Arthur Scargill was the gift that went on giving; so too a divided Labour Party led from the left and abandoned by the Social Democrats. So Thatcher drained a sea of fudge, brought the unions to heel, reasserted the case for markets and enterprise, opened the chance of home ownership to tens of thousands of council tenants, and re-established the governability of the country. For the rest, a damaging ideological experiment was succeeded by pretty traditional market-oriented policies which favoured consumption and pre-election booms.

In 1990, Margaret Thatcher argued, 'Do not say it is time for something else! Thatcherism is not for a decade. It is for centuries!' Well, actually, no. There were for example two departures from traditional Conservative philosophy that had shelf-lives which were in the first case passing and in the second balefully long-lived – surviving at least until today. Any regard for the importance of intermediary institutions in society – for example, universities, the BBC, local government – was thought a denial of the government's democratic authority. Margaret Thatcher's government was a ruthless centralizer. No one should stand in the way – from Ken Livingstone to the professions to university Vice-Chancellors. The way in which opposition to these government policies was sometimes conducted demeaned those who understandably took up the cudgels against them: denying Margaret an honorary degree from her own university discredited it; rioting against the poll tax was inexcusable. But both actions reflected real, sustained and understandable opposition to bad policies.

The poll tax was a crazy policy devised by a group of very clever men. Quite how it ever survived from the scientists' laboratory to the light of day tells much about the servility which had become by the late 1980s a dominant characteristic of the way the government did business. Certainly no new tax should survive without the agreement of the Treasury, and Nigel Lawson was one of the few ministers who opposed it. Having done so vigorously but unsuccessfully, he retired in a grumpy huff to his tent from which he only occasionally re-appeared, for example to dress me down for trying to get the Prime Minister to understand the horrendous political consequences of what the poll tax would do to Conservative fortunes. I wanted her to intervene either to abate the financial consequences for ordinary fam-ilies by capping individual losses, or by introducing the tax bit by bit. Nothing happened: a politician usually hypersensitive about the impact of tax or interest changes on people's pocket books, she was then distracted by rows over Europe. My main meeting with her about this, shortly after my appointment in 1989, was the only one at No. 10 of which there appeared to be no minutes. The poll tax came in and Margaret went out: it was a much more important reason for her downfall than rows about Europe, although it was more than self-indulgent to lose both Nigel Lawson and Geoffrey Howe to res-ignations over European policy. No one close to her had the gumption to tell her that what she was doing was reckless.

It was partly because she had gone out on a limb before, risked pretty much everything, and been proved right. It was during the Falk-lands campaign that Thatcher's qualities as a leader who could blow a trumpet and bring the walls of Jericho (or Port Stanley) down were best demonstrated. She was exactly the sort of brave leader that gener-als and admirals, and those they commanded perhaps, admired and even loved. She was clever, decisive, supportive, courageous, unsqueam-ish and a doubt-free zone. Unfortunately, one of the triggers for the campaign may have been inadequately considered public spending cuts (especially on the navy), and she had some difficulty in displaying any magnanimity in the wake of victory. Good soldiers are often excellent at this since they have witnessed the horrors of war, the large and small acts of decency and courage, close up. (Remember *The Surrender at Breda*.) Nevertheless, the Falklands campaign was her finest hour.

Margaret Thatcher's courage had been honed over the years. At every rung in her clamber up the political ladder, the grocer's daughter must have felt the weight of people – mostly, but not exclusively, men – patronizing her. At Oxford, it probably felt worse than it was. She had only just scraped into Somerville to read Chemistry, and even her college head (a woman) was subsequently witheringly condescending about her intellectual abilities. Her north London constituency (for which she was chosen as Conservative candidate by a stroke of more than luck) enabled critics to associate her opinions with a suburban world view, as though there was something intellectually diminishing about living in Finchley with a privet hedge. I doubt whether many of the Conservative MPs who voted for her as leader thought she could win an election: for them the important thing was that she was not Ted Heath. Even after that victory, her gender and her self-confident – sometimes overbearing – advocacy of positions that often challenged conventional wisdom (not always itself wise) created patronizing resentment. She responded by developing a battling Boadicea personality, and a brittle carapace of opinions on everything under the sun. In practice, she was mostly more cautious and politically smart than her language and attitude suggested she would be, at least until her retirement meant that there were fewer practical consequences to what she said. She was undoubtedly a luckier politician than either Heath or Major. But she was brilliant at spotting when the currents were running in her favour, and brave in taking them in full flood.

In person she was a strange mixture of kindness and occasional bullying. I was fortunate, despite sometimes disagreeing with her publicly as well as privately, to be the beneficiary mostly of the former and very seldom of the latter. She was particularly graceful and courteous towards waitresses, drivers, lift attendants and the like. She remembered partners' and children's names. When I was director of the Conservative Research Department and writing conference speeches and pamphlets for her, one of my daughters had an accident. Margaret was particularly solicitous, especially when she discovered that she and Laura almost shared a birthday. She used to send me home after party conferences bearing one of the cakes that her well-wishers had baked for her.

Later, when I was in Hong Kong, she visited quite often. She was always impeccably mannered, was pretty well the only house guest we ever had who made her own bed, and relentlessly spoiled our greedy terriers, Whisky and Soda, feeding the little buggers smoked-salmon sandwiches and chocolate bourbon biscuits in her sitting room, where they invariably spent most of the time when she was staying. She was always supportive of my work in Hong Kong despite the efforts of some to squeeze a few words of criticism out of her, and even when provoked by the identity of some of my other visitors. For example, she came to stay one summer on the way back from a conference she had been addressing in Hawaii. She arrived late in the evening, exhausted from the long flight, while we were finishing my birthday dinner with a group of friends. Kindly, she said she would come down and join us for a celebratory drink after she had 'powdered her nose'. Nose powdered she joined us in the drawing room, was poured a whisky, and fell fast asleep on a sofa, her feet tucked up characteristically under her. The rest of us were chatting away, and one of my friends asked me how a visit earlier that week to Hong Kong by Helmut Kohl had gone. (Answer: Mr Kohl's consumption of Chinese food did not let Germany down.) At the mention of Chancellor Kohl's name, Margaret awoke with a start as though an electric charge had been passed through her. Without drawing breath, she went straight into a not-so-short lecture on the history of Europe out of which neither France nor Germany emerged with much credit. 'And,' she said at the end, turning to my wife as though denouncing a crime against humanity, 'I believe that you have just bought a house *in France*.' Her charming private secretary came gallantly to Lavender's rescue. 'Well, Margaret, you can't hold that against the Pattens. Peter Lilley [an intellectual ally of Mrs T] has bought a chateau in France.' She paused for a nano-second and then continued her advance, guns blazing. 'Yes,' she said, 'but it's in northern France.' Oh, for the days before Calais had to be inscribed on Queen Mary's heart.

This was one example out of many of Thatcher's truncated sense of humour, on which in retrospect I look more kindly than I do on Heath's. She occasionally got, or even came close to making, what my mother would have called a 'broad joke', mildly lavatorial or related to the reproductive organs. But subtlety was a very rare visitor, and she had no self-knowledge of how absurd she could seem; hence I suppose 'We are a grandmother', her breathy announcement to the press in Downing Street of the birth of a grandchild. One illustration of this incapacity came when in 1977 Ronnie Millar and I were doing duty again on the speech-writing front, passed down like baubles of office from Ted to Margaret. At party conferences these were dire occasions. We would work in a hotel room – I remember with particular horror the Arthur Askey Suite at the Imperial Hotel, Blackpool, complete with a green shagpile carpet rather like an unmown lawn. Each day we would write most of a new speech, which would be torn to pieces late into each night by our diva, while we made desperate efforts to save a few bits for the next day's offering. Worst of all were the occasions when she would arrive late at night clutching a draft that some aspirant for her favour had pressed on her, full of the sort of stuff that her instincts would have liked her to utter but which her political intelligence would usually eventually reject. One year we were writing the speech not long after Jim Callaghan had become Prime Minister and announced his conversion to monetarism. This was greeted by his son-in-law, the economic journalist Peter Jay, who was about to go off to Washington as British ambassador, as a spectacular example of leadership, tantamount to Moses leading his people into the Promised Land. Ronnie and I wrote a passage for the speech welcoming this conversion and concluding, 'So my message to Moses is this: keep taking the tablets.'

Night after night – and these drafting sessions would go on until near dawn – Margaret stopped at this line, her red pen poised to strike, and said she thought it made no sense. Night after night we fought successfully to retain it. On the last night, we seemed to have completed the speech to her approval right down to the R. C. Sheriff type peroration in which Ronnie specialized (these passages usually brought stout Tory ladies close to tears). Then she suddenly struck. Putting down her whisky she said, 'Can we go back to that Moses line? Wouldn't it be better not to say 'keep taking the tablets', but 'keep taking the pill'.' Grimacing in horror at one another, we managed to convince her that this would not be a good idea. The following day she delivered the line as we had drafted it. There was a roar of laughter. I do not think she ever knew why.

Britain could at least be governed again after the Thatcher years.

But was what emerged from the ideological struggles of this era, often fought over very muddy terrain with few intellectual peaks in view, the sort of cultural shift in Britain that was her aim? Did she help to change Britain's soul? She would undoubtedly have hated some of the results of her decade in office. She was a committed unionist, but the United Kingdom faced the growing threat that Scottish nationalism would break it up. She usually believed strongly in traditional middle-class values – prudence, saving, looking after your family against a rainy day, and would have had no time surely for 'loads of money' triumphalism, from city yobs to retail slobs – but she did not seem to comprehend that if you banged on the whole time about price the notion of values could easily go for a burton. Some go further and question whether she made it more difficult in Britain to conserve anything any more. I do not agree with that. It should always be pos-sible to conserve in a wet sort of way while conceding sufficient change to keep things much the same. Margaret's intellectual hero, Hayek, would not have approved of this idea. In the book she said that she most admired (*The Constitution of Liberty*), he explained at the end why he was not a Conservative at all. Conservatism, which he thought was far too close to nationalism, could never be more than a brake on the wrong journey. 'Conservatism,' he concluded, 'may often be a useful practical maxim but it does not give us any guiding principles which can influence long-range development.' She surely cannot have believed this; perhaps she skipped that chapter.

Thatcher's departure from the leadership was sad. Tears were shed, often by crocodiles: 'dust to dust, and ashes to ashes'. All of us in the Cabinet had been required to see her individually after she didn't do quite well enough in the first leadership ballot. I do not think that many urged her to fight on with promises of abiding, strong support. For my part, I told her that I thought she would lose if she went on and that it would be humiliating. Better to go now than to face this. When she decided not to fight on (Denis's advice too) and a new bal-lot for the leadership was held, I worked with several of my friends for Douglas Hurd, making it clear (for example, to the inquiries of Norman Lamont) that I would not myself be a candidate. I did not think I could win and have always found sentiments like 'it's sensible to put down a marker for the future' pretty risible. The imagined future rarely comes. I would have been happy with either John Major or Michael Heseltine as leader, but Douglas was the man in the Cabinet whom I most admired – both clever and wise, a senatorial figure and a great delegator. At last, I reckoned, we would have a Prime Minister who was pretty normal.

We actually got one in John Major, by a comfortable margin, though not as a result of the myths about matricide spread by the right wing of the party. They convinced themselves that Margaret had been brought down by a coup, triggered by disloyal left-wing Cabinet ministers and their henchmen and henchwomen, largely on account of her tough views on developments in Europe. It is true that Thatcher's rows with her close colleagues Nigel Lawson and Geoffrey Howe, over whether Britain should join the Exchange Rate Mechanism and link sterling informally to the Deutschmark as a way of disciplining the economy, contributed – through their shrill antagonism – to a feeling that she was losing her grip. But the biggest reason for her fall was hostility to the poll tax, the unpopularity of which stuck to her like fly paper. Moreover, as has invariably been the case, it was right-wingers who were the flakiest when it came to trying to keep the ship afloat through choppy waters, though some of her most ideologically loyal praetorian guard did continue to support her long past the moment when her position was lost.

John was elected leader partly because she was thought to favour him rather than anyone else. Above all, he was not Michael Heseltine, whom she regarded as regicide-in-chief. John had been advanced by her rapidly from one great office of state to another as the casualties of her eccentric man-management fell by the wayside. No one had any reason to know what his views really were. Margaret herself did not seek to block him, as she did Heseltine, and even gave the impression that she could manage the direction and speed of travel from the back seat of the car. She implied that she might need to be disloyal in some higher cause, and more than lived up to this once John had been elected. She became even more stridently right wing, albeit usually in semi-private, than her political instincts had ever allowed her to be in office. So, while she had certainly helped to save Britain, she paradoxically also came close to destroying the Conservative Party. Her legacy may still achieve that, all these years afterwards. She injected a virus of disloyalty into the body of the party which had given her more loyalty than she sometimes deserved – for example, during the Westland helicopter company row, when her closest advisers behaved pretty dubiously to save her skin.

So John inherited a party many of whose members were sullen and vitriolic about her departure. These mutinous sentiments were given a sharper edge following John's extraordinarily successful negotiation of the Maastricht Treaty in 1992. What emerged from these discussions was an outcome full of opt-outs from European policies like economic and monetary union which Britain did not like. Maastricht was a great achievement. We remained members of the EU on pretty much our own terms. Tristan Garel-Jones was European Minister at the time. Years later, when he was becoming a member of the House of Lords, he asked whether he could take Maastricht as his territorial designation. It was explained to him that foreign places could usually be used only if they were the scene of a great British victory. (El Alamein etc.) 'Precisely,' said Tristan. But the authorities made him settle less romantically for Watford.

After Maastricht we had to settle down to plan the General Election campaign. When John became Prime Minister, he moved me from the Environment Department, to become party chairman, to run his re-election campaign, his closest political colleague. We had first discussed the election as the Gulf War drew to a close. I was in John's flat the evening that Saddam Hussein's army was streaming home north to Iraq from Kuwait. John talked to President Bush on the hotline to Washington about calling off the so-called 'turkey shoot', the continued destruction of the Iraq forces now unable to defend themselves. I was impressed by John's assurance in raising the right military strategic questions. Later that evening, we agreed that it would be wrong to use the successful aftermath of the campaign to call an election. It would seem like taking partisan advantage of a national military success.

As the succeeding months brought more and more bad economic news, the timing of the election – despite John's successful dismantling of the poll tax – became increasingly difficult. Eventually, we left it until very nearly the last moment and fought and won the election – with over 14 million votes, the largest number ever cast for the victorious party in a British General Election – principally on two issues: John's quiet competence and authority as Prime Minister, and the likelihood of economic trouble and tax increases if Labour under Neil Kinnock won. Losing my seat in the campaign and going off in the late summer of 1992 to Hong Kong, I was on the other side of the world in September when Britain crashed out of the European Exchange Rate Mechanism, which we had eventually agreed to join in 1990 at the wrong time and – thanks in part to Margaret Thatcher's insistence – at the wrong rate. Despite the later success of the Major government, with Kenneth Clarke as Chancellor of the Exchequer, in getting the economy back on an even keel and laying the basis for future economic growth, the events of the early 1990s had lost the Conservatives the most important ingredient in politics: the benefit of the doubt.

Clarke, Chancellor for four years, gave Britain the steadiest and most successful period of economic management for a quarter-century or more. He led the recovery from recession, brought down unemployment and interest rates, reduced the budget deficit from £50.8 billion in 1993 to £15.5 billion in 1997, and cut the basic rate of income tax. He passed on to the successor Labour government a golden legacy of sustainable growth. No wonder Labour stuck to the letter of Clarke's spending plans for two years. Rab Butler, Roy Jenkins and Ken Clarke were the most successful Chancellors since the war; it was a pity that Clarke did not have the chance to build on a foundation that he had laid in adversity.

John's difficulty as a leader came principally from two causes. He was elected to follow an unusual leader who had ridden her Cabinet hard, centralizing policy making and delivery on herself and her immediate entourage. She had driven the coach at breakneck speed along winding mountain roads; the result was inevitably a crash. John was a much more conventional leader, with an admirably collegial style. He actually listened to other opinions. At the first Cabinet meetings with John in the chair several of us felt as we were invited to contribute to the discussion a little like the prisoners in *Fidelio*, staggering up out of the dark into the light. A brilliant negotiator, within government and abroad, John often got his own way because of hard work (he always knew the brief better than anyone else in the room), charm, courtesy, a phlegmatic determination to go on until he got an acceptable outcome, and a brilliant ability to read body language. But the party and its senior members had got used to being roughed up, and seemed to find it difficult to summon the grace to behave well when they were themselves treated like grown-ups, for example when Major set out for debate in the Commons his negotiating stance at Maastricht before the European Council began.

The second reason for John's difficulty was Europe and the antics of his predecessor, who not only tried her hand at back-seat driving but aimed the car at the oncoming traffic. A largely invented Thatcherite history of her own views on Europe destabilized her successor. She gathered around her standard, openly raised with increasing regularity, a cabal of dogmatic subversives whose views on Europe she would have trampled into the dust when as Prime Minister she was driving through legislation on the Single European Act which made the single market possible. The combination of her own behaviour and the ejection from the Exchange Rate Mechanism gave opponents of the government's European policies open season to attack Major and the Cabinet and to render the smooth management of business all but impossible. I watched this play out from Hong Kong, talking to John when I could by telephone or during my quarterly visits back to London. I felt bad not being around to help. This had not been the plan before 1992. Like Thatcher, John Major was patronized, but he did not develop a thick enough skin to deal with it comfortably. He should have regarded these critics, and their mock tweedy ways, with the contempt they usually deserved. But he allowed them to cause him pain.

John was one of the most decent people ever to lead the Conservative Party. Moreover, despite so little formal education, he was formidably clever and worked harder than any of his contemporaries. He was rarely not working. When he was Chief Secretary to the Treasury and I was negotiating my departmental budget with him, he asked me if I would be happy to do it with him alone without civil servants on either side. I swallowed hard, agreed and went into the lion's den with a man who appeared to know at least as much about the complications of my brief as I did. While I was alone with him, contending with his grasp of housing benefit and local-government capital-spending controls, my team of civil servants chatted in his outer office with his Treasury officials. In the office there was a long row of photographs of his predecessors in the job. One of my team, pointing at the photographs, asked, 'Who was the best of all of them?' 'Easy,' came the reply. 'This one.'

John's sensitivity about his background and identity had three effects. First, he was always careful about what he would look like. Would he be wearing the right clothes? To his credit, he would have been mortified to show a builder's cleavage when clambering into a lorry in a way that never seems to embarrass Boris Johnson. The image of wimpishness – shirt tucked into his underpants as Alastair Campbell mendaciously suggested – was the reverse of the truth. He had a strong personal presence and could be surprisingly physical with a very firm handshake. He was also conspicuously good dealing with the women who worked for him, taking their views as seriously as was deserved. He was not one of those men who look for other men to talk to at dinner. Second, he never turned the rise from Brixton into the rather heroic story of social ascent and mobility it could have become in the telling of other more populist politicians. Third, he was horribly sensitive to criticism in the press, the amount of which increased as some of the bullies of Wapping discovered how much they could hurt him. 'Don't read the bloody things,' we would all say to him. But he did – even poring over the first editions so that he could worry himself to a bad night's sleep. Even when I was chairman of the Conservative Party, I was extremely reluctant to telephone a newspaper editor or journalist to complain or argue about something I did not like. I thought it a bit demeaning. This probably took things too far in the opposite direction to that taken by John. He would have been happier if he had had some of Margaret Thatcher's homemade iron cladding. This combination of (mostly) strength and (a few) weaknesses made up a man I liked and inordinately respected. I was proud to work for him and to call him a friend.

John Major was the only member of my age group to lead the Conservative Party and the country. He was Prime Minister for seven years, longer than Brown, Macmillan, Douglas-Home or Heath, longer in fact than most holders of the office. History may not sufficiently celebrate his intrepid qualities; he was a rather quiet hero who had to manage the country through a difficult period. But on one issue after another he has been shown to have taken the right decisions and to have been on the right side, not least over European policy, especially the eurozone and the Schengen area. He led Britain in wartime; dismantled the poll tax; and somehow kept a truculent Conservative Party more or less afloat – having had to put to sea in stormy waters and in a pretty leaky craft. When I think about his years in No. 10, I just wish that he had enjoyed the experience much more.

7

Crazy Irish Knots

We have always found the Irish a bit odd. They refuse to be English.

Winston Churchill

A person from Northern Ireland is naturally cautious.

Seamus Heaney (2008)

My first ministerial job introduced me with all the thunderous reverberation of a Lambeg drum to the violence that identity politics often breeds. One particular incident (which I will describe later) combined the prosaic with the stomach-turning. How did it come about?

After re-election in Bath with a much increased majority in the 1983 General Election, I was offered a junior job in her government by Margaret Thatcher. In my first four years in Parliament, I had blotted my copy-book with party managers by occasionally speaking out against some of the more bruising, ideological aspects of the government's economic policy, as described in a previous chapter, especially the quasi-religious reverence for reducing the Public Sector Borrowing Requirement. The odd abstention vote or slightly coded but critical article or speech, and a pamphlet written with my closest political friends, had caused some teeth-sucking in Downing Street. While originally tapped for rapid promotion, I had plainly been relegated to the slow lane on account of being a trifle too independent-minded, even ornery. So in my first Parliament I saw members of my peer group taking their first steps on the ministerial ladder well before me. Was I jealous? Yes, a bit. But I think I understood that you had to lie on the bed that you had made. It was simply not in my constitution – maybe vanity or naivety came into it – to lickspittle my way to the top, or just play cautiously 'shtum' from time to time. Before the 1983 election, Alan Clark, who seemed to think that he had spotted a fellow anarchic rebel with few conventional careerist instincts, suggested that we should organize a lunch after the election for all those like us who had been passed over. Somewhat to our embarrassment, come the lunch, Alan and I found that we had been invited to take on junior posts in the government. The truth is we were both more ambitious for office than we let on.

The call from Downing Street in June 1983 sent me to what wags called, rather revealingly for what it said about national priorities, the Siberian power station: Northern Ireland. This seemed to have become a place to which those whose Thatcherite sympathies could not be wholly trusted were exiled. The Secretary of State was Jim Prior, one of the last 'wet' critics of government economic policy left in the administration; his deputy was Nick Scott, an attractive, left-wing Conservative, once tapped for great things. It was suggested that since I was keen on public spending, I should be given lots of money to distribute in Northern Ireland before being weaned off it with some future return to a domestic, mainland department.

This fairly cynical approach to the Northern Ireland Office rather bore out the contention of the Irish Taoiseach, Garret FitzGerald, that the British government and public did not take the issues that Northern Ireland had to confront sufficiently seriously. By the time the Blair government brokered a peace deal in Northern Ireland in 1998, more than 3,500 people (about half of them civilians) had been murdered during the euphemistically called 'Troubles'; thousands more had been maimed, economic prospects ruined, businesses destroyed, civil liberties curtailed and mayhem brought to the streets of Northern Ireland – and to some cities in mainland Britain. Yet it often seemed as though political initiatives and imperatives could be put on hold provided an 'acceptable level of violence' (as the senior Conservative minister Reginald Maudling once called it) could be achieved. Northern Ireland had once been dubbed 'John Bull's political slum'; often it appeared to have morphed into 'John Bull's forgotten tragedy'. Maudling himself, after paying his first visit to the Province as Home Secretary in 1970, got on the plane to fly home and demanded 'a large scotch!' He went on, 'What a bloody awful country.'

Amnesia about Northern Ireland was more or less a continuation of the way it had been treated since the partition of Ireland in 1923. The struggle for Irish independence had been increasingly complicated by the results of the colonization of some northern counties in the seventeenth century by English and Scottish Protestants. The so-called flight of the earls and subsequent fighting between the Catholic aristocracy in Ireland, King James I and later William of Orange drove Catholics off much of their land, and replaced them with Protestant settlers whose loyalty to monarchs in London could be guaranteed by ties of religion and possessions. John Hewitt, progeny of this plantation, was one of many fine Northern Ireland poets who emerged during the second half of the twentieth century. It was as though their creativity had been precipitated by the bloodshed around them. In his poem 'Ulsterman' Hewitt wrote:

> Kelt, Briton, Roman, Saxon, Dane, and Scot,
> time and this island tied a crazy knot.

Elsewhere he noted:

> This is my country. If my people came
> from England here four centuries ago,
> the only trade that's left is in my name . . .

While he was appalled by the violence and hatred that ran through the history of some of his Protestant co-religionists, he could never disavow his own country. His heritage was not the violence inflicted by others, but he warned that he would 'not be outcast in the world'. Another Protestant poet, Louis MacNeice, expressed a similar sentiment:

> I can say Ireland is hooey, Irelandic
> A gallery of fake tapestries
> But I cannot deny my past to which my self is wed,
> The woven figure cannot undo its thread.

Where did that thread lead? The partition of Ireland and the creation of the statelet to the north was a direct result of the Easter Rising in 1916. Home Rule could not incorporate the whole of an island, whose northern, Protestant citizens remembered 1916 not principally for the martyrdom of Irish Nationalists who had called for independence in the Post Office in Dublin, but for the sacrifices of the battle of the Somme. The huge losses sustained by the largely Protestant soldiers in the Ulster Division at Thiepval were in fact later followed by the deaths of many Catholic members of the 16th Irish Division at Guillemont. But for the north the Easter Rising looked like an Irish and Catholic stab in the back, supported by Germany, which could lead not to Home Rule but Rome Rule.

So what was this 'Northern Ireland' that turned its Britishness into a sacred identity that most of the rest of Britain could barely recognize or comprehend? What, for a start, should we call the place? Northern Ireland itself is something of a misnomer. There are three counties of historic Ulster's nine which are left outside the state completely because the boundary was drawn with some political guile. One of the three counties of the Ulster Province, Donegal, excluded from the north and included in the Republic, is actually further north than the other counties of the Northern Irish State, or perhaps the Almost-Northern Irish State. The 'Six County' state is a term, mostly out of fashion now, which was originally used by moderate anti-partitionists who would not go so far as many Republicans in talking about British-occupied Ireland. This business of names is something of a minefield, one that crosses the whole northern Province, and nowhere more so than in what ministers informally used to call 'Stroke City' on the banks of the Foyle. The city and its county are called Derry by most Catholics and Nationalists, and Londonderry by Protestants and Unionists. Derry is derived from the Gaelic name for oakwood; the prefix 'London' was added in the seventeenth century. The name of the city became an absurdly contentious issue when the Troubles began in Northern Ireland, hence the absurd but neutral 'Stroke City', though I used myself whenever possible to avoid the problem by talking vaguely about 'this beautiful part of Northern Ireland'. What made this argument (to which I will return later covered in bruises) even more absurd is that the principal ceremonial organization of local Protestants was called 'the Apprentice Boys of Derry'. Sportsmen somehow seem to get round this turbulence over names: both rugby and soccer players have clubs named after Derry and play in leagues in the Republic.

So in Northern Ireland – or whatever you want to call it – after

1923, what went wrong in communities which though divided by religion had certainly not regarded ethnic cleansing as an acceptable mode of behaviour? The blame for what happened is mostly Britain's, but the Republic played its own significant role too.

Britain largely ignored the creation of Orange, Unionist myths about their offshore statelet, and generally tried to forget about it as it marinaded in its own prejudices, bigotry and victimhood, a less and less significant part of the wider United Kingdom economy as the textile, heavy engineering and ship-building industries declined. Just as decent Americans in the north of the United States in the 1930s, 1940s and even later tried to look the other way when segregation in the southern states came into view, so Britain pretended that there was nothing wrong with Ulster. But there plainly was. Votes were rigged; constituencies were gerrymandered; public spending was skewed towards Protestants; policing kept the 'taigs' – slang for Catholics – in their place with the excuse of occasional terrorist activity by Catholic Republicans. Housing and employment heavily favoured Protestant communities. The Prime Minister of Northern Ireland, Lord Brookeborough (who presided over a mini-Westminster parliamentary system), said in 1937, at a meeting to mark 12 July and the victory in 1690 on that day by King William over the Jacobites at the Battle of the Boyne, that many Protestants employed Roman Catholics even though Catholics were set on destroying Ulster. He appealed to all Unionists to 'employ good Protestant lads and lassies'.

Arguably things did not get much better even in the 1960s. Terence O'Neill, a Prime Minister who was swept from office in 1969 for being too much in favour of inter-community reconciliation, noted approvingly in his autobiography that the typical Belfast Protestant working man was 'strongly anti-Catholic, but decent'.* And could the Protestant, Belfast working man or his Catholic peer tell who was on the other side

---

* O'Neill was a Unionist Prime Minister who tried to improve relations with the Republic and with the Catholic community. He did not last long since his Unionist support drained away faster than Catholic support increased. Greatly daring, he visited a Catholic school. Photographers for the Unionist papers waited to snap something shocking, alas finding no nuns to horrify their readers. One photographer struck lucky. He managed to get a photograph of O'Neill with a crucifix behind him, which crafty juggling in the darkroom was made to look as though it was hovering

of the divide? Names helped the instant forensic quest; looks, sometimes; streets, schools, pubs and communities certainly. A crucifix or painting of the Blessed Virgin Mary glimpsed through a window would provide proof certain, a reason for keeping drawn what a Belfast mayor once described to me as the 'Vietnamese blinds'. But usually you didn't need any of these things. You just knew who was topdog and who came along behind. One Catholic writer claimed he could detect a sort of Protestant swagger or show of self-confidence; they – the 'Prods' – looked as though they owned the place. And so they did. A friend of mine who lived south of Belfast in a rural town called Downpatrick remembers the time when he heard the children of a Catholic family, driven out of their home in Belfast by intimidation, playing in their neighbouring garden. He heard one little girl saying to her sister, 'Now I want to be the Prod.' He leant over the fence and asked what she meant. 'Well,' she replied, 'I want a go on the swing now.'

So was the problem really religion? Was there some doubt about interpretations of the Nicene Creed? Did the doctrine of justification through faith stir political passions? Did transubstantiation irk members of the Orange Order? In fact, the main idea of religion in some Unionist homes was simply to tell the Bishop of Rome to piss off. Rome and Catholicism were at the kernel of Nationalist and Republican identity. So religion, shorn of any idea of Christianity, provided the kindling for the blazing struggle because it encapsulated land, power and ascendancy. What was at stake were not articles of faith or liturgical rituals but the role of master, and the idea of who 'we' were. Sure, Catholicism itself provided lots of targets – incense, lace, Latin prayers, devotion to the Pope's slipper, not the Queen's crown, the example of the Republic (to which I will also return). But this was not a Protestant cri de coeur, not Luther or Calvin howling at the gates or nailing manifestos to them. This was simply about centuries-old prejudice.

The tawdry pageantry of Protestant dominance in Northern Ireland continues to amaze British mainlanders and foreign visitors, who are told it is all about showing loyalty to the notion of Britishness.

---

over his head. The tortured Christ could thus be used to question whether O'Neill knew his own identity any more.

Perhaps these days the followers of Nigel Farage and other Brexiteers find it easier to embrace and support these manifestations of the Protestant make-up. They start with the kerbstones painted red, white and blue, the end walls of terraced houses decorated with memorials to the massacre of Protestants in 1641, the 103-day siege of Derry in 1689, the Protestant Apprentice Boys who shut the gates of Derry against the army of the Catholic King James, the Protestant victory under King William of Orange at the Battle of the Boyne in 1690, the Ulster Covenant of 1912 signed by just under half a million men and women against Home Rule. This is the remembered narrative of identity. It is the iconography of the so-called Loyalists' anthem, 'No Surrender' – 'no surrender' to Catholics, Republicans, Nationalists; 'no surrender' to the twentieth century let alone the twenty-first.

On the high days and holidays of Loyalist celebrations, to the gaudily painted streets – 'a by-word of offence', in John Hewitt's words – you add the bunting, streamers, flags and bonfires, built to burn effigies of the Pope and other Nationalist villains. Then come the marches of the Orange Order, with each lodge celebrating its loyalty to their own version of Queen and Country. The lodge from each town – Portadown, say, where the Orange Order began, or Ballymena, constituency of the late Ian Paisley – is led on a march along traditional routes that mark out the geography of Protestant ascendancy, like dogs cocking their legs against favourite lamp-posts. Wherever possible, these routes allow for Orange hate to be shoved in the faces of Catholics. At the front of the march to Drumcree, say, in Portadown are the grand masters of the lodges in navy blue suits, bowler hats and sashes, carrying bibles or ceremonial swords, and behind them come the bands of fifes and horn pipes, with at their heart the great Lambeg drums, a foot in depth and three in width, lashed with canes as they warm the Pope's ears and cover the towns through which Loyalists march with what Bernard MacLaverty called 'a canopy of dark noise'. With their banners showing Queen Victoria sitting on a Union Jack or handing a bible to a grateful black man, or the burning of Latimer, they remind us of the days when the Penal Laws allowed lower-class Protestant settlers to lord it over indigenous Catholics, before the Catholic Relief Act of 1829 began the long and slow business of restoring some sort of political and economic balance. This is the history acknowledged by Hewitt in his brave poem 'The Colony':

> We took their temples from them and forbade them,
> For many years, to worship their strange idols.
> They gathered secret, deep in the dripping glens,
> Chanting their prayers before a lichened rock.

And, of course, in their glens and their slums, they plotted revenge. That is one reason why those parades needed, as Seamus Heaney said, 'policemen flanking them, like anthracite'.

So Catholic areas, too, bore the gaudy paintwork of their own remembered history, all exploitation, outrage and martyrdom, the kerbstones in Nationalist colours of green, white and orange, the frescoes of the hunger strikers and of masked men with balaclavas and Kalashnikovs. The worst example of this was perhaps Crossmaglen, a murderous centre of IRA activists near the Irish border. As you approached this grim town, a military stockade at its heart, there were posters urging British murderers to go home. While the north dug itself ever deeper into its sad and divisive history, the Republic, at least until the 1980s, pretended that it was resolutely set on uniting the island and fulfilling the northern Republican dream.

The candles of this mythology were regularly re-lit with Articles 2 and 3 of the Irish Constitution (eventually amended in 1999 after the Good Friday Agreement) claiming the whole island as one national territory. John McGahern described Ireland in the 1930s, 1940s and 1950s living through 'a very dark time' in which 'an insular church colluded with an insecure State to bring about a society that was often bigoted, intolerant, cowardly, philistine and spiritually crippled'.

Until globalization, feminization and membership of the European Union set it firmly on the road to modern and prosperous pluralism, the Republic as a whole behaved as though its script had been written in the Orange Lodges of the north. It gave Protestant Loyalists all that they wanted to hate. Under de Valera, Ireland became (as McGahern suggested) a confessional state, policed by Archbishop McQuaid and other narrow churchmen. The Protestant community dwindled to 3.5 per cent of the total population, partly because to marry a Catholic a

Protestant was required (as my mother did) to embrace the partner's beliefs, at least nominally. With contraception, abortion, homosexuality and divorce all illegal, the community was trapped in a world of dark confessionals and the rejection of modernity. Emigration continued to drain the country of some of its best. Colm Tóibín, one of the Republic's fine modern novelists, wrote in *South*, 'If you know anything about the country, you wouldn't ask me why I left.' Put on the spot by the violence against the human rights covenants in Northern Ireland in the late 1960s and 1970s, and then by the growing communal violence there, with the British army turned by bloodshed from defenders of the Catholic minority into the targets of armed Republicans, southern politicians initially resorted to Fenian conspiracies – like Charlie Haughey's support of gun-running – and to rhetorical sympathy for down-trodden Catholic cousins in Ulster. All this was sustained by an idea of Irishness which played well to the Irish American diaspora, mixing the suffering of a crushed colonial country with the twinkling toes of step-dancing and mildly risqué humour about priests, whiskey and horse-racing. All this was broken down by economic growth (the sort that would have horrified de Valera), membership of the European Union, the ability of Ireland's well-educated work force to attract inward investment, the return home to a now prospering country by many immigrants, the brave campaigning of the two female presidents, Mary Robinson and Mary McAleese, the political leadership of politicians like Garret FitzGerald (a real hero of our time) and Dick Spring, and Irish cultural achievement from popular music to literature. Moreover, the tight grip that the Catholic Church had on Irish life was destroyed by its terrible moral failures shown in the child abuse and related scandals. That the Irish Catholic Church could still be civilized, thoughtful and relevant – think for example of Archbishop Martin of Dublin – was too often forgotten, not least because Rome's disapproval of how the Church had behaved in its authoritarian prime was less clear than it should have been. Gradually, both London and Dublin came to realize that a problem they had both caused could only be solved by working together across a border that geographically wriggled over Ulster, without it being clear some of the time which side was in the north and which in the Republic. Happily, the border was also flattened psychologically and politically by both countries' membership of the EU and by the arrival in Ireland, rather late, of the twentieth century.

As late as the 1980s, when I arrived in Belfast as a junior minister, Northern Irish identity still compartmentalized the tribes, a point noted in a parody of Gilbert and Sullivan's 'Tit Willow' by Robert Johnston. In this poem, addressing British, Irish and Ulster drinkers in a bar, the poet concludes:

> As I left, I called out, 'Sure our family tree
> Is part Scottish, part Irish, part English.
> I don't give a toss about identity,
> Whether Ulster, or Irish, or British.
> For each of your gods I have only a curse!'
> At this the three of them looked fit to burst,
> And they all there agreed that agnostics were worst,
> Whether Ulster, or Irish or British.

The new Parliamentary Secretary was of British Irish heritage and Catholic, plainly not agnostic so far as local media were concerned but a little odd. Lavender is a member of the Church of England and at an early press conference a journalist asked me about my 'mixed marriage'. She sounded as though she thought my wife and I were from a very distant planet, disciples now of strange and alien rites. Our children at the time were very young – Kate ten, Laura eight and Alice three. We decided immediately that we were not going to cocoon them, keep them at several removes from a new life full of real excitements and enjoyment but also of potential threats and armed bodyguards. Security is not something you should be casual about, but nor should you allow it to dominate the way you live: that way lie madness and a victory for the violent. So we took our children to Northern Ireland when I was on duty (once a month) over weekends and for two Christmas holidays. We used to stay in a modern flat next to the old Governor-General's house at Hillsborough, a handsome Georgian building in beautiful grounds twelve miles from Belfast. I was looked after by four charming police officers, two in my ministerial car and two in the follow-up vehicle. They all became friends, as golfers, sailors, pint-sinkers. They were (I think) all Protestant, with not a hint of bigotry about them. They were prepared to die for me, and you cannot ask any more of men than that, especially when they are not maudlin about it. On our first weekend at Hillsborough, my youngest daughter hit the inviting red panic button within five minutes of arriving in our flat. 'We'd taken a bet on how long that would take,' said one of the police guards with his gun cradled across his chest. Later that day we saw Alice being swung between two armed police officers – automatic weapon in one hand, three-year-old in the other. The only time my children were a little spooked was when, after I had left Northern Ireland, they were watching BBC News and the first item was a story that an IRA bomb factory had been found in London; among the items there was a terrorist death list of ten targets, including me.

Back in London I was not provided with any security beyond a reinforced front door, a panic button and curiously a mirror which Lavender was advised to use to check under the car every morning in case of a bomb. While it is possible that she might know what a bomb would look like, the same could not be said of me. I think I can tell an exhaust pipe when I see one and that is about it.

The civil servants who worked with me in Belfast were uniformly helpful, mostly drawn from the Northern Ireland civil service; some in the London-based Northern Ireland Office were typically former Home Office, Defence or Foreign Office officials. I only had difficulty with one rather officious civil servant in London and that was over our determination to spend the weekend together – good for us, and apparently appreciated by the locals. He said he would have to report any weekend family visits to the Inland Revenue as a taxable perk. The Inland Revenue were more sensible and I heard no more about this.

My regular routine – weekends apart – was to spend two or three days a week in Northern Ireland, the rest of the week in Parliament or the department's London office in the old Admiralty Building on Horse Guards. We would usually fly backwards and forwards to Belfast in a small chartered plane from Northolt. This was a bizarre consequence of Treasury accounting rules. As we trundled down the runway, we would pass small, unused RAF passenger jets, which were more expensive to take than privately hired planes, apparently because the Treasury computations for its sister department capitalized virtually every aspect of air travel. Our flights in these small private planes were the worst part of the job, especially in winter, when the journey seemed both endless and very bumpy; they became quite spiritual occasions in my life. Once safely arrived in Belfast, we stayed in the old Speaker's House near the Stormont Parliament Building, a residence more strongly fortified than Rorke's Drift. We were looked after by Ulster's best providers of fries and protein was not in short supply. The whole experience was described unfairly (because the staff were all very kind) by one ministerial colleague as Stalag Fawlty Towers. I guess it had to be like this. We would give regular dinners to talk about the political way forward with local politicians. The wine flowed (except when Dr Paisley's Democratic Unionist Party was present), and we circled over and around the same points of dispute less warily as the night wore on. Ulster men and women talk well, if often about the same old things.

My denomination – my essential manifestation for many in Northern Ireland – continued to attract interest. At an early municipal lunch in 'Stroke City' I made the sign of the cross after the Catholic bishop pronounced the Grace. I had been doing this since I was about five. It marked me out, 'taig' through and through. Usually on Sundays, I would go to mass at Riley's Trench near Hillsborough, at a little church named after St Colman. My bodyguards liked it, as did the local men of the parish, who usually stood outside smoking until mass was well underway. Part of the reason for its popularity was the fact that the priest (as one policeman noted with enthusiasm) took less than twenty-five minutes from take-off to touch-down, sermon included. Alternatively, we would sometimes go to the Church of Ireland (Anglican) church in Hillsborough, an eighteenth-century building with a tall spire from whose gardens there were long views across the Lagan valley to the Belfast hills. We used to sit in the Governor's seats, but I did not take Communion (something I have usually done in the Church of England at home) lest it cause offence. Ecumenism may be a matter of individual conscience but it does not always travel very well.

With direct rule from London since 1974 – a result of the violence of the early 1970s – ministers had to lead the departments formerly run by Northern Ireland's devolved administration. The Secretary of State did the big stuff – politics, negotiation, security; Nick Scott helped with security and took on education and the budget. An amiable peer, Charlie Lyell, looked after agriculture. I did most of the rest grouped in two large departments – the environment and health and social security.

Environment covered housing, transport, planning, local government and urban renewal. The housing portfolio covered a massive public housing programme, an effort to remove the legitimate grievances which Catholics and some working-class Unionists had about the poor state of their homes. The quality of new social housing in Northern Ireland was way above the general standard in Britain; the costs were high both for this reason and because the construction business (like the drinks business) was under pressure from paramilitary organizations on both sides of the community divide, which extracted extra loot from protection rackets. One of my first decisions – which confronted my initial liberal sentiments that this society could not possibly be divided as much as I was told – was to agree to add another metre and a half to the height of an already high wall which divided the housing in a new Belfast estate between Republicans and Loyalists. The wall constructed was higher than parts of the one that divided contemporary Berlin.

The most difficult part of the job intellectually was visiting the more than two dozen local councils for question-and-answer sessions. A regular feature of political life in Northern Ireland was the refusal of one political party or another to meet ministers because of some mortal sin allegedly committed by the government, though sometimes its precise nature had been forgotten. In 1983, we were just coming out of a period in which we had been sent to Coventry by some of the Unionists for one of these imagined assaults on their principles. Connecting with local councillors was thought to be a way of rebuilding bridges, though for how long and for what great purpose was never entirely clear. Anyway, it involved me touring the town halls of Ulster with huge files packed with briefings on every aspect of the local council's life. I had to learn details of road schemes from places I had never visited to other places that I had hardly heard of; the finer points of local planning disputes; the reasons for damp ceilings in new housing estates; and on and on. Fortunately I have a good memory – or at least had one then. Some of my visits to local councils involved more cheerful duties. I was asked, for example, to visit Newry to open the mayor's new drinks cabinet. When I got there it was discovered that someone had already broken into it, so we had to send out for more bottles of gin and whisky. Before visiting Dr Ian Paisley's constituency in Ballymena (where there was no drinks cabinet), I met the Democratic Unionist Party leader with a delegation from his town. I had been well briefed, but did not want these local councillors to think I was showing off about how much more I knew about their community than they did. I said to Dr Paisley, 'I must confess at the outset that I have never visited Ballymena'. 'Confess?' he said, well aware of my religious affiliations. 'Not to me you don't.'

The most enjoyable work was the attempt to breathe new life into Belfast and Derry, both of which had been heavily targeted by IRA bombs. I got to like both cities despite the way that intimidation and violence had shunted populations from one set of streets to another. Like Glasgow or Liverpool, Belfast remained a segregated city where the industrial landscape – the shipyards, the linen mills, the tobacco factories – was the heart of where people lived; in the Falls Road, for example, Catholics lived close by the mills where they worked. Not far from the Falls Road and the police barracks at Hastings Street was a terrible reminder of the worst sort of 1960s and 1970s housing development – the brutal concrete architecture of the Divis Flats, whose balconies and walls gave cover to the IRA gunmen. Within a few hundred yards of the Falls Road was the Protestant Shankill; the roads in between were as dangerous for a foolhardy wanderer from the wrong tribe, 'taig' or 'Prod', as they were for soldiers.

The way in which murder squads had re-planned Belfast to suit themselves was an additional unconventional challenge for redevelopment. Like the Lagan river in Belfast, Derry had its river too, the Foyle, curling around the hill on which the old city stood. The communities were probably more clearly divided there even than in Belfast, Catholics in the Bogside and the Creggan making those areas at one time no-go areas for the British army. Redevelopment in both cities required imagination, patience, lots of government money (my admirers in the party were right about that) and resilience, as the bombs continued to explode even while the new buildings were being constructed. The work which we began in the early 1980s was brilliantly continued and expanded by my successor, Richard Needham, an Irish earl of unusual talents. Richard is a justification for having politicians; he made things happen in the manner of Michael Heseltine, one of his mentors. Good civil servants liked to work for him, because he knew what he wanted to do and gave them brave leadership in doing it. Inevitably, a plate or two occasionally got broken, which prevented him rising as high in politics as his talents deserved – he peaked as a very good trade minister outside the Cabinet. Richard is another example of the perils of identity pigeon-holing – the son of an Irish peer and a Jewish mother, he is married to a beautiful German whose family was not wholly put off him by the fact that at their first meeting with this strange mélange of a suitor he somehow contrived to shoot his would-be father-in-law's gun dog.

My civil servants at the Northern Ireland Department of Health were led by two exceptional Permanent Secretaries. The first was a Lancastrian, from Burnley, who had found his way to the Northern Ireland civil service partly because of ill-health. Norman Dugdale was reserved in manner and just a little courtly. He insisted that he should have the last sight of any piece of paper that came in to me; fair enough, because he wrote as well as any civil servant with whom I ever worked. He was a fine, published poet, who translated C. P. Cavafy and introduced me to that brilliant poet of public affairs. It seemed a very long way from the Alexandria of Cavafy and his sometimes homoerotic verse to wet and grey Ulster. Norman wrote one poem ('*Provincia Deserta*'), clearly directed towards the succession of young British politicians who passed through his able hands. It was a little melancholy and tartly observed:

> Well, here it is: not Botany Bay
> But a penal settlement all the same,
> The sentence life without remission – saving,
> Of course, Sir, such as yourself, gentlemen newly sent
> To live here at the Governor's Lodge. Two years from now
> You will be safely home again and dining out
> On your bizarre experiences, which cannot fail
> To please your hostess and amuse the company.

Norman was one of the very best members of what he called 'the well-trained squads that clean up the carnage'. He was succeeded by another star, Maurice Hayes, the most senior Catholic in the

Northern Ireland civil service, a polymath, Gaelic speaker, friend of Seamus Heaney, a county hurler and great figure in Gaelic football, and writer of two magical volumes of autobiography describing growing up a Catholic in County Down (*Sweet Killough: Let Go Your Anchor* and *Black Puddings with Slim: A Downpatrick Boyhood*). Maurice went on to become the Northern Ireland Ombudsman, an Irish senator and chairman of the Republic's National Forum on Europe. He is as well-read as anyone I have known, witty and very wise, and became one of my best friends. It was rather a stroke of luck to find engineers like this in the Siberian power station.

It was the Department of Health which provided the stomach-churning shock with which I began this chapter. Visiting a hospital a couple of days after my arrival in the job, I chatted to a young nurse in the Accident and Emergency ward. Hands behind my back, the young copy-cat Duke of Edinburgh, I bent over a tiny nurse who smelt of Lux toilet soap, and asked her gravely whether there had been many recent patients as a result of the Troubles. 'Oh yes,' she replied, 'Two nights ago, we had to look after a couple of Catholic knee-cappings.' 'Now, come on,' I admonished her. 'You can't tell me that you can distinguish between a Protestant and a Catholic knee-capping.' I heard my private secretary and bodyguard sucking in their breath. 'Of course we can,' she replied, clearly astonished by my naivety. 'Catholics use a shotgun; Protestants use a Black and Decker drill.' Welcome to the world of identity knee-cappings.

Two other incidents came to symbolize for me the horrors of identity politics in Northern Ireland. First, a well-meaning youth leader organized a mixed team of elementary school pupils to play a team of Catholic boys in the Republic. The coach picked up one group from near the Falls Road and then the other near the Shankill. The boys got on really well together and won their game. They sang all the way home. The coach dropped off the Catholic half of the team, but as it drove away a crowd of small boys began pelting it with stones, including the boys who had been in the team. 'Any kiddies in my school can live like a fool, / But hating, my boy, is an art', says Ogden Nash.

A similar goodwill gesture was made by a Belfast schoolmaster who organized a match for his Protestant pupils in Dublin. As a gift at the end of the match the boys were each presented with a statue of a woman whose identity they didn't know. Arrived home, one eleven-year-old showed it to his father who exploded, dragged his son down the backyard to his work shed and thrashed him. He then took his big hammer and smashed the plaster statue of the Blessed Virgin Mary to smithereens. The weeping boy, who was abused when he sought consolation from an older friend, was later one of the victims questioned by the inquiry into notorious allegations of organized paedophilia at the Kincora Boys' Home.

I do not think that these 'bizarre experiences' will amuse the company, or please my dinner hostess. For me they simply underline some of the nastier consequences of the abuse of identity. But for Northern Ireland as a whole I formed considerable affection, first for the many friends we made there, not least the aristocrats who gave us hospitality from time to time, like the Duke of Abercorn at Baronscourt in Omagh and the artist Lindy, Marchioness of Dufferin and Ava, at Clandeboys in County Down, full of the gubernatorial collections from Canada to Burma of a former Marquess. We were also generously taken on occasional picnics by Enoch (a local MP) and Pamela Powell, travelling with my armed bodyguards. From Enoch's careful study of the Ordnance Survey the Powells would find perfect places to lunch in the Mournes. Wine Society sherry would be followed by cold Ulster beef, a lesson on Ulster's topography for my children, and home for tea at their simple cottage to eat one of Pamela's delicious sponges. One Sunday Alice, our youngest daughter, was sick all over the back seat of their car. They could not have been nicer about it, commenting kindly that one of their daughters used to do this regularly on their journeys to his Wolverhampton constituency. Come the following Monday morning Enoch would cut me dead in the House of Commons corridor.

The last time I talked to Enoch and Pamela was in Italy in the 1990s. We had taken a family holiday in the Marche and were putting our car on the train in Bologna. Looking in my rear-view mirror I spotted their familiar faces in the car behind. I went back to talk to them and offer to drive their car onto the train, a slightly hazardous enterprise. We chatted afterwards. Enoch explained that he had wanted to make one last visit to Italy before he died to see some of his favourite churches and paintings. In particular he was keen to confirm his view (shared by many scholars) that the frescoes in the Basilica in Assisi were probably not by Giotto but by Cavallini. He was pretty sure about this, but then he was pretty sure of everything: for example, that Jesus Christ was not crucified but stoned to death by the Jews. He was closer to the mark with his Italian pictures.

From these hosts and other friends, not least my police guards, I got to see much of the beauty of Northern Ireland from the granite of the Mournes to the Causeway coastal route and the golden beach at Portstewart on the North Atlantic coast. I loved the white thorn and the fuchsia hedges, the waters of Strangford Lough and the Fermanagh lakes with their sandpipers, blackthorn and Gueler roses, the whitewashed farmhouses (preferable to the hacienda-style bungalows that spring up everywhere) and the incomparable bluebells of late spring followed by the magnificent rhododendrons and in late summer the plump raspberries.

My ministerial job was demanding and enjoyable. I was running most of the life of the ordinary government of Northern Ireland, under two secretaries of state, Jim Prior and Douglas Hurd, who left me to get on with it. They were both kind to me and Lavender. We built houses, opened health facilities, conserved buildings, ran a railway and spent the public's money pretty well. I had little to do with security issues or the big political questions, though I was sometimes asked my opinion and required to canvas the views of Ulster's politicians, with whom I had a lot of day-to-day contact over what were generally constituency issues. They were not too bad a bunch, with some very decent and brave ones like the Unionist Ken Maginnis and the moderate Labour Nationalist Seamus Mallon.

The only real trouble I got into was over the name of 'Stroke City', or rather of its district council. When the political composition of the council changed from Unionist to moderate Nationalist (the Social Democratic and Labour Party), the new councillors announced that they wanted to alter the name of the council from the Londonderry District Council to the Derry District Council. This was meant to be provocative to both the moderate Unionists and the Paisleyites, the Democratic Unionist Party, and it was. You could argue that the Unionists had not been beyond provocative gestures themselves, but that was not the point. The point was the law, which made it clear that councillors had the power to change the name of the district council though not of the city which it covered. It remained London-derry, within the territory of the Derry District Council. You could not make it up – nor the explosion of Loyalist/Unionist rage when I announced the legal opinion. But the law was the law, rather an important part of the British way of life. This earned me for a time the sobriquet 'the Minister of Treachery'. I awoke one morning at our government hostel at Stormont to the sound of the Lambeg drum as Orange Lodges gathered to march on the house in a protest to denounce my decision. It passed off smoothly enough, though it doubtless reinforced the Loyalist view that you could not trust a 'taig' minister who crossed himself and went to mass on Sundays.

I was sad to leave Northern Ireland, not least because it was a job in which I was largely left to my own devices and did not have to attend too many Cabinet committee meetings or engage in rows with Treasury ministers. My family too missed the beauties of Ulster. But I was never seduced into thinking, as some seemed to believe, that these six counties were so uniquely beautiful as to explain or justify people killing to control them, a downright absurd and rather offensive argument. There were also beautiful parts of Scotland, Wales and England which people did not kill one another to run. Paris might have been worth a mass at the end of the sixteenth century, but Ulster was certainly not worth a car bomb, let alone hundreds of them, at the end of the twentieth. We ruled it because that was what the overwhelming majority of its people wanted us to do, and we will continue to do so until they don't.

I had never expected to go back with any meaningful responsibilities to Northern Ireland, though I continued to be concerned about what happened there and returned occasionally to do a broadcast or speak at a university. So far as I was concerned it was definitely not 'Provincia Deserta'. Then, a few months after I left Hong Kong in 1997, I was telephoned by a friend to be told that Mo Mowlam (Northern Ireland's relatively new Labour Secretary of State) was anxious to find out whether I might be at all interested in taking on the chairmanship of the Independent Commission on Policing in Northern Ireland, which was to recommend how the police service should be reorganized to reflect the recent Belfast Agreement. The Agreement had been concluded through the brave and sensitive leadership of Tony Blair, Bertie Ahern (the Republic's Taoiseach), Senator George Mitchell and Mowlam herself (all building on work begun by John Major for which he got too little credit). It appeared to have brought peace and reconciliation to the Province, and for once London, Dublin and Washington were all on the same page. Washington's contribution was important – too often, American politicians had played to the Irish diaspora vote, ignoring the advice of some of their best diplomats, like the US ambassador in London Ray Seitz. The one thing that the Northern Ireland politicians who accepted this new deal could not agree was what should happen to policing. This issue went right to the poisoned heart of politics in Northern Ireland. To the surprise of Mo Mowlam, though not I think my friend, I said yes to this offer straight away. When Mo talked to me on the phone (I was in New York giving a lecture), she asked, 'But don't you want to think it over for a bit with your wife?' I replied, 'She'll say yes too' – and she did. Some right-wing Conservative suggested that I should not help get the government out of a difficult corner. The issue after all had not come close to resolution during the main talks. This argument seemed rather a departure from customary attitudes to public service. Norman Tebbit went further and said I was just doing the job for the money: thirty pieces of silver and all that. Norman is a bit of a card and one can forgive him his views on Ireland given what the IRA did to his wife, whom he has looked after for decades with such devotion. As it happened, the per diem was a bit more than that, though I cannot imagine anyone regarding it as sufficient to give its recipients a reason for following the example of Judas Iscariot.

I had little say in choosing the members of the Commission which emerged from negotiations between London, Dublin and (I am sure) Washington. I was lucky to have two very good police officers, one an outstanding policewoman from Boston, Cathy O'Toole, the other a retired Deputy Commissioner of the Metropolitan Police, Sir John Smith. Even greater fortune came in the shape of the principal Northern Ireland members, Maurice Hayes and Peter Smith, a wise and brave Unionist barrister. As things turned out Peter took much of the heat in Northern Ireland for our eventual proposals; he was a man of unquestioned integrity who took the view – uncomfortable for some Unionist politicians – that the Belfast Agreement and our terms of reference meant what they said. For the post of secretary of the Commission, I persuaded the Foreign Office to loan us the young diplomat who had been my main diplomatic adviser and negotiator in Hong Kong, Bob Pierce, one of the most intelligent people who has ever worked for me.

Our terms of reference – agreed by the parties to the Belfast Agreement – could not have been much clearer. Taking account of the Agreement we were required to 'bring forward proposals for future policing structures and arrangements ... Our proposals should be designed to ensure that policing arrangements, including composition, recruitment, training, culture, ethos and symbols, are such that in a new approach Northern Ireland has a police service that can enjoy widespread support from, and is seen as an integral part of, the community as a whole.'

We described the heart of the problem we had to tackle at the beginning of our report. The composition of Northern Ireland's police – the Royal Ulster Constabulary (RUC) – had always been disproportionately Protestant and Unionist. While more than 40 per cent of the population in Northern Ireland was Roman Catholic only 8 per cent of RUC officers were. We argued that 'in the past, when the police were subject to control by the Unionist government at Stormont, and more recently in the period of direct rule from Westminster, they had been identified by one section of the population not primarily as upholders of the rule of law but as defenders of the state, and the nature of the state itself has remained the cardinal issue of political argument. This identification of police and state is contrary to policing practice in the rest of the United Kingdom. It has left the police in an unenviable position, lamented by many police officers. In one political language they are the custodians of nationhood. In its rhetorical opposite, they are the symbols of oppression. Policing therefore goes right to the heart of the sense of security and identity of both communities, and because of the difference between them, this seriously hampers the effectiveness of the police service in Northern Ireland.'

We observed that the problems faced by the police were similar to those confronted by police in other divided societies. It was impossible to have fully effective policies 'when the police have to operate from fortified stations in armoured vehicles, and when police officers dare not tell their children what they do for a living for fear of attack from extremists from both sides'. Police had frequently been burned out of their homes when they tried to live in the communities they served.

The Commission invited written submissions, conducted a survey, researched through focus groups, met police services and experts in other countries and held open public meetings throughout Northern Ireland. When we announced that we were going to do this, some suggested that it would be a waste of time since no one attended public meetings these days. In fact, about 10,000 people came and over 1,000 spoke. They were pretty harrowing occasions: Omagh – not long after the Republican terrorist bombs there killed thirty-one people; Portadown – a raw little town where the meeting was kept just on the peaceful side of very heated debate by a Catholic solicitor who not long after was murdered by 'Loyalist paramilitary car bombs'; the same evening on to Craigavon, where four police widows spoke in turn, including one whose alleged IRA murderer had been got off on what seemed a technicality by the solicitor from Portadown. To make these occasions possible, but also to add to their tension, I decided from the outset with my fellow commissioners that we would work without security. How, after all, could you examine the history and behaviour of the RUC while being guarded by its officers? We depended on the word of the paramilitary terrorists on both sides that they would give us safe passage. We would occasionally gulp on our way into community halls at some of those clearly providing their own version of security for the occasion. But they kept their word with only one or two scares.

The political difficulties were clear enough. Whatever they had signed up to in the Belfast Agreement, the leading political figures wanted irreconcilable outcomes. Gerry Adams and Martin McGuinness and their Republican colleagues wanted the RUC to be scrapped. Any reformulated police force should include only those who had gone through a human rights test to prove they were suitable. This process went by a rather liturgical sounding name – 'lustration', they called it. The idea that terrorists who had murdered their fellow citizens, including policemen, should be given a veto over who could join a new force was clearly a complete non-starter.

Loyalists like David Trimble were not at all clear what they wanted except that there could be no change which suggested that the RUC had been less than pluperfect or that those who had died had done so in vain. This broadly meant that issues like the name of the force and its symbols needed to be preserved at all costs. Lustration to the left, status quo to the right. Given these views, it was difficult to see how the politicians had signed the Agreement. Trimble's opinion – more hardline than that of many serving police officers – suggested that he had not comprehended the underlying bargain that brought about peace. The Nationalists had accepted that change in the nature of the Northern Ireland state (the end of partition) would only come democratically through the ballot box. In return, they should not be required to demonstrate loyalty to a state which they wanted to change, albeit peacefully. Both sides would retain their own sense of who they were. One state, two identities.

We decided that there should be five tests for our recommendations. First, would they promote effective and efficient policing? Would they deliver fair and impartial policing, far from partisan control? Would they provide for accountability both to the law and to the community? Would they make the police more representative of the society they serve? Finally, did proposals protect and vindicate the human rights and dignity of all?

Our report, advocating 'a new beginning' for Northern Ireland's police, contained 175 recommendations covering accountability, human rights, management, public order policing, recruitment, training, co-operation with other police services, ethos and symbols. The greatest controversy touched on balanced recruitment and on ethos and symbols. To make the police service more representative we argued that for at least ten years new recruits for the police should be drawn on a 50:50 Catholic and non-Catholic basis from a qualified pool so that within ten years 30 per cent of the force would be Catholic. Second, to promote impartiality we recommended symbols 'free from association with the British or Irish states'. The name, Royal Ulster Constabulary, was not neutral and would have to go; instead, police officers should be part of the Police Service of Northern Ireland.

Its badge and symbols should change, just as those of the Northern Ireland Assembly had changed by political agreement. The Union Flag should no longer be flown from police buildings.

When the Commission had been established there had been a tacit acceptance that the government would accept whatever we could agree. By and large, our report was pretty well received, except by some members of the police service and Loyalist politicians led by David Trimble. He argued, among other things, that I had promised to show him our report before it was published to check it over with him. The idea that I would have done this with him or any other political leader was plainly absurd, though the party leaders all got sight of it just before it was published. Trimble stuck to his guns, denounced me and the report at every turn, and went through all the usual pantomime tricks of refusing to shake my hand and so on. I am prepared to believe that he must be a nicer man than he seems. His outrage was sufficient to knock the government off its stride. Despite the assurances we had been given, Mr Blair and his new Secretary of State, Peter Mandelson (Mo Mowlam had alas moved on), thought they could square the circles that we had recognized were 'unsquarable' and tinker with our recommendations (especially on recruitment, name and symbols) in the legislation required to implement the report. I concede with alacrity that Peter Mandelson is a clever fellow and is usually much too transparent to deserve being called 'the prince of darkness'. He was a good Business Minister and the Labour Party would have been better off if it had listened to him more. But I have never believed that Mandelson is quite as clever as he thinks he is. When he started to water down our proposals to keep Unionist critics quiet, there was outrage about what one serious newspaper called the 'travesty of a bill'. The cry went up from Nationalists – 'We want Patten, and nothing but Patten.' This sentiment was also expressed in some surprising quarters, by Republicans who not many years before had been minded to kill me. So Patten is what the Blair government concluded it had to accept. Opposition died away. The Police Service of Northern Ireland (PSNI) was instituted and soon settled down. The police were removed from the heart of the political dispute and the violence which had accompanied it. Our report was regarded by many others in divided communities elsewhere as a model. Today the proportion of Catholics in the PSNI is over 30 per cent. Since the Belfast Agreement there have been very few police fatalities. Why did it all work out so well? Above all, I reckon, because we did not duck trying to do the right thing in a moderate way.

I took with me a particularly strong memory from one of our public meetings. It was in a small village on the coast in the beautiful Mournes. The village was half dependent on agriculture, half on fishing; it was half Catholic and half Protestant. We met in the village cinema, a little like the one in *Cinema Paradiso*. I recollect that it had just been showing the James Bond film *Tomorrow Never Dies*. Here it was yesterday that seemed never to have died. We were sat up on the stage, three of us, as the audience told us their stories of suffering and complaint, one lot of stories contrasting like so many antonyms with the others. I eventually called an end, and gave my usual pretty little peroration about the need for generosity, reconciliation, healing and hope, thinking as I offered these clichés about the large malt whisky that awaited me back at Hillsborough. A little old lady at the back of the hall in a hat and coat of many colours put her hand up insistently. 'Before you go,' she said loudly. 'I've got just one thing to say to you. It's all very well coming over here and giving us all that stuff about generosity of spirit. You go home after this is over. We have to stay with our histories and experience all around us. For example,' she said, leaning forward and touching a young man in front of her on the shoulder, 'this man here murdered my son.' It was true. He was a murderer let out of prison as part of the Agreement. His victim's mother lived on with the intimacy of violence, so often in all its bragging insolence, the stuff of her daily existence. That was and in a sense still is real life in a small and beautiful village in the United Kingdom of Great Britain and Northern Ireland.

8

Out East

The most important political office is that of private citizen.
Justice Louis D. Brandeis, *Boston Record* (1903)

I don't actually believe in a clash of civilization. I believe in a
clash of the civilized and the non-civilized.
Madeleine K. Albright, *Bloomberg* (23 December 2002)

Not the least peculiar irony in the history of democracy in Hong
Kong – a story still far from its final pages, whatever President Xi
may think – is that the collapse of the Labour Party vote in the British
constituency of Bath resulted in 1992 in that city's defeated MP
becoming the last Governor of Britain's last major colony. Conservative success in Bath had for years depended on the Opposition vote
splitting between Labour and Liberals. In 1992, Labour voters
deserted the red rose and voted tactically to defeat me, encouraged
by an effective and expensive campaign funded by David Sainsbury, the supermarket multi-millionaire and (later) Labour minister.
It was painful. I felt hurt and, for a time, sick at the humiliation. My
wife and daughters, who had worked hard in my campaign, were
shocked at its nastiness as well as the result. But that is political life.
Expect garlands and petals scattered before the wheels of your char-
iot and you are bound to be in for a rude and salutary shock. I had
been the chair of a successful – in national terms – General Election
campaign, but as the slave accompanying the victorious general
during his Roman triumph used to whisper, 'Remember you are
mortal.'
Fortunately, I had expected this outcome (which did not make it

any less unpleasant) and had even told the Prime Minister, John Major, that he would win the election overall but that I would lose my own seat. I tend to pessimism at the best of times and I think John believed that I was exaggerating the difficulties. In any event, I had plenty of time before and during the campaign to consider what I wanted to do if I lost. When that happened, I was not attracted to the idea of trying to continue my political career in the House of Lords, though the opportunity was offered to me. So was the possibility of being parachuted into a rapidly vacated constituency in a by-election. Kensington and Chelsea was suggested, apparently gift-wrapped. This struck me as unseemly, and a further unfair burden on my wife and children, who had already faced the heat of an occasionally vicious campaign in Bath.* I resisted some well-meaning pressure to pursue this course, or at least to hang around the political scene, a wallflower at the ball, waiting for someone to ask me to dance, an embarrassment to everyone. Despite occasional second or third thoughts I never really regretted this decision. I was thinking about looking for a post outside politics in the field of development assistance. Then John Major offered me the chance to go to Hong Kong as the last British Governor, a politician to end a line of Colonial or Foreign Office appointments. Recent policy seemed to have driven London into a diplomatic cul-de-sac, in which routine humiliations by China (not least of the Prime Minister, John Major) never seemed to bring any benefit for Hong Kong or Britain. The diplomatic object was simply a smooth transition to Chinese sovereignty in 1997. Smooth was defined as meeting Chinese demands, after a few ineffectual objections and a bit of hand-wringing. But what price a successful and honourable transition? One of my advisers used to ask mischievously whether you could describe a funeral as 'a smooth transition'.

The offer was made and, after talking to Lavender, I accepted. It was quite a sacrifice for her. Her career as a family lawyer at the Bar

---

* It was moreover a dangerous political choice with some dark precedents. Patrick Gordon-Walker had lost his Smethwick seat in 1964, fought a by-election in Leyton as a seat-less Foreign Secretary in Harold Wilson's government and promptly lost it, thus virtually terminating his career at the top.

had taken off. We were happily settled in London with teenage daughters. As ever, she supported me at some personal cost. This has happened throughout our marriage. In Hong Kong she worked immensely hard to give leadership to a number of charities, like hospice care, street children, prostitution, mental handicap and AIDS, that for local cultural reasons had not attracted much public support in the past.

I was not a complete stranger to Hong Kong and China. I first went to the colony in 1979, when I was a young backbench MP. On my return I wrote an article for the *Guardian* advocating the introduction of elections for local government there. This did not please the then Governor, a stern chieftain, who thought that popular political pressure could best be dealt with by housing and welfare programmes. He drove through ambitious schemes with great energy and determination, dealing with floods of refugees from the mainland. Lord Maclehose was a clever man, no one's stooge. It used to be said when he was Governor that he and the Maltese Prime Minister, Dom Mintoff, were the most unpopular men in the Foreign Office; that spoke well for his independent mind. But he was not at all interested in anyone's democratic aspirations to run their own affairs. He was a civilized, unbending Scot who thought he knew what was right for Hong Kong, and that he could best manage its relations with Beijing. How much his own initiative, eighteen years before the hand-over, in raising quite so explicitly with Deng Xiaoping questions concerning Hong Kong's position after 1997 reflected the Cabinet's views has never been wholly clear to me. I liked him – after all he was another Balliol man with a taste for dry martinis – but I was never under any illusion about what he would think about even modest efforts at democratic reform. Unlike some others, however, he did not seek to bad-mouth me or stab me in the back.

I had also been to China on a number of occasions, particularly when I was Minister of Overseas Development. In that role I attended the Asia Development Bank (ADB) meeting in May 1989 in Beijing. We were there until about a week before Deng and the other elderly Communist Party leaders sent in the tanks to crush the demonstrators in Tiananmen Square and elsewhere in China. With the square and other public spaces overflowing with demonstrators during our

ADB meetings, the atmosphere felt like a Glastonbury Festival of freedom and democracy. I have never before or since felt so close to history being made. Sadly, it turned out to be the wrong history. I played one very minor role in the proceedings. The senior ministers attending the ADB meeting were invited to a discussion with Zhao Ziyang, the reform-minded party secretary-general. We sat around asking polite questions about agricultural reform and the role of market forces in China, while our thoughts were on what was happening outside on the streets. Eventually, after an hour or so of these slightly surreal routine exchanges, I asked the question on all our minds: what was happening outside and how would it be resolved? Zhao pulled a card from his pocket and gave a short, passionate lecture which sounded very like the speech that he subsequently gave to the students in the middle of the night in Tiananmen Square, and which would expedite his downfall. He expressed sympathy for the students and workers, hoped that they would give up their hunger strike before they damaged their health, and promised a dialogue with them. Alas, events took a brutal turn. The tanks rolled in; many were killed; and the subsequent crackdown on any dissident activity was tougher than anything that has happened in China until the recent repressive measures of Xi Jinping. As was the case with the much later democracy protests in Hong Kong in 2014, it is difficult for demonstrators in what are strategically unplanned events to know when to back off, having won not just a place on the moral high ground but a position from which, a little later, further advances could probably be made. To activists, tactical withdrawals and regroupings look like appeasement and surrender. But, though difficult to time and to organize, they are often the sensible short-term course, and sometimes the sensible long-term one too.

So I had some bruising and disappointing experiences of Chinese politics. The effect of the murder of Chinese students and others in 1989 – called by one of the Communist Party's businessmen poodles in Hong Kong 'the kerfuffle' – was to raise the alarm in Hong Kong about what the return to Chinese sovereignty there only eight years later might presage. The movement to speed up the democratization of Hong Kong became understandably much stronger. The Joint Declaration, an international treaty signed by Britain and China in 1984, with a fifty-year life from 1997, and the Basic Law, which was a Chinese constitution for Hong Kong based on the treaty, were supposed to guarantee Hong Kong's freedom and the way of life of the colony after Beijing had resumed sovereignty. What would ensure that the Chinese complied with all this? This must have been of special concern to Sir Percy Cradock, a former ambassador to China, who had assumed a role as the Cardinal of the Holy Office on all matters affecting 'the middle kingdom'. Cradock had once said of Chinese Communist Party officials, 'They were thugs, are thugs and always will be thugs.' So what do you do with 'thugs' (not a noun I have ever used about Chinese leaders)? Do you pay them off whenever they come calling reminding you, as they tend to do, of all those who had not paid a 'pizzo' and now slept with the fishes? That seemed to be the Cardinal's view. You accepted a regular shakedown as part of normal diplomatic practice, trying to make it through your own demeanour a little less unbecoming.

Intellectually and politically, Sir Percy resisted what his political masters assured the world, and especially Hong Kong: that Britain would make certain that Hong Kong retained its pluralism and its freedom. He was not the only mandarin who wanted to be emperor or at least exercise imperial authority from behind the throne. Though he was a very clever man, he was one of those quite rare officials who never really accept where a civil servant's authority ends and a democratically elected politician's takes over.

After signature of the Joint Declaration, whatever had happened before, the British government's policy was now clear. Hong Kong was to become democratic. Democracy would steadily take root and give people the means to defend themselves against any erosion of their liberties. This was said publicly and privately in Parliament and outside. I have always been surprised by those who suggest that we should take no notice of promises made in the House of Commons. The declared British policy was the all-purpose reply to those who worried that Britain's last imperial gesture was to be the handing over of a free society to the last great totalitarian power in the world, with more sleight of hand in the process than transparency. This was the backdrop to my arrival in Hong Kong as the last Governor.

I have already set out in truncated form some of my experience as

Governor of Hong Kong, the most interesting and worthwhile five years of my life, and I do not intend to beat through the shrubbery over all these issues again, despite the continuing occasional squawks of rage from the Cradock acolytes who still carry a torch for his approach to China. To them any alternative attitude has to be demolished lest its success, or even partial success, raises questions about the effectiveness as well as the morality of what went before. But it is important to sketch out the bare bones of the story of the thwarting of democratic development in Hong Kong because of its relevance to my arguments about identity. First, there is the question of whether so-called Asian values include any concern for political accountability and human rights or whether there is an inevitable 'clash of civilizations' between the East and the West. Second, there is the matter of whether civic values can become an important part of identity, helping to shape it. Third, it is worth considering how far the Chinese leadership's incomprehension about the meaning of a free society limits its clout in the world, despite the size of its population and hence of its economy.

Why was Hong Kong not already well on the road to democracy, let alone to being a fully democratic society, well before Britain's departure from responsibility for this great city? One characteristic of efforts to introduce more popular accountability and more involvement of Chinese citizens in Hong Kong's government, during the nineteenth century and the first half of the twentieth, was the resistance of the British business community. Events in the region – wars in China and the military adventurism of Japan – also argued against political change in a colony that was always regarded in London as rather different from Britain's other dependencies, more trading post than settled community. A big push for democracy under Governor Young after the Second World War was thwarted by nervousness about the consequences of the collapse of the Kuomintang (KMT) government in China and the advance of the Communist Party. Local business, colonial officials and Whitehall readily accepted the argument that introducing democracy in Hong Kong would divide the community along the lines of the communist–KMT conflict on the mainland. Beijing itself was unsurprisingly nervous about any democratic moves in Hong Kong too. For instance, in 1958, with decolonization picking up speed in Africa, Zhou Enlai sent a message to the then British Prime Minister, Harold Macmillan, expressing the worry that Britain might be pushing the colony along the road to independence like Singapore. Britain should not change Hong Kong's constitutional status, which America (the Chinese believed) would welcome as a means of weakening China. Beijing's apprehensions helped strengthen the hand of those in the colony and in London who advised against change.

The 1960s and 1970s were dominated by an influx of refugees to Hong Kong from the mainland, riots in 1966 against colonial government, and Maoist riots in 1967 in organized sympathy for the Cultural Revolution. But these decades also witnessed Hong Kong's increasing economic vitality, the result of free-trade policies, surplus cheap labour and the booming Asian economies in its neighbourhood. As the countdown to the inevitable transfer of sovereignty in 1997 began to dictate the pace of events, the arguments about democracy resurfaced. They became part of the basis of the negotiations on the Joint Declaration with the promise that Hong Kong would have a legislature constituted by elections to which the executive would be accountable. The then Governor, Teddy Youde, tried bravely to push through practical ways of achieving this in 1984–5 with the introduction of a steadily increasing number of directly elected legislators. He was thwarted by opposition from Beijing, the local business community and the Cradock votaries. Youde died in 1986 and in a subsequent consultation exercise, allegedly to discover the Hong Kong public's wishes on the pace of introducing direct elections for the legislature, a clear majority in favour of a faster pace for democratization was morphed, with not very well-disguised sharp practice, into a victory of the minority for going slower. If the 'thirty-year rule' leads to the release of all the papers and telegrams for this period, I do not believe that London will emerge from this episode with much credit. Perhaps some of these papers have already slipped down the back of a sofa. Summarizing in my Hong Kong diary the questions that I put to the Foreign Office in 1997 about the papers for this period that I had seen while clearing out old government material for return to London, I wrote, 'we told the Chinese that they shouldn't underestimate the pressure for direct elections just because the consultation exercise purported to show there wasn't great support for them. The whole business was an essay in trying to avoid a row with China rather than respond to the demands for more democracy in Hong Kong. If we'd done more then we'd have had almost a decade of developing representative government under our belts before the hand-over. At best the exercise was cynical.' In short, Britain behaved badly because it wanted that 'smooth' transition and no rocking of the boat.

When I went to Hong Kong in 1992, my briefing on the question of democratic development was pretty limited. Naturally I read the parliamentary debates about the negotiations over the transfer of sovereignty in Hong Kong. I was struck by the weight of argument that it would be the steady introduction of democracy that would really guarantee Hong Kong's future freedom. One of the strongest proponents of this point of view was Edward Heath. In the history of decolonization, he said, we had always tended to go too slowly in pressing ahead with democratization. In Hong Kong we should go faster than the government seemed to envisage. He repeated these arguments after the Tiananmen killings in 1989. But I am afraid that, at some stage between then and my arrival in Hong Kong in 1992, other counsels – I wonder whether they could have been Chinese – had overwhelmed Heath's democratic spirit. When I was Governor, he would regularly invite himself to stay so he could spend a week going around Hong Kong telling everyone prepared to listen how stupid and confrontational I was being in my dealings with China. He would then depart, with a wintry expression of gratitude, for Beijing, before repeating the whole tiresome exhibition of unhelpful ill-manners the following year.

Before leaving for the colony I also had a large amount of rather general briefing about the agreed electoral arrangements. For his part, Percy Cradock in two or three discussions simply told me in his austere but lordly way that everything was clearly set out in the Chinese Basic Law for Hong Kong. This specified what should be done, including the number of directly elected legislators to be allowed. In the proposals I set out when I arrived in Hong Kong I did not try to overturn this but simply attempted to use every bit of flexibility allowed to make the electoral arrangements as broadly democratic as possible. So, for instance, I greatly enlarged the numbers who could vote in the so-called functional constituencies which represented business and professional interests, and made the District Boards (local government) fully democratic. Shortly after I announced these plans, Lee Kuan Yew gave an interview in which he applauded my deepening of democracy and the ingenious way in which I had filled in the spaces left in the Basic Law and the Joint Declaration. When I had seen him on my way to Hong Kong he told me to set out my agenda very clearly at the outset and stick to it. This is what I tried to do, and also to entrench Hong Kong's rule of law and protection of human rights. In response to this rather modest advance in account-ability (well short of the demands of local Democrat Party legislators), Chinese verbal pyrotechnics turned me into a champion of democ-racy akin to Tom Paine. It was not meant as a compliment, and it would certainly not have been deserved. But China's barrage of abuse secured some traction, gaining the surprising approval of both Prime Minister Lee and much of the British business community (though not the American) in Hong Kong. My greatest crime, I have reflected subsequently, was to decline to be either a lame or a Peking duck. Moreover, in a constant and deliberate effort to engage in what a member of my Executive Council called 'tutorial government', I constantly emphasized the relationship between Hong Kong's civic values and its economic success. I also tried to take the stuffiness out of the gubernatorial role, did public question-and-answer sessions on radio and at public meetings, gave broadcasts once a month on issues related to governance, and made speeches about Hong Kong's way of life and what made it special.

Did the rows with China over pluralism damage Hong Kong? The economy continued to grow. Every year we cut taxes, increased spending not least on social programmes, saw our reserves increase, developed our infrastructure, almost completed a new airport (paid for largely out of revenues, not borrowing), created more jobs, and brought inflation and crime down to ten-year lows. Hong Kong remained stable; there was no social breakdown or political chaos. Any demonstrations against the government – and there were few – involved hundreds not thousands of people. We left Hong Kong without the territory or Britain facing international obloquy. Most of my local and expatriate advisers in 1992 and 1993, when I first arrived, argued that we should stand fast on the commitment to

democracy. They had been obliged to negotiate for years without a
bottom line and had seen the consequences. Their conclusion after all
these dramas was that, whether you have a bottom line or not, the
Chinese behave in the same way. I described it in my diary in September 1996 after one of our negotiators had suffered what he called a
'grisly' encounter with his opposite number. 'Others, while wanting
to get the best for their own side, do at least search for some acceptable compromise or accommodation. But the Chinese were only
interested in getting their own way. They'll hold on, even if they
intend to do a deal, until the eleventh hour and beyond trying to
extract last-minute concessions. And if they can't win everything,
they'll try to ensure that the text of an agreement gives them enough
elbow room to reopen every matter they want subsequently . . . The
rest of the world should really know how to play hard ball with them.
At present they get away with a negotiating style that combines the
tactics of the Mafia and of every barrack room lawyer with a good
dollop of straightforward duplicity thrown in for good measure.'

This is called 'the struggle school of diplomacy'. Struggle or not, I
concluded that at least if we had a bottom line we would be able to
hold our heads up and make it easier to govern Hong Kong. So we
struggled diplomatically, but not in governing the territory: a better
all-round bargain. As we got closer to 1997, one of my advisers used
to argue that Hong Kong was like a Rolls-Royce. The Chinese wanted
to tinker with the engine and change the tyres, but all they really
needed to do was turn on the ignition and away she'd go.

Some argued that this whole approach hurt Britain's business interests in Hong Kong and in China. Even some former Conservative
ministers like Lord Young, now working (not always hugely successfully) as company chairmen or directors, were not above telling
whoever wanted to listen in Hong Kong or London that democracy
was not all that it was cracked up to be and that rows with China
undermined business opportunities. Democracy was often blamed
when the culprits were actually bad management decisions. Local Chinese companies ran rings around some of the old British 'hongs' and
mainland Chinese officials regularly took their distinguished British
visitors to the cleaners. (A good piece of advice from those at the sharp
end of commercial negotiations was never to allow the company

chairman near the talks.) Douglas Hurd, the former Foreign Secretary, once noted, 'There are people who stay at the Mandarin Hotel and listen to a few people and think they know Hong Kong. They don't see that what is actually happening inside that amazing society is change. And when it is put under their noses they don't like it because life would be much easier if everything went on as before and there were no politics in Hong Kong. There are politics in Hong Kong and ministers have to take account of that the way that taipans don't have to.'

The toe-curling lack of any sense of honour or decency in some of the political and commercial lobbying was more than matched by the efforts made by some local commercial bigwigs to curry favour with mainland officials. The weather was changing as we got close to 1997, and the toads croaked. But these panjandrums could miscalculate badly. One concerned a local businessman with spectacularly Neanderthal political opinions. He ran an investment bank that crashed in flames in the Asian financial crisis of 1997–8. He had courted controversy on a number of occasions. In what many assumed was a joke, he had allegedly once offered the Conservative Party five million pounds to get rid of me; I was never sure whether he thought shooting me might be an option. Anyway, addressing the Hong Kong alumni of an American Business School one day in spring 1997, he attacked democracy fiercely, noting that the USA had done well until thirty years before it had become a real democracy, which seemed to mean when segregation was ended and black voters were registered. Few others went quite this far, at least publicly.

Controversy about the relationship between courting China politically and success in, for instance, exporting to them or attracting Chinese inward investment continues to this day. It very rarely generates serious efforts to see whether there really is such a relationship. I have always believed that the Chinese do business on much the same basis as most others. They buy what they want and need at the best price with the best terms they can get; they invest where they can see a profit or a long-term commercial opportunity. If they can get away with putting the frighteners on potential trading partners by threatening dire consequences if a government supports criticisms of their human rights record or a Prime Minister meets the Dalai Lama, then I suppose one should not be too surprised at them for deploying this bit of triad-like protectionism. The criticism should be directed more against those who bow to bullying. When Michael Heseltine told John Major that taking a firm line with a Chinese visitor about Hong Kong risked destroying our trade relations with China, I noted in my diary in November 1996: 'Fact: exports to China fell 25 per cent in the four years before my trade-wrecking arrival in Hong Kong. Fact: exports to China rose by 75 per cent in the four years since then. What does this prove? Not much. Only maybe that kow-towing doesn't make much difference.'

Having nosedived in the years preceding my arrival, Hong Kong's exports did indeed gallop ahead after 1992, with our share of OECD exports as a whole growing faster than the average for this group of countries. All this proves is that, for all the threats, over time politics rarely has all that much effect on trade.* On the relatively rare occasions when unacceptable commercial retaliation happens, the democratic partners of the offended country should work together in or outside the WTO to retaliate against, and put pressure on, China. They are usually too feeble to do this. Trading with China is always difficult, whatever the political situation. But you do not have to borrow from the Cradock rule book in order to succeed. According to journalists accompanying the Prime Minister and Cradock to China on the miserable and humiliating post-Tiananmen visit in 1990, undertaken in order to secure China's support for building the new Hong Kong airport (with the territory's own money), every time that John Major mentioned human rights Cradock told them afterwards that this was not serious but just for show. That behaviour does not win bigger trade deals. The Germans export a lot more to China than Britain does because the Germans make more things that the Chinese want to buy. It is high time for Britain and others to grow up about this issue, though China will not much care for it when we do.

The verbal bombardment of Hong Kong by Chinese Communist

---

* One exception that I would concede is direct Norwegian salmon sales to China after the Nobel Peace Prize was awarded to the Chinese writer and dissident Liu Xiaobo. But as one businessman in the fish industry opined, 'History has shown that salmon always finds its way to market.' Almost overnight after the Chinese ban, sales of Norwegian salmon to China's neighbour Vietnam rocketed. Who knows how much of this salmon found its way rather rapidly to China?

Party officials clearly had little effect on the territory, whose economy cruised serenely on. Nor did it seem to have much effect on me, save (as I noted earlier) to make me appear a braver champion of democracy than I really was. I did not complain but observed others, like the Democratic legislators Martin Lee and Emily Lau, or Bishop Zen, who was to become the Catholic primate, who deserved the praise a great deal more. When I left Hong Kong, and became the European Commissioner for External Affairs responsible among other things for the EU relationship with the Chinese, that country's officials as ever showed their pragmatism and treated me with considerable respect. At my first meeting with the Chinese foreign minister (Tang Jiaxuan) at the UN General Assembly in 1999, he said to me, 'This time we should co-operate.' 'That's what I wanted to do last time,' I replied. A nice and chirpy man, he came to see me in Brussels on a kiss-and-make-up mission. The meeting got off to a bad start when he cracked a joke. I had a collection of photographs on the wall of my daughters. He took one look at them, guessed who they were and asked, 'How come such beautiful young women have such an ugly father?' His ambassador, reeling from what he feared might be taken at face value as an insult, interjected nervously, 'It's a joke, it's a joke.' I knew that, and it was quite a good one. Later in the meeting, the minister read word for word from a brief to announce that the leadership had considered my position and concluded that I was 'a force for concord not discord'. Just to make sure that we had got the point, the Chinese embassy to the EU checked with my 'Chef de Cabinet' afterwards to ensure that he had taken the words down correctly.

During my time in Brussels, I had a good, constructive relationship with Chinese officials, who always – such was my ancient infamy – knew who I was and usually wanted what we did not then call a 'selfie'. I particularly enjoyed meetings with the premier Zhu Rongji (one of the most impressive officials I have ever met), usually about WTO access. At EU meetings with the Chinese, I was usually landed with handling the more contentious issues like human rights and – ridiculously, because it was really a matter in which member states were in the driving seat – arms sales to China, which had been suspended after Tiananmen. I recall Zhu recounting a conversation with a Falun Gong demonstrator, and his incomprehension at discovering that this believer put so much emphasis on what Zhu thought was spiritual 'waffle' rather than personal economic circumstances. His officials were horrified by the admission that he had even had this conversation. Even more memorable was a dispute about capital punishment, which turned into a sort of no-holds-barred students' debate.

I was invited for a private official visit with Lavender to China by the President, Jiang Zemin. After our meeting, mostly spent discussing old movies and Shakespeare, one of his staff asked me if I would sign a copy of my book *East and West* for him. This secretary had got hold of a pirated copy, printed in Taiwan, I noticed. I seemed to get on well enough with the last President, Hu Jintao, a very polite man, and am always greeted enthusiastically by Chinese groups in airport terminals and the like, which is good for my morale. But in recent years my critical remarks about China's handling of Hong Kong affairs have fired up the communist vocabulary of abuse once again, not least on the part of China's ambassador in London, who plainly dropped out of the class on charm and tact during his diplomatic training. It is rather worrying to assume that he goes on behaving as though he was taught by the Corleone family on the grounds that he normally gets away with it. All in all, however, it is still my view that trying to establish an open and mutually positive and beneficial relationship with China is fine; kowtowing to Chinese Leninism is not fine. Whether the arrival of a Trump presidency will smooth Chinese diplomacy at the edges will be a defining issue in international affairs in the next few years. On the face of things one needs to be an optimist to think that President Trump and President Xi will bring the best out in each other.

The argument that democracy itself is alien to Asian culture is much more damaging to communities like Hong Kong than threats to limit trade if too much support is given to the indigenous development of pluralism. Hong Kong has invariably been caught up in the arguments about so-called Asian values, the claim that there are fundamental differences between cultures. The Asian identity brings with it, so it is said, a much weaker concern about individual rights and accountability, and a greater awareness of the importance of obedience to the family and the state.

The distinction drawn between different civilizations obliges us to put on one side the overlaps and the cultural cross-fertilization between countries and continents. Anyone with an awareness of Christian history knows that the first thrust of Christian evangelism was from Palestine east into western Asia. Medievalists have taught us how much Islam shaped European society and learning. Many of the founding classical texts of Christian society in Europe came to early-Renaissance cities and universities through the agency of Arabic scholarship. Similar stories can be told about other civilizations. Asia itself – 30 per cent of the world's total surface area and over 60 per cent of the world's population – is actually a European concept and indeed word, from the initial involvement of Herodotus and other classical writers. Over the years this European view has changed from seeing in Asia an other-worldly disdain for utilitarian matters of commerce and technology, to regarding the continent as a world-beating global workshop. Reflecting the earlier views about 150 years ago, Matthew Arnold wrote:

> The brooding East with awe beheld
> Her impious younger world.
> The Roman tempest swelled and swelled,
> And on her head was hurled.

> The East bowed low before the blast
> In patient, deep disdain;
> She let the legions thunder past,
> And plunged in thought again.

Arnold's view of Asian culture and values was a long way from today's Shanghai or Singapore. There is today more commercial thunder in the East than thoughtful disdain.

The rather silly argument about Asian values, much devalued by the Asian financial crash of 1997–8, was given some intellectual heft by the father of the Singapore city state, Lee Kuan Yew, and his acolytes. Despite other Asian politicians and thinkers like the Korean Nobel Peace Prize Winner, President Kim Dae-Jung, the Nobel Economics Laureate Amartya Sen, and the disgracefully incarcerated Malaysian political leader Anwar Ibrahim, putting the contrary view, Lee's arguments secured for a time a good deal of support. Today, long after his death, they are still repeated in Singapore as an act of filial loyalty. These nostrums provided a useful cover for authoritarianism, both soft and hard, and an excuse for Western businessmen and politicians not to allow issues like torture and the suppression of freedom of speech to get in the way of trying to do business. For these disciples, the Asian-values argument was that human rights and democracy were bad for economic development and that keeping them in chains had been the reason for Asia's booming economies. The undoubted success of Lee's own small economy was taken as the necessary, almost sufficient, proof of the truth of these propositions. There was, it was argued, a preference in Asia for the collective and for harmony over individual initiative and endeavour. Figures of authority deserved and received loyalty and respect. Civil and political rights were matters which Asian communities should deal with themselves without external interference. In Singapore, the British barrister Anthony Lester said they liked the forms of democracy but not their values. This was not Confucian. Nor was it uniquely Asian. It was just authoritarian: a touch of Sparta in the Orient.

I have never been convinced that Singapore's success depended on vigorously refuting any criticism of its first leader and his family. Singapore pursued effective economic and social policies with a lot more social engineering and central direction than I would normally find attractive. It had a great port and a hub position in a booming region. Given my economic liberalism, I was pleased by those American economic studies in the 1990s that showed a higher rate of return on investments in Hong Kong, where there was no industrial strategy but a free economy, than in Singapore, and that our Interpol crime figures were better than Singapore's (even though we did not hang or cane offenders). Lee Kuan Yew was a remarkable man and I have never doubted Singapore's success. But I do not believe that this validates an inherently absurd argument, nor that the Singapore model would necessarily have worked on a larger stage.

I presume that Lee Kuan Yew developed the 'Asian values' argument for four reasons. First, he was keen to fend off criticism that Singapore was an American poodle in the region. Second, he wanted to deflect criticism of his authoritarian style and the extent to which the institutions of plural governance that he created had some of the characteristics of Potemkin villages. Yes, there were parliamentary elections but what chance a government defeat? Yes, there were courts but how strong was the rule of law?* The third reason was that it enabled him to warm up his relations with China, even while staying on friendly terms with Taiwan, which had embraced democracy. Fourth, he claimed ancient confirmation of his approach by digging up the roots of his philosophy in a somewhat partial perusal of the *Analects of Confucius*.

Just consider for a moment some of the absurdities of the overall argument. Marketed as Asian values, it has to cover an awful lot of political and cultural ground from dictatorships in Central Asia to the largest world democracy in India to Stone Age totalitarianism in North Korea. Inconveniently, India is not only a rumbustious democracy but, as Amartya Sen has pointed out, embraced political tolerance under King Ashoka in the third century BC and Emperor Akbar in the sixteenth century AD. India had already established a rich tradition of tolerance and debate when Europeans still believed in the divine right of kings. Even if you narrow the field and look at East Asia alone, you have to contend with totally different sorts of government from (to be polite) guided democracy in Singapore, to Leninism with capitalist characteristics in China to democratic South Korea, Taiwan and Japan, and to aspirations for democracy in Hong Kong. Are the Taiwanese democrats or the Hong Kong aspirants for democracy less Confucian than get-rich-as-quick-as-possible capitalists in Beijing or Shanghai? What are the principal Confucian values exemplified in Shenzhen or in the spectacular number of those helping the anti-corruption police with their inquiries in the People's Republic? In the *Analects*, Zilu asks the Master how to serve a prince. Confucius replies, 'Tell him the truth even if it offends him.' The

---

* When I was staying in Singapore in 1992 on my way to Hong Kong, and much enjoying conversations with the city's sage (it was after this that he wrote suggesting we should be on 'Harry' and 'Chris' terms), I asked him how he had dealt with the triads. 'We used one of your colonial ordinances. We locked them up at Changi.' 'How many?' I asked. 'About a thousand,' he replied. 'All triads?' I inquired. 'Probably,' he said, nodding ruminatively. Not long after I told this story to one or two colleagues in Hong Kong, I heard that it had been repeated by one of them to show how superior was Singapore's idea of the rule of law to Hong Kong's.

subtleties of Confucius are ignored by those who want to turn him into an excuse for iron-clad patrician authoritarianism. The governor of She says to Confucius, 'Among my people there is a man of unbending integrity. When his father stole a sheep he denounced him.' 'Among my people,' replies the Master, 'men of integrity do things differently; a father covers up for his son, a son covers up for his father, and there is integrity in what they do.'

The central fallacy in the Asian-values clash-of-civilizations argument is that it denies the universality of human rights. As the UN Declaration on Human Rights asserted, after the barbarities that preceded it and took place during the Second World War, human beings have the same individual rights, regardless of race, religion, nation or location. They are entitled to a fair trial, to due process, to free speech, to freedom from torture or enslavement. It hurts the same to be tortured in an Asian police cell or to be water boarded in a US military base. Denial of free speech leads to the same calamities in every society – to corruption, bad government, economic crimes and further abuses, all of which China has conspicuously suffered under communism (and some of which it suffered before). The most successful societies are those that combine inclusive economic policies and inclusive political structures.

There is a further reason for throwing the arguments about Asian values overboard. They assume that democracy and human rights are principally Western (European or American) concerns and by implication they suggest that this is how the West always behaves. But we know that the West's record on all this is patchy. No one can look back at the history of the first half of the twentieth century and regard it as a successful example of the West's practice of pluralism, accountability and the rule of law. The West has no monopoly of virtue in governance. Nor does the West avoid hypocrisy in the way it stands up for what it purports to believe. We are often all as bad as one another. Looking through my Hong Kong diaries I can find references to French ministers appearing to put cognac sales above 'les droits de l'homme' and Germans giving priority to car exports. Were they joking? And what about Britain, recently launched (so ministers claimed) on an apparently 'golden age' of relations with China. President Xi Jinping, lauded on a state visit to London, while he cracked down on any sign of dissent at home? Did any British minister protest loudly enough to be heard? The Joint Declaration and Basic Law have been breached – for example, with abductions of Hong Kong citizens by mainland officials and some erosion of the territory's legal autonomy – yet there have been very few squeals of disapproval from London.

A question near the heart of the Asian-values debate is whether you have to be Western to be modern. I have never believed this to be true, partly because so many of the physical manifestations of modernity are designed and manufactured in the East. Visit the most sophisticated computer laboratories or back-office outsourcing companies in Bangalore or Poona and count the saris; look at the modishness – their very own hipsterism – of young Japanese in Tokyo and the sophistication of their retail industries; visit a school in Shanghai or Seoul and admire the intellectual firepower of the students, their familiarity with every aspect of information technology. The issue is not 'modernness' but the sustainability of economic success, of competitiveness and of a decent society where individual rights are protected and the public good is at the same time asserted. In the years after the Second World War these attributes were more frequently found in Europe, North America and Australasia. But they were not exclusive to these countries; nor were civic values their intellectual invention. A civic consciousness, a sense of what it is to be a good citizen, and what government should do to protect and develop that notion, helps to shape a country's ideal of itself. This is far more a hallmark of identity than some largely made-up idea of civilizational behaviour.

In the 1990s, Hong Kong had all the freedoms and protections of a plural society except the right to choose its own government. Sooner or later this had to come as well. People were taught about freedom, and, moreover, they practised it – not in an abstract way but freedom specifically to do this and to do that. They were never going to accept that the one thing they could not do was to choose how accountability could be assured. It was absurd for some, especially but not exclusively in the business community, to argue that a colonial Governor had introduced politics to a previously apolitical community. Hong Kong is sophisticated and well-educated with two or three of the fifty best universities in the world. A large part of its community comprises refugees from the often savage politics of mainland China. Political demands were not foisted on Hong Kong. What is true is that they were sharpened by fears of the Chinese Communist Party's plans for Hong Kong, and that a moderate movement for democracy was to a limited extent radicalized by attempts to suppress it.

Efforts since 1997 to politicize Hong Kong's fine civil service, and to bend the equally good police force to securing political objectives, must have had some effect, even if only to blur ideas of the meaning of public service. The rule of law and the independence of the judiciary have nevertheless survived despite some minatory noises from Beijing. Civil society also remains strong, the churches too. Yet freedom of speech has been snipped away by commercial manoeuvres and physical assault. Citizens have been abducted from Hong Kong streets and taken to the mainland because they displeased the authorities there. Recently questions have been raised about both university autonomy and academic freedom, partly because of the extent to which the democracy movement in 2014 (the so-called Umbrella Revolution) appeared to spring from universities and schools.

This extraordinary display of democratic zeal in the autumn of 2014 was triggered by Beijing's imposition of control over the arrangements for the election of Hong Kong's chief executive, the restriction of the candidates for this post to people the Chinese leadership thought they could trust to toe the line. The Chinese Communist Party was determined not to risk losing its handle on the process twenty years after the change in sovereignty which had been accompanied by Beijing's clampdown on the development of democracy in the legislature. Most of the world – except in China where the news was blocked – watched the demonstrations with surprise and admiration. The young people who formed the core of the protests acted on the whole with courtesy and restraint. They helped one another with their homework; they drew up rosters of duties to make the demonstrations as acceptable as possible to others; they cleaned up the litter. Some of the policing of the demonstrations and the organized use of triads and paid-by-the-day bullies to break up the demonstrations brought shame on the authorities.

It was a slur on the integrity and principles of Hong Kong's citizens to assert, as the Chinese government's propaganda machine did, that they were being manipulated by outside forces. What motivated Hong Kong's tens of thousands of demonstrators – many if not most of whom had grown up after the reversion to Chinese sovereignty – was a passionate belief that they should be able to run their affairs as they were promised, choosing those who govern them in free and fair elections. These peaceful demonstrators, with their umbrellas, their refuse collection bags, their passionately held beliefs, could not be swept off the street like garbage, or permanently bullied into submission by tear gas and pepper spray. Young and old, they represented the city's future. Their hopes were for a peaceful and prosperous life in which they could enjoy the freedom and rule of law that they were promised. This is not only in the interests of their city. It is in China's interest too. Although it did not of course intend this, what the Chinese Communist Party has done is to bake into Hong Kong's life a real sense of citizenship. Increasingly, Hong Kong's feelings about its own identity have not been to accept or even reject Chinese-ness but to assert Hong Kong Chinese-ness. This has been a real and lasting development which the Communist Party needs to recognize. The fact that it finds it so hard to do this strikes at the heart of China's biggest existential problem, the lack of a civil ethic which draws together economic interests, political aspirations and patriotism. Unfortunately but predictably, China's garrison mentality not only strengthens the idea of Hong Kong citizenship, but pushes this idea so far as to drive some more radical voters over the edge into unwise calls for independence. This further enflames the situation.

Just before I visited Hong Kong in November 2016, two years after the extraordinarily impressive democracy demonstrations, I rediscovered the whole text of the diary that I had kept when I was Governor, and occasionally referred to earlier in this chapter. Rummaging through the stories of old administrative adventures, political news, meetings with world leaders, and accounts of the sheer enjoyment of living in Hong Kong, as in effect the mayor of a great Asian city, two things struck me forcefully.

First, in the summer of 1996, I record one or two minor incidents of hostility towards expatriates on the part of the local Cantonese. The wonder was not that there was some hostility, but that there was not more. Yes, we had done much good, creating institutions which worked. Colonialism could not be defended at the end of the twentieth century, but in Hong Kong we British had been pretty decent. We had provided a haven for all those refugees from the tumultuous events on the mainland after the revolution – the totalitarian brutalities, the cultural revolution, famine, and so on – but even the least sensitive Chinese must have encountered behaviour that offended them, being patronized by a small ruling minority, from time to time. Why was there not more of this quite mild bitterness? Presumably the answer is that there were many more British people who behaved well, who were not patronizing, who did not humiliate others, and who loved the community of which they were a part, who loved it as much as I did and my family did, and who knew how much we had to be grateful for. Hong Kong was not British, but we had played a part in creating it and we thought it unique. Chinese Hong Kong with some British attributes.

The extent to which this was implicitly recognized in Deng Xiaoping's famous aim for China and Hong Kong – 'one country, two systems' – perhaps underlines the failure of Beijing to understand its own principles and policy. Yes, Hong Kong was and is part of China; its citizens are Chinese citizens. But what exactly is the system that gives them a distinctive identity? It is a belief in pluralism under the rule of law; an enthusiasm for accountability; a recognition of the relationship between civic freedoms, security, stability and prosperity. People in Hong Kong have this sense of citizenship. Beijing communists cannot both assert the existence of two systems and then contend that men and women in Hong Kong have exactly the same political personality as the Chinese on the mainland, that they are carbon copies. If that were true then 'one country, two systems' would be wholly meaningless.

As modern colonialists, we had tried to safeguard these differences. I do not believe that in the 1990s we deserved to be run out of town with abuse ringing in our ears for failing to do so; nor did this happen. But going back in 2016 I found myself being asked again and again what should happen next to Hong Kong's governance. Denied a sensible dialogue about the political future by a pretty hopeless, cloth-eared government, aware of increasing pressure on its autonomy from the mainland's communists, some in the Democratic camp had moved the debate on from calls for rather greater democracy to demands for independence for Hong Kong, an impossible and (for Beijing) incendiary demand that would dilute support for democracy, play into the hands of the communist hardliners and throw away international understanding. I spoke in these terms, not least to hundreds of university students. They were polite but firm: what will happen, they asked, if they got nothing from Beijing except more interference in their autonomy? What would Britain and others do? What, one bright student asked, had we done in the past for previous generations of democracy activists? I blundered through an unconvincing reply. When I got home to England, I recalled a passage in my diary about one of the democracy activists with whom I had had to deal, 'X annoys me – with those savage sound-bites denouncing Britain, but I admire the guts and eloquence – X has at bottom a devastating strong moral case.' Did we ever have a real sense of our moral responsibility? Is any idea of honour old-fashioned, something a country loses when it is in inevitable decline, unsure of its role and values? At the very least those of us who loved Hong Kong and did not behave too badly when we had the privilege of being its transitory citizens should feel some responsibility for its liberty and welfare in the future. Those students deserve that of us; but, then, so did their parents. As this book was in preparation in March 2017, a new chief executive was chosen by Beijing's trustees, who was drawing only half the support of one of the other candidates in the polls. His fault in Beijing's eyes was plainly that he had advocated dialogue with the democracy activists. One country, with Beijing increasingly hell-bent on one system.

The sheer size of China, once it rejoined the world economy in the 1980s, has inevitably led to a tilt back towards Asia in global affairs, particularly since it follows hard on the heels of the economic rise of Japan and of the Tiger economies of Taiwan, South Korea, Singapore and Hong Kong, and the slower, less steady opening of India to the rest of the world. When over 60 per cent of the world's population starts to get richer, the effects are dramatic. Europe has about 7 per cent of the world's population, Asia over 60 per cent, America about 5 per cent. Sheer aggregate numbers multiplied by growing figures for

GDP per head really started to shift things towards the East even when country by country the GDP per head was and is usually much higher in the West. Perhaps we are at or even past the moment when the world starts to spin off in another direction; maybe modern history has just started anew.

Looking back, there was a huge tipping point in the world after 1500. Until then India and China represented about 50 per cent of the world's output. Between then and the Industrial Revolution in the early nineteenth century, the West began to overtake, and through the nineteenth and twentieth centuries India and China fell far behind, partly because of their own acts of omission and commission and partly because of colonial exploitation by Europe, Japan and even America. By the 1970s, China and India together accounted for less than 10 per cent of world output. Since then the figures have changed dramatically, especially for China. This has resulted in bookshops full of volumes predicting the End of the West and the Triumph of the Rest.

To borrow Samuel Beckett's favourite word: 'perhaps'. I accept that America and Europe no longer rule the roost in the way they did in the nineteenth and twentieth centuries. But I find it difficult to accept that exponentialism is about to hand the century ahead to Asia, especially when so much of the argument depends on the continuing hectic growth of China. But let me start with the back half of the Chindian colossus: India, a country which I regard as the most interesting in the world, unlikely as it is to become a conventional superpower any time soon.

India has a population of 1.3 billion, second only to China. This is predicted to exceed China's population of 1.38 billion by 2022, and to hit 1.6 billion by 2050. India's population is younger than China's: more than 50 per cent of Indians are below the age of twenty-five. As China's workforce ages – moving from labour surplus to labour shortage faster than any economy ever before – India will have many more economically active men and women. India encompasses a dazzling variety of ethnic groups, religions and languages. It is also home to the largest number of poor people in the world: over one fifth of its total population, more than half its households, have no modern sanitary facilities. After independence in 1947, India's government drew up a constitution which incorporated democracy, secularism and socialism. The democracy and secularism have worked pretty well. While there have been religious flare-ups between racial and religious groups – especially Hindus and Muslims, who murdered one another in large numbers when Pakistan and India split apart – overall India has coped with potentially explosive tensions through the safety valve of democracy. Without this, in all likelihood, it would have shattered. Socialism did not have a good record in India, condemning it for about four decades to what Indians themselves called the Hindu rate of growth, much lower than what was being achieved elsewhere in Asia. Since India started to strip back the over-regulation and bureaucracy associated with the 'licence Raj', growth has picked up, as it needed to, and from the 1990s on India has become steadily more integrated in the global economy. In 2015–16 the World Bank placed it at the top of the table for global growth and forecast a slightly higher figure for the future. Services are growing especially strongly: for instance, in the IT and software sectors. After independence, India was overtaken by China. In 1960, India's per capita wealth was higher than China's; today it is between a half and two thirds of China's. Yet, if it continues, Indian growth will make it the third-largest economy in the world by the 2020s.

India has been very successful at creating world-class global brands with a far higher standard of corporate governance than exists in China. Firms like Reliance, Ranbaxy, Infosys and Tata (the largest manufacturing employer in the UK) have risen to the top of their industries; overall, IT outsourcing, pharmaceuticals and the automotive industry have performed exceptionally well. India now invests more in the UK than the UK invests in India. But India is hampered by a number of problems. While their scale varies considerably from state to state, infrastructure everywhere requires huge investment to bring it up to the standards – for example, in transport and the power sectors – required in a modern economy. Corruption and clientelism are rampant in politics and the political class is dominated by family connections. The legal system is slow and also weakened by corruption. The governing Bharatiya Janata Party, led by the Prime Minister, Narendra Modi, may be rather more business-friendly than its main opponents in the Congress Party, but it teeters on the edge of promoting extreme Hindu nationalism. For its part, Congress – the original party of Indian independence – seems trapped with a dynastic leadership in an out-of-date socialist cul-de-sac. Other regional parties thrive in this political atmosphere. Meanwhile a Maoist guerrilla campaign – the Naxalites – continues to affect about nine states. Yet India's very effective technology sector, its extremely successful diaspora, its growing middle class, its cultural successes in literature and cinema, and its booming media sector promise an exciting future. There are huge challenges. Should the economy be mishandled or regional and sectarian problems ignite, a demographic boom could easily turn into a demographic bomb with huge numbers of poor men and women without jobs.

A real difference between India and China is that Indians are usually very open about the problems that affect their country. Not so mainland China. Most Chinese follow the former and much criticized Hua Guofeng (Mao's unsuccessful chosen successor) in being 'whatever-ists' – whatever the party says is happening is happening. Overall, of course, the story has been a pretty amazing one. Alongside the fall of global communism – as distinct from Chinese Leninism – this has been the most important development of my political lifetime, and the Chinese economy has doubled in size every eight years for three decades since I first clapped eyes on the country in 1979. China now produces more in two weeks than it did in the whole of a year in the 1970s. It is the world's largest exporter and manufacturer, the biggest maker of steel. Its demand for energy has gone up by well over 200 per cent since 2000. Everywhere you look there is Chinese money, from the purchase of famous Château wine estates in Bordeaux, to investment in crucial Western infrastructure, to buying up vast tracts of African and other continents to get access to mineral and agriculture supplies. So is the red east – to borrow from the old Maoist song – about to ensure that the Communist Party's sun will shine on the rest of us?

It is not in our interest that China's success should turn into a story of failure, but in my view it is profoundly unlikely that (to borrow from the title of a book by a British ex-Marxist) China is about to rule the world. First, there are the perils of exponentialism to which I have already referred. The line never, ever, just continues up the whiteboard and through the ceiling. As the American economist Herb Stein used to say, things that can't go on for ever, don't. Larry Summers, the former US Treasury Secretary, while noting the humbling of past predictions of continuing helter-skelter growth in the USSR and Japan, argues that China's growth will flag as has happened previously with rapidly growing economies. These reversals are sometimes pretty dramatic. There has been a median decline of 4.7 per cent in the rate of growth of the twenty-eight countries that had previously sustained more than eight years of super-rapid growth. If China followed this pattern its growth would snap back from its present faltering 6.5–7 per cent figures to much less than 4 per cent.

China may yet defeat all the odds, and anyway what is really happening in China is difficult to fathom given that even the Chinese Prime Minister, Li Keqiang, has told us that he does not believe the figures; they are not just 'man-made' but 'Chinese communist official-made'. When a Chinese leader departs from 'whatever-itis' and tells us that China faces a four-part challenge then we should perhaps take some notice. Li's predecessor, Wen Jiabao, expressed his own doubts about China's prospects when he set out the four 'uns' confronting the country after the National People's Congress as far back as 2007. The Chinese economic model was, he said, unsustainable partly because of environmental costs. It was uncoordinated, with an imbalance between investment and consumption, manufacturing and services. It was unbalanced across the country between the sea-based provinces and the interior. Finally, it was unstable because of growing inequity. Not much has changed to manage an escape from this four-cornered trap.

All Wen's 'uns' seem today to have grown and at their heart is the existential problem created by Leninism. For the economy to grow in a sustainable way, the party has to surrender much of its control over the economy: for example, the state-owned enterprises which consume the lion's share of state investment but produce less than the output of the private sector. If the party does this, hardliners argue, it will sooner or later lose control of the state. If on the other hand it does not do this, it will certainly lose control of the state as the economy slows down with more and more credit being pumped into producing less and less growth. This is what cannot go on for ever. China's dilemma is how it can square this circle.

President Xi's response is to take more power to himself. He has become stronger than any leader since Deng and probably since Mao. His henchman Wang Qishan (a clever man now in charge of a wide-ranging attack on corruption, dragging in at the same time the President's potential adversaries) draws some parallels from the history of the French Revolution. He distributed copies of Alexis de Tocqueville's *The Ancien Régime and the Revolution* to members of the Politburo and to cadres at the Central Party School, noting with Tocqueville that economic growth could increase insurrectionary pressures and that authoritarian regimes were at their most vulnerable when they began the process of reform. So Xi has cracked down on every sort of dissent. Propaganda has been stepped up. Western countries are blamed for stirring up trouble in China and other countries. Hong Kong is regarded with greater suspicion. The influence of the West is denounced, both today and historically, as though no one apparently recalls where Karl Marx was born and where he worked. Lawyers and human rights defenders are imprisoned; freedom of expression and civil society organizations are stamped on; more and more repressive legislation is passed; abductions are carried out and regional aspirations suppressed. The behaviour of the leadership does not suggest great confidence in the stability and strength of the system. Any real reform has been replaced by state thuggery, to return to Sir Percy's language.

This is where Leninism always leads eventually, with the rich getting their money and children out of the country and trying to find bolt holes for themselves. 'We are the Communist Party and we will decide what communism means.' The one thing that it does not seem to incorporate is much in the way of real communism: while the numbers removed from absolute poverty rose after Deng's reforms, the share of China's growth that has gone subsequently to the workers has slumped. The party cannot show that the achievement of communist goals (a fair, more equal society) legitimizes its hold on power, so it has to fall back on Chinese nationalism to try to justify control of everything. Morally bankrupt and no longer communist, the party must at least show that it is Chinese.

This probably accounts for China's aggressive behaviour in the South and East China seas and its rejection of UN arbitration in settling these disputes. The old Chinese proverb that two tigers cannot exist on the same mountain has worrying implications for Japan and India as well as the United States (and its allies like Australia). Managing these relationships, as well as China's dealings with its smaller neighbours, is likely to produce some of the most sensitive issues in international politics over the next decade.

Hong Kong is likely to be one arena in which China's trustworthiness and preparedness to act as a responsible world citizen are severely tested. Do Chinese Communists really keep their word even when their word is included in international treaties? If over time they slough off their legal and moral obligations in Hong Kong, where else should they be trusted to hold to them? It used to be said by some of the 'old friends of China' – diplomats and businessmen, mostly, who could always be relied upon to put the best spin on whatever Chinese Communists did – that however tough it was to negotiate with them, once an agreement was reached they stuck to it as though it was fly paper. I was never entirely sure why the old friends should encourage us to ignore our own experiences in this way. Perhaps, whatever has happened to date – only a few major breaches of the Joint Declaration, the steady erosion of Hong Kong's autonomy and rule of law – President Xi will go out of his way to make it plain that, in Deng Xiaoping's words in 1984, he is 'convinced that the people of Hong Kong are capable of running the affairs of Hong Kong well'. That would certainly help to put unsettled minds and hearts in this city at rest. It is difficult to convince Asia and the world that you have a model of governance for others when you cannot even run this part of your own country where you have made a pledge to its seven million or more citizens which it is essential for you to keep. 'One country, two systems' still means what it has always meant; never more so. We should all enormously admire the young men and women in Hong Kong with their yellow umbrellas and their bravely asserted principles who have made that so pellucidly clear.

So there should be no doubt that though China is big enough – and potentially awkward enough – to shake the world, it currently provides no model for running the world. The Communist Party has enough of a problem running China without taking on a more ambitious burden. Its foreign policy is focused on historical issues of territorial integrity (like Taiwan), its own continuing dominance in domestic politics, and securing the economic resources it needs. It has no model of good, sustainable governance to offer the rest of us. Its principal friends tend to be basket cases from Venezuela to Zimbabwe to North Korea. Compared to its economic strength, it has little soft power. In that respect it punches well below its economic weight and leaves a very light footprint. Chinese Leninism is not an identity that attracts followers. I hope that Chinese behaviour changes, and that China does not itself trigger the snapping shut of what is called the Thucydides trap.

The American political scientist Graham Allison has written about the rise of new powers throughout history, drawing first on an early example that Thucydides wrote about in his study of the Peloponnesian wars, namely the fight between Athens and Sparta. Sparta turned to force when it thought that its supremacy in Greece and the eastern Mediterranean was being challenged by the Athenian building of its own navy. President Xi has himself referred to this, clearly pointing a finger at the United States. He argues that it should accommodate the rise of China peacefully, rather than challenge it as Sparta challenged Athens, and as France and Britain just over a hundred years ago confronted the rise of Germany as it built its own naval force to take on the older imperial powers. Before making this speech President Xi might have asked himself who looks like the provocateur today. Which country is building up its naval strength? Which is spying on other great countries and assaulting them in cyber space? Which rejects rulings by UN arbitration?

President Xi's reading list should perhaps not only include Thucydides and Tocqueville's *Democracy in America* as well as *The Ancien Régime*, but also China's most famous philosophical work, *The Analects of Confucius*. Tsu-kung asked about the necessities of government. The Master said, 'Enough food, enough weapons, and the confidence of the people.' Tsu-kung said, 'Suppose you had no alternative but to give up one of these three, which would you relinquish first?' The Master said, 'Weapons.' Tsu-kung said, 'Suppose you definitely had no alternative but to give up one of the remaining two, which would you relinquish first?' The Master said, 'Food. From of old, death has come to all men, but a people without confidence in its rulers will not stand.' More important than presidents, premiers, monarchs or even party secretaries are citizens.

Whether President Trump and his appointees will encourage a peaceful escape from the Thucydides trap and an atmosphere in which China confronts its internal dilemmas successfully is an issue which will determine peace and well-being for all of us in the future. They will also need to enlist China's assistance in dealing with the menace from the rogue state of North Korea. As in classical mechanics, rampant American nationalism in East Asia is likely to produce an equal and opposite reaction.

Trump, Xi and growing nationalism in China and America seem a long way from sailing away with my family from Hong Kong in 1997 on the Royal Yacht, surrounded by flying fish, dolphins and the navy of an old Empire in which we had just turned off the lights. Yet twenty years since we left it, Hong Kong still represents the same enduring values, as relevant to Asia as to the rest of the world. It is likely to be a city and community where some of the ideas that shape the century ahead are fought over and resolved.

9
The Loneliness of the Long Distance European

'You should think about nobody and go your own way.'
  Alan Sillitoe, *The Loneliness of the Long Distance Runner*

'Of course, if we had succeeded in losing two world wars, wrote off all our debts – instead of having nearly £30 billion in debt – got rid of all our foreign obligations, and kept no force overseas, then we might be as rich as the Germans.'
  Harold Macmillan

During what was called 'the new Elizabethan age' – the middle of the 1950s – we used as a family to go regularly to our suburban cinemas in Ealing with their art deco and Alhambra facades. 'Don't be disappointed if we can't get in,' Dad would say every Friday evening as the family piled into the car. There were cheerful films like *Doctor in the House* and *Genevieve* but also movies to remind us of our wartime heroics. (Now they are invariably shown on the television, early in the day, on bank holidays.) There were *The Cruel Sea*, *The Dam Busters* and *Cockleshell Heroes*. But the content darkened as we moved past former wartime heroes as in *The Bridge on the River Kwai* into gritty kitchen sink dramas in the 1960s like *Saturday Night and Sunday Morning* and *The Loneliness of the Long Distance Runner*. We were indeed on our own, running uphill, through woods and across streams, trying to retain the illusion that we were still a global leader, our winner's status guaranteed by our lonely wartime bravery when we stood and ran alone, except for our friends from what we still called the British Empire.

Outside the cinema, our imperial dreams died at Suez in 1956. Our trade with the Commonwealth (as we struggled to recover from near bankruptcy) was less then than with Europe, even though the latter was still recovering from a devastating war. America did not see its role as sustaining us in our post-Churchillian dotage. Brave as we had been in the 1940s, no one owed us a pension. Though we were one of the wartime victors, we had to face the unpleasant truth that the European Economic Community, as it was then known, was more likely to protect us from decline than the small group of Scandinavian and Alpine countries that we spatchcocked together as a possible alternative to joining the more integrationist club formed after the Messina conference in 1955. So, with the threat of becoming irretrievably the sick man of Europe, we swallowed our pride and applied, eventually successfully, to join the European Economic Community. We decided to run with the pack rather than try to make our way solo; we had tried 'lonely' and it did not work too well.

The challenge to our national psyche was profound. Whilst Winston Churchill wrote with greater European commitment after the war, two sentences he had written in the 1930s seemed to describe our position even after we were members of the European club. 'We are with Europe,' he wrote in the 1930s, 'but not of it. We are linked but not combined.' Maybe that has always been the problem. Did we ever really join? It was not just that, for us unlike most of our fellow members, the economic case for belonging usually trumped the political, though we definitely recognized the importance of a Western Europe which combined its strengths to secure peace and greater influence in the world. More important still was the difference between the foundation myths and ground zero moments for the principal members of the European adventure. We thought back to *The Dam Busters* and *Cockleshell Heroes*, to standing alone, and committing ourselves to the amazement and admiration of the rest of the world to fight for Europe's freedom on Britain's beaches. We thought of the bravery of 'the few' in 1940, and still heard the Churchillian cadences which had sustained the nation in its 'finest hour'. For the French, their sense of identity and the importance of turning the European continent away from aggressive xenophobic competition (from which they had suffered so much) were tied to memories of defeat and humiliation in 1940 and of General de Gaulle struggling through indignities to secure a place at the top table with the Americans, British and Russians. For Germany, ground zero was the physical rubble of 1945 and the moral rubble of the death camps where the Nazis' previously unimaginable genocide was carried out. Against this background the wonder is not that the European Union was in many respects such a rickety construction, but that it was assembled at all. Its early successes perhaps persuaded some of its members subsequently to try for too much. To invoke another film of the 1960s, there was *A Kind of Loving* in Europe, but the devotion was often awkward and sometimes feigned.

Despite the fact that I held views such as these, which would have been regarded as heterodox by many of my future European colleagues, part of the British media still regarded my decision to move to Brussels as a European Commissioner in 1999 as an act of perfidy. The *Telegraph* opined that, in accepting this post, I had 'turned my back on the British way of life'. The article might have been a little more accurately focused, certainly in more recent times, if it had equated Brussels with hostility to the nationalist English, rather than the British, way of life. After all, both Scotland and Northern Ireland were to vote by large margins to remain in the EU in the 2016 referendum; hardly then a lion's roar for Britain. The elision of Britishness and Englishness, something for which we have long criticized Americans and other foreigners, has been pretty dramatically splintered by the issue of Europe. Our own Union in the British Isles, whose largest member (England) is a nation but not a state, is itself a possible long-term casualty of the vote to leave the EU. The Scots ponder whether or when to call for another referendum on independence; citizens in Northern Ireland apply in droves for passports for the Republic in the south and the future of the border which separates them will cause big problems for Brexit negotiators.

What exactly was it that the dear old *Telegraph* thought I was abandoning? Ideas of Britishness and of Englishness are not identical. They have rather different narratives at their heart, narratives occasionally wound more tightly together: for example, in the days of Empire and in times of conflict against an external adversary. Maybe the fact that, while English by birth, I am in part Irish by descent makes me warm most to the sense of being British. I regard Scotland as a different country but an invaluable part of a unified state, and one that brings enormous cultural and political quality to Britain. I worry about Scottish independence not only because of what Scotland would lose by separation from the rest of Britain but, perhaps even more, because of what the rest of us would lose. Edinburgh and Glasgow always feel like slightly foreign cities, yet magnificent ones that I am proud to share as a British citizen. If Scotland were to declare for independence I would feel that the national community of which I am a citizen had suffered serious amputation.

One thing that Britain and England have very much in common is that we are comprised of a mix of European and non-European identities, plainly more so in England than in Scotland, Wales or Northern Ireland. We are a jumble of pedigrees – to borrow from Daniel Defoe, a nation of mongrels. We also have histories, taken together, shaped by our island geography which has separated us from the European mainland and opened up the world to our travels, imaginations and trade; this was one of the reasons why General de Gaulle thought we were unsuited for membership of the European Common Market. Today, when you look at the size of our commercial fishing and naval fleets, you might find it hard to believe how important the sea and these wider horizons have been to us. Our relations with our European neighbours have been intimate, sometimes hostile, often friendly and always culturally close. Our Royal Family is as German as I am Irish. When, in 1914, war between Britain and Germany broke out, Oxford University dons scurried about to get hundreds of German students home before the shooting started; earlier that summer distinguished Germans had starred in the list of honorary degrees at the university. The university did not offer degree courses in French and German until shortly before this on the grounds that anyone intelligent enough to study at Oxford would naturally have a good knowledge of these languages. It was a common assumption among politicians that the peace, economic rejuvenation and stability of Europe after the Second World War were national interests of our own. While we had once to stand alone, we now had to build together.

Which of the things that are emblematic of our island home are British and which English? Where would you place roast beef or chicken tikka masala, now apparently the nation's most popular

20. The Governor shares a joke with the senior service at the Tamar naval base, Hong Kong.

21. Trying to keep an eye on the dragon on a visit to Kwun Tong.

22. Stepping out with Margaret Thatcher in Hong Kong. She strongly supported our efforts to preserve its unique way of life.

23. Signing Chinese New Year Lai See packets for enthusiastic residents of Sham Sui Po, 1997.

24. With Lavender in Hong Kong. Partners for life, not just on the dance floor.

25. Time to say goodbye: my ADC has just presented me with the Hong Kong flag.

26. Not a dry eye on *Britannia*. Lavender, Kate, Laura, Alice and the Prince of Wales.

27. 'The Prince of Wales and Mr Patten' (as the protocol instructions called us) wave farewell to the colony. Until midnight Patten took precedence as representative of the sovereign.

JUNE 9 1997

EYEWITNESS REPORT: MASSACRE IN AFGHANISTAN

TIME

The Last Governor

Was Chris Patten Good for Hong Kong?

28. I hope that the answer to *Time*'s question was 'yes'.

. At Buckingham Palace after being made a Companion of Honour. All smiles now.

. Listening hard to evidence from the DUP in 1998 about
licing in Northern Ireland. The report is being read by a
lice officer.

31–32. Arriving in Macedonia with Javier Solana, the European High Representative for Foreign and Security Policy, in September 2001. Bombed churches are just one of the consequences of the extremes of identity politics.

33. With Yasser Arafat, Romano Prodi and Arafat's advisor Nabil Shaath in May 2001 – a handshake which helped keep the Palestinian Authority alive.

4. Meeting a very Holy Father in St Peter's, 2014.

5. It's off to work we go – the Encaenia procession passes in front of the Radcliffe Camera in Oxford, June 2015.

36. Hope for the future: left to right from the top, Elodie, Isabella, Samuel, Max, Willow, Francesca, Noah and William, on the steps of our home in France, with Phoebe the springer spaniel.

37. Old man with book, in a garden in the Tarn.

dish? Where manicured front gardens or hybrid tea roses? Where beer or whisky? Where sponge cakes or bran biscuits? Where hedgerows or moors? Where the rule of law or habeas corpus? Where parliamentary sovereignty – difficult because England does not have a parliament? On the other hand, here is an easy one – what about Nigel Farage and his Brexit posters? Or Iain Duncan-Smith and his right-wing sidekicks? Are they more English or British? See what happens if you dare ask these questions in Glasgow.

When I arrived in Brussels in 1999, feeling both English and British, there was not much of a culture shock. For a start, despite the number of member states, all with their own language, English was the language most commonly spoken and written. I could have worked in my own mother tongue the whole time I was there, though occasionally I essayed a meeting in French, inevitably displaying my inadequate grasp of the subjunctive. The French worked hard, as we would have done in the circumstances, to protect the use of their own tongue, the historic language of diplomacy. I remember one meeting in Helsinki of European heads of state and government and their equivalent officials from candidate countries. At the 'tour de table', most present spoke English. At one point, President Chirac crossly interrupted the Italian President of the Commission to demand 'langue maternelle'. Romano Prodi continued to speak in English. For most, this was the easiest thing to do. The European house magazine was a British newspaper – the *Financial Times*.

Institutionally, the European Commission reflected the French influence from the early years before Britain's membership. I was supported by what was called a 'cabinet', in practice a large private office, staffed by men and women from several countries whom I picked myself. They helped me to run a directorate-general led by an official who was doing the same sort of job as a British Permanent Secretary. The main difference from running a British government department was that there was much more jockeying for position and for promotion in Brussels, a fight to put flags on jobs, encouraged by some of the member states, Spain and Italy to the fore. There was also a much more explicit obligation to build consensus across the Commission and with member states. The officials I worked with in Brussels were excellent and the process of accountability was in some respects tougher and more transparent than back home. You had to manage your relationships with colleagues in the Commission, the ministers and ambassadors of member states, and the European Parliament. This is an institution about which it is easy to sneer, particularly if you are a well-paid, expenses-consuming Eurosceptic member of that body, choosing to spend your life in an organization that you are intent on destroying. The Parliament works in every EU language, which makes its interpreted proceedings pretty clunky. It travels from Brussels to Strasbourg at great expense to satisfy French amour-propre, which is of course administratively crazy. The Parliament's role and members are too little known in most member states. It tends to be fired up by extremes of integrationist sentiment. But the Parliament and particularly its committees do much good work, largely unnoticed, and it is home to many genuinely expert parliamentarians. I found my British parliamentary experience a useful asset in dealing with it. As with Westminster, it wanted to spend a lot of its time debating issues over which it had little or no control. Since my brief was External Affairs, this affected me considerably.

When I arrived in Brussels there were two commissioners for each of the larger member states – France, Germany, Spain, Italy, the UK – and ten for the remaining smaller member states. (In the summer of 2004, ten new commissioners were appointed from the countries such as Poland and Hungary in Central and Eastern Europe which had joined the Union. The new Commission formed later that year had one commissioner for each country.) The twenty-member Commission from 1999 to 2004 contained some real heavyweights, as good as any Cabinet ministers with whom I had worked in London. Mario Monti, who dealt with Competition, was a distinguished Italian economist, with impeccable manners and a strong commitment to socially responsible market economics. Frits Bolkestein was a crusty, clever, old-fashioned European Liberal who would have graced any Conservative Cabinet in London. Pascal Lamy, who covered Trade, was an outstanding product of the Ecole Nationale d'Administration (ENA); he had been the head of the private office of the previous Commission President, Jacques Delors. He was steeped in European politics and just about as clever as it is possible to be, but dwelt well beyond the vulgarities of politics. He went on to be the secretary-general of the WTO. Pedro Solbes, who returned to Spain to become finance minister in the socialist government in 2004, ran Economic and Monetary Affairs. The Portuguese Commissioner, António Vitorino, was intellectually first rate and adroitly gave the member states the impression that they were driving the Justice and Home Affairs agenda, whereas in fact he was himself doing all the heavy lifting. I mention them, not because some of the others were not equally good, but primarily because they were the ones with whom I mostly dealt. It should be added that they all spoke perfect English, and in some cases other languages too. Virtually every Commissioner had good English and French. Northern European commissioners tended to speak German as well.

The President, Romano Prodi, was a genial Italian economist who had previously been Prime Minister of his country. He did not have a very high profile, which was partly a result of his disinclination to interfere in the departments of his colleagues. It was to his credit that he captained a pretty contented crew. Romano had an early, bruising experience of British politics and tabloid journalism. Shortly after I got to Brussels, Neil Kinnock, my fellow British Commissioner, telephoned me to suggest that I should join him in discouraging Romano Prodi from an initiative he was determined to take. He intended to go to London to see the editor of the *Daily Mail*, Paul Dacre, to tell him what he wanted his Commission to do over the next five years. He thought he could persuade Dacre to give the Commission and its policies fairer coverage. I agreed with Neil that this was a terrible idea, born of Romano's perhaps other-worldly view of the quality of British tabloid journalism and its interest in the truth. We both failed to dissuade him, even though we argued that the word 'fairness' became oxymoronic when used in the same sentence as Dacre's name. He duly went to London, Dacre received him courteously but told him succinctly that his position on the EU was very clear. His newspaper, he said, had two 'stringers' in Brussels. They were there to ferret out every bad story they could find about Brussels and the EU. That is what his paper would publish. He was not interested in anything else. Romano returned, chastened, to Brussels, his belief in the British commitment to responsible free speech and liberal values considerably dented. I mentioned to him a line of Tom Stoppard's: 'I am passionately committed to free speech, it's just some newspapers I don't like.'

Nothing in my new life in Brussels put any great strain on my sense of identity; indeed in many respects I felt able to assert strongly felt aspects of my Britishness. I paid a lot of attention to the Parliament, flattering its own idea (not always vain or wrong) of its own importance. I stood up for promotion on merit. I resisted pressures to parachute particular national choices into jobs for which the candidates were not especially suitable. I tried (as did members of my cabinet) to argue my corner in forceful, clear English, not Brussels bureaucratese. This occasionally gave us the reputation of being blunt, not just unambiguous. Moreover, what I was trying to do plainly mattered to Britain as well as to its EU partners. We were developing and implementing policies of international co-operation from the Balkans to China, from Colombia to Palestine, as efficiently as possible. The surrender of any of my national affiliation didn't come into this, unless of course you take the view that organized co-operation with other European, or indeed any other countries, is by its very nature a quasi-treacherous activity.

I am a Conservative who has never believed that everything my party does or stands for is right. I am a Catholic who has occasional doubts and disagreements which have not persuaded me of the merits of agnosticism or atheism. In a similar if not quite so important a spirit, I have always been in favour of Britain's membership of the EU without thinking everything about it is hunky-dory. Working in the Commission made me more aware of some of the inadequacies of the EU, as well as some of the myths, exaggerations and lies that we allowed in Britain to erode trust in the whole institution: 'allowed' because we usually tried to avoid confronting these for fear of standing up to the tabloid press or, in the Conservative Party, taking on the right wing. I will try to avoid what follows turning to a lengthy Lenten meditation, and divide my criticism into two parts – the way the European Union works and what it seeks to do.

A fundamental principle of Catholic social teaching is the notion of subsidiarity, which has become attached, not by accident, to the philosophy of European activity as well. The idea is that decisions should be taken and policies implemented at the lowest manageable level.

This is obviously a sensible guide to action in a collection of nation states used to running most of their own affairs. What it means in practice is that many – arguably most – of the non-economic functions of government are left to the member states to run. It would have been foolish for Europe to try to run welfare, health or education policies, though from time to time an initiative that the European Union wants to take collectively may have an impact on an area of policy reserved to national governments. For instance, a public health issue which is not contained within national frontiers may affect national health policies. But overall the principle is clear and sensible. There are times, including recently, when subsidiarity has been pursued with a modicum of enthusiasm. There has inevitably, however, been a tendency (as in most bureaucracies) to develop the equivalent of imperial over-reach. When I was a Commissioner, I used to think this was given a curious sort of moral impulse by the feeling in the very bowels of the institution that everything would be done better if it was done on the European level. This was a sentiment that could easily be given a push by the fact that so many things done at national level as a part of European initiatives were done so badly. Most of the auditors' queries about Europe's accounts concerned mistakes made by national governments, not by Brussels institutions.

So the rule on subsidiarity was more likely to be honoured in the breach than in the observance. The case for forgetting about it was invariably contained within the notion that this or that area of activity cried out for 'more Europe' not 'less'. Sometimes this was true; one could see the case for it in relation to many aspects of energy policy for instance. Yet while the single market, to take the most important example, needed to be completed, with 'more Europe' in areas like e-commerce and services, pushing back the frontiers of commerce did not necessitate drawing in as much as the Commission could acquire of the social policies of member states. The Commission took on too many tasks that it should not have been doing and could not do well. More functions meant more meetings, with more staff and more interpreters. Inevitably, as ever, Hendrickson's Law began to apply: 'If you have enough meetings over a long enough period of time, the meetings become more important than the problems they were intended to solve.' It was at such a meeting, the subject of which has long since escaped me (though there is probably a directive on it), that I tried to work out what proportion of the rest of my life was being consumed by it. I mentioned this fairly straightforward arithmetical problem at a private dinner for Conservative Members of the European Parliament that evening. Fool! Inevitably it got on to the front page of the *Telegraph* the following day as an example of how bored I had become in Brussels. It was true of that meeting, but overall I found being a Commissioner rather more interesting than being, say, Secretary of State for the Environment, with endless meetings about the mostly incomprehensible arcana of local government finance.

So the Commission suffered from a form of mission creep that was part of its DNA. There would always be someone in a meeting or hovering just outside who wished to make the case for 'more Europe'; 'more' answerable to whom? To the Council of Ministers, and through that body to national parliaments, and to the European Parliament. But these forms of accountability were pretty opaque, though probably not much more so than the parliamentary process in Britain. We tend to assume not only that our island home is governed by a flawless parliamentary democracy but that its mechanisms are widely understood. As I write this sentence, the House of Lords, of which I am a member, is poised somewhere between the Second and Third Reading of a bill on universities and research which will have a profound impact on both. I doubt whether this legislation is being followed with close attention on our buses or even in the common rooms of English universities. We have always been happier to criticize the imperfections of the 'demos' – even the lack of it – in Europe, while rather romanticizing its role in our own country.

In political as in other areas Inverness probably has more in common with Plymouth than Seville has with Reykjavik, and probably always will. So Europe tries routinely to do too much and, as a result, exacerbates the problem of clarifying accountability. This becomes much clearer when the great purposes of the EU are considered. Europe's history determined what the organization set as its main priorities. It wanted to anchor the reconciled France and Germany at the heart of a co-operative, rules-based venture that would secure the development of welfare democracy among the ruins of post-war

Western Europe. Britain's greatest contributions to this were to pioneer the establishment of the single market so as to maximize European trade, and to lead the campaign to enlarge the borders of the EU so that we could accept as members the not-long liberated countries of the old Soviet Empire. There was a good deal of politics in both these ventures. Enlarging the single market – one of Margaret Thatcher's great achievements, driven through in the mid-1980s by the British European Commissioner, Arthur Cockfield – involved political rows in Britain over the necessary extension of majority decision making in Brussels, and arguments in other European countries which saw market competitiveness as a threat to national commercial interests. Germany and France, for example, both threw up roadblocks against the opening of service and retail sectors to greater European trade. Professional services were always protected by national governments. In these fights for a more liberal, market-oriented approach to Europe's economic challenges, Britain regularly argued for 'more Europe' not 'less'. London was probably too reticent, fearful perhaps of provoking domestic opposition, in pointing out to European colleagues how much leadership we were trying to give in an integrationist way on this issue, which, if we had been successful, would have raised Europe's growth rates and productivity levels.

Inevitably there was a lot of politics about the enlargement process, which was in many respects a triumph for Brussels management. The politics lay principally in securing the democratic stability of countries which had only recently been under the thumb of Moscow's communist empire. Helping these countries to be free and democratic naturally took them out of any Russian sphere of interest. They were independent and able to chart their own course. Where the politics went too far was in rushing the process for some countries, out of a desire to get as many countries as possible into the Brussels lifeboat as quickly as we could manage. Sometimes Brussels was plainly inclined to pretend that the would-be member states were conducting reforms or had already done so when in practice this was far from the case. (The same happened, as we shall see in a moment, over membership of the eurozone.) Had Romania and Bulgaria really complied with Europe's demands over the rule of law and the suppression of organized crime, for instance? We knew the answer but pretended to believe their assurances. We were even prepared to allow Cyprus into the EU with the promise that if we did so its Greek leaders would work with Turkey and the Turkish community on the island to end its by then three-decade-old division. It would have been perfectly possible to condition Cypriot accession on an agreement, rather than allow (as happened) duplicity to trump diplomacy in order to inflate the EU accession numbers. A divided Cyprus became and remained an EU member with its Greek leaders initially actually campaigning against a UN-brokered agreement, despite all their former promises. A besetting sin in the EU (and in most diplomacy, it has to be said) is to duck hard questions in order to secure soft answers.

The most damaging example of politics triumphing over other considerations was the introduction of the euro. The case for economic and monetary union and the introduction of a single currency was essentially political. The economic case was that the euro's arrival would boost inter-EU trade (which it did to some extent, alongside the reduction of barriers in the single market) and prevent competitive devaluations which would damage the integrity of the market. The results have been economically and politically terrible for most members of the eurozone, particularly the weaker ones, and it is at least worth considering how much stronger and much more competitive Europe's economy would be today if as much political effort and energy had gone into completing the single market as has gone into keeping the euro afloat.

Initially, I supported the case for Britain joining the euro, although mindful that it was primarily a political project driven by France in particular. For Paris, German abandonment of its own currency, the Deutschmark, in favour of a new European currency was the price demanded by President Mitterrand for supporting reunification of Germany in 1990. Germany at the time must have been a little unnerved by the fact that both France and Britain were opposed to reunification. In Margaret Thatcher's purported recollection of a remark by the French novelist François Mauriac, 'We like Germany so much that we want two of them.' Thatcher had explicitly told President Gorbachev in 1989 that Britain did not want a united Germany. The hostility of both France and Britain to reunification must have been a powerful point of pressure on Chancellor Kohl to persuade his government and party to surrender their own beloved currency, the hardest of the hard, for a sickly infant. No wonder some German politicians still argue that this grand bargain did not occur, despite the evidence published by the news periodical *Der Spiegel* and the corroboration of French officials like the former Mitterrand adviser and foreign minister Hubert Védrine. The way the euro has developed must make French officials these days wonder whether an initiative which made Germany even more central to the running of the European economy was such a bright idea.

It was not too long before my views on the euro came into line with those of John Major. From the start, he had argued that there was a strong case for a common, not a single, currency running alongside national ones. In time the strong would drive out the weak. But the launch of the euro, a single currency, was fundamentally flawed. First, it treated all the members of the zone as though they were at similar levels of competitiveness and needed a single interest rate to deal with similar levels of cost push inflation. This could not have been much further from the truth, particularly since Germany under Chancellor Schroeder had just driven through painful reforms to lower costs. In the early years, there was a flood of money from northern banks into southern economies in pursuit of wholly implausible returns which mostly depended on unlikely levels of competitiveness. For a number of years, flying into Madrid or driving out of Dublin, the amount of construction activity made you think for a moment that you must be in an emerging Asian economy. What made the situation even more damaging was that some members of the eurozone – Greece was the prime example – were only there because of politics; in Greece's case indeed it only qualified as a euro member because it fabricated, with the help of a well-known global bank, the figures necessary for membership. Presented with the evidence that Greece did not really qualify to become a member of the eurozone, President Chirac famously observed, 'But how could we exclude the country that gave Europe Plato?' Very easily, actually, if the eurozone was to be taken as a serious economic policy rather than a genuflection to the roots of Western culture. This was level one economics, not the beginning of a philosophy course.

So a collection of countries of varying degrees of economic vitality and competitiveness was brought together in a monetary union which was, in effect, formed on the assumption that they could all accept the same disciplines as the most powerful among them like Germany and the Netherlands. But where was the evidence that you could have a single currency without a fiscal union, and was it really conceivable that member states would be happy to have other states, or some super Commissioner in Brussels, deciding their tax-and-spend policies? To take one obvious example, would one of the principal impregnators of this idea, France, be happy to have its budget set by German politicians? What level of VAT on restaurant meals in Paris does Herr Schäuble think we should pay this year? As if this was not enough, if you were to have a fiscal union or even a pale imitation of one, you would need a transfer union as well. Money would have to be sent from stronger countries to weaker ones, from Berlin to Athens for example, even as Athens or another less competitive economy was having to pay back northern banks for the money they had been lent and then lost in the days after the eurozone's creation. In order to remain in the eurozone, southern countries in particular were obliged to make sacrifices and cuts in social programmes which produced public convulsions. At a conference in Rome in the early years of Greek blood-letting, the Greek education minister (a friend of mine) told me that she had been obliged to close 2,000 schools that week. The euro, badly conceived and badly managed, has almost torn Europe apart.

It was all very well scolding the Greeks or Italians for being too idle, too corrupt, the French for being too dependent on a bloated public sector, the Portuguese for being too far down any queue of economic comparators. That might all be true. But for sure you could not wave a wand or offer a blessing and save these sinners overnight. They each sinned in their own chosen way and however tiresome that might be, you could not make them all into Germans. If you believed in fiscal responsibility, you sympathized with German policy. But if you wanted the European project to survive without the political tumult of protests with banners showing photographs of Angela Merkel with a Hitler moustache, if you wanted a Europe which thrived partly because it took account of diversity and frailty as well as economic power, then change was essential – whether substantive or cautiously fudged. The problem was that Germany, which saw itself as the principal guardian of the European vision, and which wanted to be seen to bury any suggestion of its nationalism in that vision, had to face the dilemma that the rest of us knew that this vision was all too comfortable for German mercantilism. Because, when you did the accounts, the euro gave Germany a cut-price exchange rate for its exports, which continued to soar. I think this outcome was accidental rather than deliberately planned. It also has roots deep in Germany's national identity. The German word for debt (*Schuld*) is the same as that for guilt. We could not expect Germany to abandon its fundamental beliefs; yet it might have better understood the need for more flexibility in pursuing its goal of fiscal virtue.

The adoption of the euro was agreed at the beginning of my term as a Commissioner; it was introduced – from ATM to wallet – halfway through that period in 2002. The management of the euro's arrival on the scene was actually a success. But not all those who worked in the Commission were convinced that it would sail safely through the storms and avoid disaster. One of the real pleasures of being a Commissioner was that you were able, as I noted, to pick your own team of close advisers for your private office. I had first thought that, as captain of my team, it might send waves around the system to select a French official. But I soon discovered the difficulties of this. Two very clever fellows were proposed, each strongly opposed by part of the Paris bureaucracy. Since I could not understand the nature of the problem – why did Monsieur X annoy Monsieur Y – I decided to play safe and choose a British diplomat as my 'Chef'. (It is said that when Roy Jenkins was President of the Commission and went for a meeting with Ronald Reagan in Washington, the latter was unable to understand why Jenkins had brought his cook along.) I had been allotted the portfolio of External Affairs and it was natural to put together a team who knew about international relations. I chose as Chef a charming diplomat – clever, well-read, funny – Antony Cary, who had sold himself to me at our interview by his articulate, forensic and unrelenting demolition of the case which I put rather vaguely for the euro. A current cliché is that good civil servants should always speak truth to power. Antony did not need to be encouraged to do this; indeed, sometimes he took a little time to recognize (given our respective positions) that my version of power might be (sometimes was) wrong, but carried more brawn than his subtler version. He was huge fun to work with, and would have gone even higher in the Foreign Office – he eventually became ambassador in Stockholm and High Commissioner in Canada – if he had been more sharp-elbowed and less determined to expose his own opinions. Together, we put together a fine team, including in time a Swedish and then a Dutch deputy, both of them safe, competent and sensible, a very clever ex-Treasury man, Patrick Child, who succeeded Antony, Edward Llewellyn (from Hong Kong) and two frighteningly smart and tough women. Miriam Gonzáles Durántez, who was Spanish, looked after Trade, Latin America and the Middle East. Provided that I did what she told me, very charmingly, to do, nothing went wrong. On one occasion, the Chef of the Trade Commissioner, Pascal Lamy, told her that his boss wanted a meeting with me to discuss the allocation of accommodation in our building. 'My Commissioner,' she responded 'was a Cabinet minister and a colonial Governor. Are you seriously suggesting that I should get him to give up an hour of his time to talk about square metres of official space?' The scion of the ENA backed down rapidly. At the time, Miriam was in the process of marrying an up-and-coming young Liberal Democrat, but woe betide anyone who refers to her now as Mrs Nick Clegg. The other clever woman, Vicky Bowman, was a Foreign Office diplomat, a fluent Burmese speaker, who went at an absurdly young age to be Britain's ambassador in Yangon. We would augment our intellectual firepower by adding each six months an intern from the ENA and another from the British civil service. The ENA interns were very bright, but slightly daunted by the informality of a British office and by the fact that they were expected to have a point of view, whether or not it happened to coincide with that of the British government. I encouraged them to follow Antony's example.

My job description (as the Commissioner for External Affairs) reflected the political and intellectual muddle over who should be responsible for the EU's foreign and security policy. Was this really a Commission task or was it a matter for the collective discussion of the member states? My own view was that it was definitely a member state function, but there was plenty that the Commission could do which though sometimes described as 'back office' often contained most of what Europe could deliver or wanted to deliver – bilateral trade, sanctions, development assistance, co-operation agreements, the linking together of those community competences – from energy to economic regulation, which had an external dimension. In some respects, provided the Commission with representative offices all around the world played its hand carefully, it was able to supply most of the beef in managing many external questions. So I had more than enough to do, with almost ceaseless travel. (A joke was told about me which had previously been attached to a French Commissioner. 'What is the difference between Chris Patten and God?' 'God is everywhere. Patten is everywhere except Brussels.') The Council of Ministers, anxious to raise Europe's foreign and security profile, had just appointed their own High Representative for Foreign and Security Policy, a former Spanish minister and NATO Secretary-General, Javier Solana. This two-headed approach to policy could have led to disaster. But Javier and I got on very well. He is a subtle, unthreatening, extraordinarily well-connected diplomat. I regarded him as my senior partner; he never treated me as his junior. In almost five years working together, no one ever managed to slip a cigarette paper between our views, a British Conservative and a Spanish socialist. A phrase at which I usually bridle is the description of an organizational relationship as not 'fit for purpose'. In my experience, this cliché can usually be circumvented when people find a way of working together. I probably frustrated Javier from time to time and vice-versa. I think he was keener on avoiding confrontation than I am. But we made the system work.

It is of course very difficult, when possible at all, to make foreign policy rapidly with twenty-eight countries, and the effectiveness of doing so declines the further you go from Europe's borders and from the functions (trade, commercial regulation, for example) which member states have agreed to run in concert. To take an obvious example, Europe's position in south-east Europe – the Balkans and Turkey – and around the Mediterranean from Morocco through to the Levant could be properly harmonized. I doubt the value of Europe trying to make a splash in say, North Korea, though I did once go there with Javier: a visit to another planet.

There were three specific issues which consumed much of our time. I moved pretty well straight from working on the brutal consequences of identity politics in Northern Ireland to spending a large part of my time in the western Balkans, accompanied on these visits first by Edward Llewellyn and later by Patrick Rock. The fighting there had bloodied and shamed Europe in the 1990s. The Kosovo War itself had ended just before I became a Commissioner in the late summer of 1999. This was a region where the crumbling empires of the Ottomans and the Hapsburgs, leaving behind the residues of their cultures and religions, had triggered conflicts which encapsulated the hostility between the West and the East, between Catholic and Orthodox. The different groups were not really very different at all. Ethnically, for example, Croats were indistinguishable from the Serbs; they were from the same Slavic race, with the same language and names. It was religion which divided Catholic Croats from Orthodox Serbs, with Muslim Bosnians trapped in the middle of this mutual hatred. The Croats had behaved appallingly as a fascist puppet state during the Second World War, especially in their barbarous treatment of Serbs and Jews. They were led then by a political movement called the Ustase, whose ideology combined Nazi views on race, Croatian nationalism and Roman Catholicism. It was a deadly cocktail. The degree to which Catholic Church leaders were implicated in their terrible crimes, turning a blind eye at best or giving a not-so-mute endorsement at worst, was the subject of much controversy after the war. In general, the identification of churches with nationalism usually leads to trouble, providing justifications for behaviour that those religions on their own would surely condemn. Corners are cut; the New Testament or the Koran takes second place to some strident anthems of tribal belligerence.

In the post-war years the Balkan states were bound together in a communist authoritarian embrace by the former guerrilla leader Marshal Tito, who recommended himself to Western countries by deliberately and successfully distancing himself from Moscow and its colonial feudatories in the Warsaw Pact. Tito, himself part Croat and part Slovene, suppressed the symbols and flags of any other national identity than that of Yugoslavia. He kept the Serbs in check; they would otherwise have dominated the state. Tito's death melted the glue that had held the country together. Though the Serbian dominance in Yugoslavia was its central problem, when that led to Croats demanding their own independence the issue immediately turned into the dominance in Croatia of Croats over Serbs.

Almost a decade of misery, horror, death and ethnic cleansing followed. Initially, Europeans could not decide whether they should try to prevent the disintegration of Yugoslavia, encourage it as peacefully as possible, or turn a blind eye until conditions had returned to those which would allow their citizens to go there on holiday. While thousands died in the fighting, in the shelling of cities like Sarajevo and Dubrovnik, in concentration camps and in besieged and pillaged towns like Srebrenica, politicians from outside faffed around ignoring three simple lessons. First, identity conflicts, like most others, require for their settlement a combination of force and politics. In Northern Ireland, there would never have been peace had not the terrorists in both communities come to understand that the British security effort was not going to run out of patience and energy. Second, in a big conflict, Europe had to work hand-in-hand with the United States. Europeans could not operate on their own. In Northern Ireland, American help – which was hard earned – had been invaluable with the Irish diaspora and moderate nationalists. Third, there had to be an offer to the warring parties of a brighter future.

I arrived in Brussels when the European Union was trying to put in place the building blocks of such a policy in the Balkans. We launched a programme which combined financial support, institution building (courts and police, for example), and much hand-holding with the offer of closer trade and economic relations with the EU. Perhaps, a long way down the road, membership of the EU would be possible for Serbia and the others, as has happened already for Croatia and Slovenia.

Javier Solana and I visited Balkan countries with wearisome frequency. I remember without much affection countless visits over the whole of our time in Brussels to Pristina, then the impoverished capital of Kosovo, a squalid colonial dependency of Serbia, only recently liberated with the end of the Kosovo War. Poor and rundown, Pristina's formerly iconic hotel, the Grand, where we often had to stay, was fitted throughout with dirty grey carpets with cigarette burns, bedding which looked as though it should come with a health warning, only occasional hot water, urine stains all over the bathroom. It had provided sanctuary for the members of mostly Serbian communist politburos over the years. Trying to get life back to something like normal in Kosovo was heroic and expensive work. I remember in particular the struggle to get the power station operational again. It came straight from a Dickensian manual of darkest industry. Gradually the resilient Kosovars got their very poor country back on the road with lots of honest EU cash and other funds rather less honestly drawn out of various European rackets.

Javier and I went with just as great regularity during one very tense period in 2001 to Skopje, the post-earthquake capital of Macedonia, to work with George Robertson, the NATO Secretary-General. We were trying to prevent the country falling back into a full-scale war between the government and its Albanian population, which lives principally in the north-west of the country. There had been heavy fighting in the city of Tetovo in 2001, ended by an agreement which we helped the Macedonian President, Trajkovski, to broker. Trajkovski was the only Methodist I met in the Balkans and was as constructive and decent as his co-religionists had been in Northern Ireland, but we had to go back to Skopje again and again to help keep the show on the road. I recall spending one long night in the presidential palace surrounded by angry demonstrators, opposed to making any concession to the Albanians. They demonstrated their anger by firing their guns in the air, at least we hoped in the air. Life for Macedonia in international negotiations was made more difficult by its name. The Greeks refused to call it anything but the Former Yugoslav Republic of Macedonia (FYROM for short) on the grounds that Europeans since Alexander the Great knew that Macedonia was in Greece. This was all made more difficult by the Macedonians endlessly naming airports and streets after famous events in Macedonian history; they naturally gave the airport Alexander's name: a tiresome but harmless tease. This is the kind of thing which happens when ideas of identity overwhelm practical politics. Our regular hand-holding in Macedonia helped end overt conflict and set the country on a bumpy road to greater stability. After Milosevic was ousted in 2000, Belgrade also had to be visited regularly. This was accomplished partly thanks to EU support for an underground radio station and for the provision of oil for Milosevic's opponents. He had proved a consummate master of some of the most effective instruments of Balkan politics: lies, cheating, blackmail, corruption, violence and demagoguery which would transport his listeners back to Serbia's fourteenth-century defeat in Kosovo by the Ottomans. The calamity of the Field of Blackbirds predated the Battle of the Boyne by a good three centuries, but it was invoked just as raucously.

The restoration of something approximating to normalcy in the western Balkans has limped along for almost twenty years now. It has been a painfully slow success story for the European Union, for NATO, for the power of European chequebooks and for a succession of excellent officials who have presided over the efforts to restore order and peace. Paddy Ashdown particularly helped to do this in Bosnia with a formidable display of leadership which made me regret that Britain no longer has an empire to provide further career opportunities for him. And, of course, we worked with the Americans. On my first visit to Sarajevo, I found that the American Secretary of State, the formidable Madeleine Albright, was also in town. We agreed to see senior members of the government together to reinforce the similar messages we were both delivering. Afterwards, the French foreign ministry complained to Brussels that I had done this and taken a joint initiative with the Americans. Europeans should have acted without the Americans. This is too often a default position for the French: keep America out of Europe's business. It is very silly, but then so too is the sight of British politicians and diplomats turning somersaults to try and get Americans to use the phrase 'special relationship'. Can we, for example, persuade President Trump to love us to bits? Do we really want to escape the alleged EU cage to take up residence in the Trump kennel?

In the Balkans as in Northern Ireland the legacy and abuse of identity, historical or imagined, has been a terrible killer. Dealing with it has required extraordinary amounts of diplomacy, commitment and applied force. In W. H. Auden's poem 'Embassy', gardeners and chauffeurs are watching as their 'highly trained' bosses take a break from their negotiations.

Far off, no matter what good they intended,
The armies waited for a verbal error
With all the instruments for causing pain:

And on the issue of their charm depended
A land laid waste, with all its young men slain,
The women weeping, and its towns in terror.

That is true from Derry to Dubrovnik, from Pristina to Portadown. We should raise a glass, more often than we do, to those who help to clear up the mess that we make when we take the idea of who we are, or who we think we are, a long way too far.

The Middle East, complete with its much discussed but mostly truant peace process, is a reminder of the importance of diplomacy consisting of deliverables and not just communiqués. Roll together all the statements by foreign ministers and others about security, the West Bank, settlements, two states, Jerusalem and so on and I guess you would have a document of Old Testament proportions about the future of the not very large Holy Land. As a European Commissioner, I became quite heavily involved in trying to make a reality of some of this writ. The Israelis had and have legitimate security interests which must be addressed if ever there is to be a lasting peace and Palestine is not to become a sort of Bantustan. The horror of events elsewhere in the region has distracted attention from the relentless pursuit of a sustainable peace. Meanwhile, the so called 'facts on the ground' – the building of new colonies (settlements as the Israelis prefer to call them), and the oppressive security presence exemplified by the Wall – make it ever more difficult to build peace on the basis of accommodating legitimate Israeli and Palestinian requirements. As ever, there is right and wrong on both sides. But a refusal in Israel and some parts of the United States to accept even this pretty minimal proposition makes the future look bleak.

The fragments of a possible future Palestinian state still exist just about, thanks largely to the money spent over the years in order to keep some sort of governance going in Palestine. The subsidies come mainly from Europe and are regularly criticized publicly by the Israeli government and by some American politicians, while Brussels is privately urged to keep them flowing. The carefully monitored support for the Palestinians at least keeps in being a notional partner for Israel. Javier and I had to visit Palestine and Israel with depressingly ineffective frequency to keep this partnership in place. We were also members of the alleged peace-brokering machinery called 'the Quartet', based on the UN, the USA, Russia and Europe. The cynical and witty former Egyptian foreign minister, Amr Moussa, used to call it 'the Quartet sans trois', reflecting the general and accurate view that it was essentially an American enterprise which gave Washington a cover for doing very little.

The last time I visited Israel and Palestine was as the president of an excellent small medical charity called Medical Aid for Palestine. During the visit I went to the Gaza Strip, a finger of land along the coast, forty-one kilometres long and between six and twelve wide. Governed by Hamas, its population of just under two million has been regarded by Israel, with some justification, as a threat. As a result of this, from time to time the Israel Defence Force has smashed much of Gaza's infrastructure and a lot of its housing to rubble, killing men, women and children, the probably guilty and the certainly innocent in the process. This is called collateral damage. I was there to try to ensure that necessary medical supplies were occasionally getting through to hospitals and doctors.

Mr Blair once told me that during his days as the Middle East Peace Envoy – the representative of the Quartet – he had been unable to visit Gaza more than once because of the security threats to his bodyguards. To get into the Strip with a visa you have to go through security checks under surveillance cameras and along wire or concrete corridors. You eventually emerge into a no-man's-land, where a scattering of men with barrows attached to their donkeys or motorbicycles are combing through the rubble and the rubbish to see whether there is anything worth trying to sell. It is like stepping into a post-apocalyptic novel, but this dystopian scene is for real. When liberal Jews criticize scenes like this, when they suggest better ways of trying to build a peaceful future, when they occasionally criticize aspects of Israeli government policy, they are described by fundamentalists and others as self-hating Jews. My own friends in Israeli politics – good and brave men like Yossi Beilin and Shlomo Ben-Ami – have been driven out of politics. This does more to discredit a noble dream than some more obvious manifestations of self-defeating policy on the ground. One day surely sanity and decency will break out and provide more effective bulwarks for the national interests of both Israel and Palestine. There is no sign of this yet. Mr Blair's activities notwithstanding, there is no peace process. There is only just a Palestinian Authority. The grim 'facts on the ground' that will make any settlement far more difficult to engineer in the future stack up remorselessly. President Trump, in the meantime, helps things to move all too perceptibly from bad to worse.

Like President George W. Bush, I have looked into President Putin's hard, cold, blue eyes, but unlike him have not been vouchsafed a sense of Putin's soul. Indeed, I noted that when Vice-President Biden met Mr Putin and questioned whether he had a soul at all, the Russian replied, 'We understand one another.' President Bush had gone further, not simply recognizing the spiritual side of Putin but identifying him as straightforward, trustworthy and frank. I met Putin on perhaps twenty occasions, mostly at Russia–EU Summits, but I also visited his office and was once invited to his dacha (I suspect it was only for show) with a group of commissioners at a time when he was trying to butter us up over the Russian wish to join the WTO. I dealt with him principally on access to Kaliningrad (after EU enlargement had surrounded the famous 'oblast' within EU territory), the extension of the existing EU trade and co-operation agreements with Russia to the new member states (like Poland and the Baltics), and the treatment of humanitarian agencies during the dirty war in Chechnya. These encounters and Russian behaviour in the Ukraine and Syria have encouraged me to take a different view from President Bush: that President Putin is a natural fit for a country where at present, in the title of a recent book by Peter Pomerantsev, *Nothing is True and Everything is Possible*. Putin's regime, in which a virtual reality is fostered in the media by the state, is built on lies, like the Soviet system before it. Putin's regard for the truth, visible from the Crimea, which he invaded and stole illegally, to Kremlin disclaimers about cyber-warfare, to the po-faced statements of injured innocence whenever a critic is murdered (in London as well as Moscow), does not make him a very obvious partner for Washington, let alone Europe, in creating a more peaceful and stable world. He presides over a rotten, petro-economy, with a modernized military, and a thoroughly corrupt political system. His ambition is plainly to create a Europe carved out into spheres of influence with the former parts of the Soviet Empire once again showing their loyalty to Moscow. The more irresolute that European countries have been in resisting this, the more Moscow has pushed and probed for advantage. President Putin was and is the most dangerous political and security threat to Europe, which will need to show more collective resolution than in the past if it is to deal with him more effectively. Washington and Brussels have not always handled the relationship with Russia with enough understanding of Russian nationalism and 'amour propre'; an even bigger mistake has been that we have not been tough enough when we needed to be.

During my five years in Brussels, in my own area of responsibility and indeed right across the board, I saw areas of public policy which were far more successfully managed because they were the preserve of a successful and not particularly expensive partnership. Coming back to London, most of our biggest problems plainly had nothing to do with Europe – from low productivity, to planning laws which throttled new house-building, to an often unsatisfactory secondary education system, to an underfunded and badly managed health and welfare system. Europe was not the problem, and again and again understandably people declined to award it in opinion polls the salience of other issues. But the whole European discussion became associated (and not just in Britain) with aggravating, not solving, the problems that crowded in on us all. Why should the public think that warming over old rhetoric about integration was the answer to new and sometimes frightening problems? The EU was stretching far too tight the thread between what it was doing and popular acceptability. Sooner or later, the cord was going to snap. And when it threatened to do so, it was not only the euro crisis but a crisis of migration in our neighbourhood and an enormous financial crisis, all coinciding, which made the challenges faced by Europe exceptionally daunting. So it became more difficult for a Britain which had always preferred psychologically to run on its own to comprehend that to play things in our national interest might mean continuing to stay a member of the pack, however difficult the terrain over which we had to travel with our fellow Europeans. Loneliness is not a very desirable condition in a world increasingly dominated by big countries and harassed by big problems. My experiences in the EU made me an even stronger believer in the importance of international co-operation, an especially important issue for smaller and middle-sized countries. But, in assembling these partnerships, it is crucial to manage national opinion so that the public do not believe that their loyalties are being rolled over. It should be relatively straightforward for political leaders to prevent national pride turning into aggressive xenophobia. The chant of the Millwall Football Club fans, 'No one likes us; we don't care', should be avoided at all costs. Patriotism in Britain and in other European countries is an inspiring notion. We have a century of experience to prove that narrow, bigoted nationalism is the path to trouble.

IO

Atlantic Crossing

'Hang on a minute, lads. I've got a great idea.'
Michael Caine's last line in *The Italian Job*

'Resentment is no excuse for bald-faced stupidity.'
Garrison Keillor, 2016

It may be about 3,500 miles wide, but the Atlantic has never been a barrier to the transmission of cults, fashions, entertainments, threats and ideas. Martini married Italian vermouth to London dry gin to create something which H. L. Mencken thought was as perfect as a sonnet, and which was soon cheerfully consumed from the Waldorf to the Savoy. Levi jeans became the world's workpants to the great benefit of the University of Berkeley, which shared in their commercial success. The sounds of Liverpool and Detroit blasted east to west and back again. Even soccer, as it's called in the States, caught on, to general amazement, with part of the American middle class, most successfully with women. And of course the western seaboard of the Atlantic could not repel the threats which are a consequence of living on the same planet as fanatical terrorists and flu germs. As long ago as 1918, the Spanish flu pandemic cut down families in New York (including President Trump's grandfather) and the children skipped merrily to the ditty:

> I had a little bird
> His name was Enza
> I opened the window
> And in flew Enza.

One belief which gained nearly as many adherents in Britain as in the United States was spiritualism, after Kate and Margaret Fox reported making contact with a spirit which knocked to attract their attention. They later confessed to making this up. I once tried to find the village in which this had purportedly happened, near Rochester, New York, where I was giving a lecture, but the hamlet had disappeared without a knock. Arthur Conan Doyle, the author of the Sherlock Holmes stories, himself became a spiritualist, but it is not his interest in the paranormal which makes him an ideal introducer to a discussion of the transatlantic migration of nationalism in 2016. What struck me as especially apposite was his wise observation that 'it is a capital mistake to theorize before one has data. Insensibly, one begins to twist facts to suit theories, instead of theories to suit facts.'

The Brexit vote in the UK and the election of President Trump in the USA have together threatened to destroy the foundations of the world order to which my political life, both at home and abroad, has been devoted. The question of whether there was some umbilical relationship between Brexit and Trump has caused big differences of opinion on either side of the Atlantic, with theories on the whole preferred to facts. President Trump saw Brexit as an outpouring of nationalist sentiment, which would soon be followed by similar upheavals elsewhere, leading to the apparently desirable disintegration of the whole supranational EU project. For him, it was a grave sin against the natural Westphalian order. Trump buttressed his analysis by putting Europe's ills down, above all, to Angela Merkel's welcome to refugees. Germany helped above anything else to trigger the Brexit triumph, he suggested: from 'Britain First' to 'America First'. Then he predicted it would be 'France First' (with Marine Le Pen) and 'Everywhere Else First'. Moreover, Trump used Brexit to give his presidential campaign a leg-up. Nigel Farage, not hitherto a household name in America, was flown in to assist the Republican campaign as a sort of intellectual character witness for 'The Donald' and all the trumpery that went with him. Every villain in the American's playbook was also in Farage's sights: experts, elites, bankers (especially from Goldman Sachs), media organizations that disagreed with him, Muslims, foreigners (except Mr Putin), immigrants and, I am sure, anyone who belonged to a tree-hugging or bleeding-hearts organization. Membership of the UN Association would of course be tantamount to a criminal offence.

Turn the telescope around, and how did America look to Brexiteers? Was there some commonality that would make it easier to understand what had happened in the EU referendum campaign and what might happen in due course in France and other countries in Europe? There was no problem in getting United Kingdom Independence Party (UKIP) supporters to sign up to this proposition. They saw in America what they saw in Europe. They pointed out a groundswell of opposition to the economic policies that preceded and followed the 2008–9 crash, to the self-serving behaviour of elites, to globalization and above all (though this should not perhaps be said too loudly) to mass migration which threatened rapid cultural change and the nation's sense of its own identity. Europe had received the largest share of international migrants in the last few years, and there were bound to be political consequences.

UKIP was perfectly happy to sign up to this analysis. It went down less well with more fastidious Brexiteers. They did not want their lofty arguments to be sullied by any comparison with the white resentment which had, as much as any other factor, got Mr Trump into the White House. Perish the thought, some of them said within hours of their victory, that it had anything to do with race or fears about immigration. They were not, we should understand, against immigration; they simply wanted to be able to say that they controlled it. This was after all at the heart of their argument: sovereignty. Nation states should run their own affairs. The European Union was a fundamentally undemocratic institution. We wanted our country back, just as President Trump wanted to make America great again. Back and great; great and back. If, in order to achieve that we had to dirty our hands with the sort of populist mendacity which also proved successful in America – the unreliability of experts, the dishonesty of the government, and so on – well, so be it; that is just part of the detritus of a democratic campaign. Anyway, if the mendacity was simply one aspect of the general buffoonery of a politician like Boris Johnson no one should get too judgemental about it. 'But you didn't actually take him seriously, did you?' Some said similar things about Trump.

There was a certain awkwardness in the outcome of these electoral upsets. No one really knew what 'The Donald' would turn out to be, but if what emerged from the chrysalis was anything like the candidate in his pupal stage, then (as the Romans would have said), 'cave', world beware. What that sort of Mr Trump would represent was not so much a butterfly as a wrecking ball swung hard if indiscriminately against the values and institutions which have been associated for over fifty years with the West and the global order it created. So will a Brexit Britain (what we are asked to call a 'global Britain' as we turn our backs on our largest markets in Europe) be required increasingly to distance itself from its neighbours and get as intimate as possible with the wrecking ball? Will Britain have to second the motion 'America First', with its corollaries 'Buy American, Employ American'?

Before trying to distinguish in Britain and Europe between theories and facts, we should consider one other proposition. Some say that what has happened in Britain and America is not so profound. In America, for instance, Mr Trump actually lost the popular vote by almost three million, despite the active help of Mr Putin. But even if Mr Trump had lost out in the electoral college as well as in the popular vote, it would have been a cause for real shock that this vulgar, abusive, ignorant man should attract as much support as he did. We would still have to scratch our heads and ask ourselves serious questions. Moreover, if Brexit had, to borrow from one of the campaigners, simply blown the doors off the van as was intended, not produced a 'quit' result, would we have been much more comfortable, waiting for the next assault? First the doors, then the passengers.

Spotting the differences in Britain between theories and facts, as Conan Doyle suggests we should, we have to begin with the growing corrosion of trust in the EU as a whole over the years. I referred in an earlier chapter to some of the reasons for this, above all the growing eurozone crisis and the sense of alienation between the public and the professed aims of the European partnership. But we also had to confront myths, exaggerations and lies about Europe which we allowed to destroy much of the credibility of the institution. We usually – nearly all of us who took a completely different pro-European view – failed to confront all this negative sentiment for fear (for those of us in the Conservative Party) of stirring up the right wing and more generally of standing up to the tabloid press. We have to take back control, we are told. It would be nice if we could for a start take back control of the political agenda from a handful of newspapers. The EU is not a corrupt, inefficient behemoth; it did not seize from us more than we gain from membership; it did not usurp our ability to govern ourselves; it did not flood our country with men and women who stole our jobs and bled dry our welfare and health systems. These claims were untrue. The fact that they were believed is partly a result of the collapse of trust in democratic politics (especially in England), the trust which should help bind us more closely together. When we ask, 'Who are we in England? Who are we in Britain?', the answer is partly that we are plainly (especially in England) not citizens of a country where the governed these days trust those who govern them. The over-whelming majority of parliamentarians wanted Britain to remain in the EU. What did they know that those who voted for them did not comprehend? Why the gulf between the ruled and their rulers? What brought together the blazers of Chichester and the blue collars of Barnsley to deal such a blow to our international reputation, credibility and interests, and to our long-term economic prospects? What brought us to vote for relegation to a lower division?

Any analysis of the vote to leave the EU should recognize straight away the differences between blue-collar alienation in industrial England and middle-class myths and truculence in more affluent areas. The former was affected as well by two powerful influences on the outcome, with the Leave vote 7 per cent higher in England than Remain, a figure which fell to 4 per cent in the United Kingdom as a whole. In Scotland, blue-collar voters still had a party with which many of them could identify, the Scottish Nationalists. But in England, though party membership has grown, the Labour vote itself has been in free fall; voter identification with its leadership and its core messages has been feeble. A healthy Labour Party, campaigning vigorously for membership of the EU, would have made a huge difference, preventing the erosion of the Labour vote which drifted away to UKIP. The Conservative Brexit vote was of course much more important than what was happening in the Labour Party. The places that voted most strongly to quit Europe shared a number of characteristics. They were older, whiter, less educated and often poorer than the places which voted to stay. They felt left behind and isolated by globalization, which was personified by EU membership. They saw Europe benefiting metropolitan Britain and particularly London. Their incomes were stuck; their public services pinched by public spending cuts and seemingly swamped by outsiders from the EU and beyond. When they were told that Britain would be much worse off outside the EU, they did not care because they believed that they would be worse off whatever happened. So (a second strong influence on the outcome) the main threat of the Remain campaign – that Britain would suffer economically from withdrawal – simply passed them by. Their electoral profile was very similar to that in rustbelt America in the presidential election.

There is not much doubt that concern about immigration was a spark plug for the Leave campaign. What mattered most was not the absolute level of immigration in an area but the speed of increase in immigration. A consequence of growth in the economy (over the years since the financial crash) was growth in EU immigration, particularly to take on low-paid jobs. While the Conservative government had a good record in creating jobs for those who had been born in the UK, many of these jobs were low-paid. EU workers were attracted to take jobs at which English workers would often turn up their noses, jobs for example in agricultural work, retail and hospitality services, and social services. The country also of course benefited from skilled workers in the health services, research and information technology. If Britain now grows less rapidly outside the EU this should indeed reduce the flow of immigration, but it will not leave people better off, rather the reverse. This divide in our society between the alienated and those who are at home with globalization is going to be difficult to heal, and the extent to which what Brexit actually brings will disappoint the alienated is a worrying point to which I will return.

The blazered rebellion against Brussels, with places like Aylesbury, Chichester, South Buckinghamshire and West Dorset voting to leave the EU, does not have all that much in common with the economic alienation of industrial England. It is even more strongly related to the state of the political party that normally represents these citizens. It also has its roots in a cultural aversion to one aspect of globalization. Where blue-collar workers in England, as in industrial states in

America, worried about the threat caused by globalization to their jobs and standard of living, the blazered vote was irritated by the undermining of their sense of their own identity. (Virtually half of all respondents to a survey before the referendum felt that membership of the EU was undermining the national idea of identity.) While the blazers were usually members of the party which championed neo-liberal answers to many of Britain's problems, they were curiously reluctant to embrace the consequences of globalization, internation-alization and the opening to an ever more interconnected world. This paradox was given personal shape in the figure of the former Conservative Mayor of London, a great international city which was a sparkling advertisement for openness and globalization. Boris Johnson helped to lead the Leave campaign while trying rather unconvincingly to persuade the world that his position was not dictated by an unflagging, tumescent ambition. During the campaign, he was unable to explain how he could both proselytize for embracing the world and at the same time turn his back on Britain's co-operation with its nearest neighbours; nowadays, as Britain's Foreign Secretary, he argues that it is somehow easier to open up to the rest of the world by leaving the EU.

Middle-class, white and on the whole older opposition to EU membership did of course encompass the narrowing heartland of the Conservative Party. It was the attempted appeasement of this shrinking regiment that brought Britain the EU referendum in the first place. It was an effort to manage the Conservative Party that went badly wrong. In a parliamentary system where the overwhelming majority of those elected favoured staying in the EU for very good reasons, the unparliamentary device of a referendum was the attempt to get the Party out of a hole, enabling it to absorb in due course UKIP supporters at the expense of the national interest. When the main cause of the result is sought, it would be unreasonable to look beyond the Conservative Party. Attempts to blame Labour and Mr Corbyn are far-fetched. About two thirds of those who voted Labour in the 2015 General Election voted to remain in the EU; less than half of those who voted for the Conservatives did so. The 2017 election was above all another attempt to manage the Conservative Party.

The persistent, growing and occasionally slightly manic Conservative hostility to the European Union began in the late 1980s and 1990s and became a real menace as a consequence of Margaret Thatcher's fall from office, Britain's ejection from the Exchange Rate Mechanism (made more certain by Norman Lamont's hapless behaviour as Chancellor of the Exchequer) and the subsequent, not always camouflaged, encouragement by the fallen leader of Europhobic disloyalty to her elected successor. It became an act of faith on the new right of the Conservative Party that Thatcher was a victim of European integration and its adherents in John Major's government. To be a proper Conservative, true blue in heart and soul, a disciple of 'the Lady', you had to oppose the EU and all its works. This mattered a lot more than any display of what used to be called the Conservative Party's secret weapon, namely loyalty. Those were the days! John Major won the 1992 election after successfully negotiating the Maastricht Treaty, which confirmed Britain's membership of the Union on pretty much Britain's own terms. There was hardly a whisper of Euroscepticism or phobia in the subsequent election campaign. But afterwards, with a small parliamentary majority and a succession of political setbacks, the right wing pounced again and again, ambushing the government, colluding with the Opposition to embarrass it and actively conspiring to bring down the Prime Minister. John Major bravely faced down the reckless ideologues – 'the bastards', he dubbed them – but they were not satisfied until they had conspired to help destroy the government they had been elected to support.

With Major gone in 1997, and a Conservative government too, the right wing redoubled their efforts. They first elected as his successor an able man who was thought to be more right wing and hostile to Europe than he was in practice. William Hague's election loss in 2001 led to the choice of two deeply Eurosceptic leaders in swift succession, first the woeful Iain Duncan-Smith and then Michael Howard, a clever former Home Secretary who at least brought greater intelligence to articulating the same critique of all things European. Howard came from a family of pre-war Romanian immigrants. As Home Secretary he was hostile to any easing of immigration or visa rules, as I found while battling to safeguard the rights that Hong Kong citizens (some of whom were effectively stateless) would enjoy after 1997. As party leader, he brought in an Australian campaign adviser who specialized in 'dog-whistle' tactics, the idea being to call up a party's base of supporters by referring however obliquely to the issues that they were thought to feel about most strongly. Conservative posters asked voters, 'Are you thinking what we are thinking?' In effect about race, immigration and crime. Perhaps we should be grateful that not enough voters turned up when the whistle was blown. During our respective political careers, I have invariably disagreed with Michael Howard while being surprised at the opinions held by a man I have never disliked.

With Howard's demise, the cupboard of available, experienced talent was pretty bare, and the party turned to a young (not yet forty) MP, David Cameron, very bright, very polished, with the gloss of someone who plainly believed that he had been born to rule and had the temperament to take this not-too-formidable challenge in his stride. Like others of his generation, he had grown up in a party where Euroscepticism was all the rage, enthusiastically pumped up by newspapers that had themselves mostly done an about-face on the question and embraced hostility to the EU for reasons which lay deep in the hearts of their proprietors and the editors they appointed.

Cameron declared himself and his closest partners, like George Osborne, who was to become an intellectually powerful Chancellor of the Exchequer, to be 'modernizers', and he advocated a number of policies that were certainly not taken from any right-wing master plan, such as a strong sense of environmental imperatives, an unshakeable commitment to raising overseas aid to the targets proposed by the UN, and gay marriage. On Europe, however, the old tunes continued to play and they did not include 'Ode to Joy'. He even took one wholly unnecessary step to shore up his support in the party leadership election: that is, a promise to withdraw the Conservative Party from the right-of-centre, largely Christian Democrat group in the European Parliament on the grounds that its instincts were too integrationist. This seemed to many at the time to be a 'nerdy' issue, of no great significance outside the thin ranks of those who followed closely the affairs of the European Parliament. In fact, it lost him friends, and sources of political intelligence and influence, when he became Prime Minister after the 2010 election.

As Prime Minister, Cameron tried – not without success – to build bridges to other leaders like Angela Merkel, and to convince them that the political postures that he was obliged to strike would not impede his continuing pursuit of the British national interest by remaining within the EU. But he found it increasingly difficult to ride two horses – in Brussels, good sense; in Westminster, the Conservative Party's prejudices. Before the 2015 election, in an effort to keep the right-wing Eurosceptics quiet and to protect his party's flank from Nigel Farage's UKIP, he promised that he would negotiate a new and improved relationship with the EU, and then put its terms to a referendum on whether Britain should remain an EU member. There are some who thought that he made this pledge not believing that he would ever have to carry it out – the prevailing assumption being that even if the Conservative Party actually won the election, it would continue to depend on coalition partners in the Liberal Party who would oppose any referendum. Others think that it was all a terrible miscalculation; and that – a clever fellow – he tended to operate on the 'essay crisis' approach to politics, believing that he was smart enough to get through the next test, whatever it was, like an Oxford tutorial essay, without taking a longer-term strategic view. But what would happen if it all went wrong? He did not believe that if he had to do it he would lose. He reckoned that as the 'victor ludorum', he would be able to hold the party together. 'There you are, the voters have spoken: now, Duncan-Smith, Fox et al, you can shut up.' Others still suggest that he had no choice save to offer the referendum. I do not buy this argument. First, you always have a choice, especially when you are proposing using as dangerous a blunderbuss as a referendum – a device which should have no place in a parliamentary democracy. It undermines the whole notion of parliamentary sovereignty, substituting a crude majoritarianism for discussion and compromise among those we elect to give us the benefit of their judgement. Before long we usually find that those who like referendums dislike all the checks and balances which go to make up a pluralist constitution, such as independent courts, and the complexities of civil society. This is exactly what has happened since the Brexit vote of 2016, with a rampant populism both stoked and policed by a few tabloid editors. Second, the reason for holding the referendum was to keep the Conservative Party together. This would certainly not have happened if Remain had won. Brexit Conservatives would have cried foul and plotted for the next assault. Even with a Brexit victory, I do not believe that the Conservative Party will now settle down to a happy old age, united and pacific; the national interest has been badly damaged in pursuit of a goal which is almost certainly well beyond reach. Sooner or later, a Conservative leader will have to face down the right wing of the Conservative Party, and it would have been better to do so before conceding the case for a referendum.

Winning the referendum vote was made even more difficult by the speed with which the leaders of the Remain campaign had to reinvent themselves as enthusiastic supporters of the EU. Mr Cameron's negotiation to strengthen Britain's sense of its own national independence was satisfactory as far as it went, but that was no great distance. He then had to wave the European flag with fellow-believing Cabinet ministers for the cynical appraisal of voters who had hardly ever heard them in the past say a good word about the EU in which they were now urged to remain. Told that they would be poorer outside the EU, they voted in England by a margin of 7 per cent to leave because they did not trust the arguments of the Remainers; instead they believed the vauntingly implausible and mendacious claims of the Brexiteers. They were not convincingly told how membership of the EU was good for them and their families in financial and security terms, and felt no connection to any pro-European story about their identity and that of their country.

Any accurate history of England and Britain, and of our national identity over the last few years, would regard membership of the EU as providing a helpful backdrop to our relative success. In what way had Europe impeded our progress? When I first got into politics in the 1970s we were widely regarded as the sick man of Europe. We had begun the years of peace in the 1940s in incomparably better shape than our liberated or defeated neighbours. Their economies were reduced to rubble. In 1947 we exported as much as France, Germany, Italy, Benelux, Norway and Denmark combined. Their currencies were pretty worthless. But by the time we became members of the Common Market in 1973 we lagged behind Germany, France, Italy and others. Now just over forty years later we have in some respects (for example, growth and job creation) one of the continent's strongest economies. Before Brexit we were on the way to becoming the biggest European economy within the next fifteen years or so. The European Union's greatest achievements – the creation of the single market and the enlargement of the Union, stabilizing Central and Eastern Europe after the collapse of the Soviet Union – had both been British initiatives. We had played a key role in bringing an uneasy peace to the western Balkans. At the same time, we had avoided becoming enmeshed in policies that we did not like; we resisted blandishments to join the eurozone. We kept out of the Schengen area of a largely border-free Europe, not least so far as internal movement was concerned. The idea that the European Union, representing almost half our export market, was a ball and chain on our progress is pretty much the precise reverse of the truth. Moreover, how many times do we need to be told by our friends around the world, including the leaders of most Commonwealth countries, that they take us more seriously as a leader in Europe than as a lone voice shouting our opinion in order to try to be heard? Leaders in the United States – presidents, diplomats, generals – told us that our relationship with Washington was underpinned by our membership of and influence in the EU. But we evidently did not care much about anyone's opinion, including that of our friends. Only Presidents Trump and Putin appeared to favour our departure from the EU. You are frequently in life defined by your friends.

Why was opinion in Scotland and Northern Ireland so different from that in England? The sense of identity north of both borders, in Britain and in Ireland, is infused with sentiments that are not particularly enthusiastic about England and far more comfortable with the notion of being European. The Northern Ireland border is the only land frontier that the EU has with Britain. A majority in Northern Ireland understands that flattening that border has brought both economic and political gains. When as a junior minister in Northern Ireland I went to meetings in Brussels, I met ministers from the Republic and we found ourselves in an increasingly normal relationship. Anyone who doubts the potency of the border in Ireland's history should read Colm Tóibín's account of his hike along its length, *Bad Blood*. Scotland has historically enjoyed a less truculent relationship with the European mainland, partly because it has distanced itself from England. While Scotland has a nationalist party and its own parliament, England has no nationalist party and no national parliament but a growing nationalist sentiment. This nationalism is not just a strong sense of patriotism. Patriotism does not require 'the other' in order to define or refresh itself. It does not draw strength from hostility to others. It does not do whistle-up xenophobia to give it some oomph. It does not sentimentalize its history, seeking to erase what might be regarded as the bad bits. It does not need to glamorize its institutions to convince itself that it has understood the secrets of good governance denied to others.

Begin there, with the most potent of the English nationalist Brexiteer slogans that 'we must take back control' of our government, our lives and (the clinching argument) our borders. What control did we lack? It is true that in return for access to the single market, we allowed Europeans to come to Britain to live and work. (We should not forget that we are talking solely about EU migrants, not those – the majority – from the Commonwealth and elsewhere). We did not apparently want to control the number from the EU who came to do skilled jobs, who more or less keep our health service running, for example. It was those who came to do unskilled jobs who worried us. We had not controlled their number because our economy had been growing and we did not want to do the jobs that they were prepared to do at the levels of remuneration which they accepted. So we needed to take control of those Romanians and others, and find someone else to stack supermarket shelves and pick peas in Lincolnshire or strawberries in Kent. Economists suggested that the resulting increases in remuneration for British-born pea pickers would be extremely modest – in the low pence – even if we could find people who would do the work. 'Why not recruit British old-age pensioners to pick potatoes?' suggested one numbskull Brexiteer. Now there's an election winner! So it was true that we could 'take control' of a fraction of our immigration numbers at a small cost in inflation (better pay for shelf-stacking) and some cost to economic growth. What will actually 'take control' of immigration figures is simple economics. Less growth will equal lower immigration, and the government will not have to lift a finger.

That tells us something about control. How much control do governments have at the best of times? I remember one weekend when I was Governor of Hong Kong and the hedge-funds launched a combined assault on the link between the Hong Kong and US dollars. Fortunately we had huge reserves and were able to see off the clever young speculators sitting in front of their screens all around the world, often manoeuvring and manipulating money that did not really exist to attack funds that did. But for forty-eight hours I did not feel very confident that I was 'in control'. I have some sympathy for the observation of James Carville, a strategist for President Bill Clinton, known as the 'Ragin' Cajun', who was purportedly stunned in the early days of the Clinton administration at the power of the bond market over the government. 'I used to think if there was reincarnation,' he said, 'I wanted to come back as the president or the pope or a .400 baseball hitter. But now I want to come back as the bond market. You can intimidate everybody.' 'Take back control' and nationalize the banks (again), the railways, the steel industry, the ownership of land. 'Take back control' and watch your economy sink as inflation starts up again, the markets mark your currency down and investors move their money elsewhere. There's control for you.

It is not only markets which have huge power and need to be managed with great care, a reason why 'blazers' presumably vote most of the time for a party committed to cut excessive deficits. We are subject to other forces which give some definition to what sovereignty actually means today, less than it did for Lord Palmerston, that is for sure. What sovereignty means in practice is the power and authority you have in relation to events at any given moment. Sovereignty is not a once-and-for-all commodity, or an incredible shrinking asset. It is not, on the one hand, like virginity, as Geoffrey Howe used to note – there one moment, gone the next. Nor is it like a great monument, probably built by some past national hero at the end of Whitehall, from which nefarious foreigners pinch precious corbels and cantilevers under cover of darkness. Sovereignty is the management of a community's affairs as the sovereign chooses and wishes. Our own sovereignty has been exercised through Parliament during the years we have been members of the EU, though this is regularly denied. 'Bring back Westminster control,' the Brexiteers demanded.

Then, when their plan was published for EU exit – a government White Paper – they had to admit that Parliament had actually been sovereign all along. One of the choices it had made using its sovereign power was to be a member of the EU. Parliament has regularly made these sorts of choice which often require partnership and negotiation with others. The choices are not boundless. That is simply a consequence of living in the modern world.

Take a choice most English nationalists, especially Conservatives, regard as fundamental, our ability to defend ourselves from threat as the financial resources available to do that dwindle. Our membership of NATO was from the outset as deliberate a pooling of our sovereignty as any other treaty that underpins international co-operation. It has at its heart a commitment to collective defence. Article 5 of the NATO treaty, to which we signed up in 1949, means that if Russia, for example, invades Latvia or Lithuania, we are obliged to go to the aid of those small Baltic states. Go further and consider our ultimate defence, the deterrent capability represented by the Trident fleet, the submarines and their nuclear ballistic missiles. It is probably true that a British Prime Minister does not have to get permission from Washington to fire a missile, nor are we dependent on US codes or satellites. But the degree of technical dependence on the US certainly raises questions about the nature of our independent control of these awesome weapons. Our missiles have to be serviced in the US and some of the components of the warheads are made there. I have always, on balance, supported our nuclear deterrent; getting rid of it has always seemed to me a risky leap in the dark. But I have never believed or argued that it is wholly independent. So while a Life Guard, breast plate, black stallion and all, may be a symbol of our nationhood, I do not believe that the defence forces of which he is a member are manifestations of our ability to make wholly sovereign decisions about our security. This is a fundamental point about sovereignty. In what sense are we sovereign, knowing as we do that we cannot defend ourselves adequately on our own? We have to some extent to depend on others. Our sovereignty is everywhere compromised. It is not an absolute.

What makes 'taking control' an even more absurd aspect of English populist nationalism is the way in which our borders have been increasingly challenged and even laid flat. I have already noted how much this is true in finance. In economics more broadly too: outside the EU our Parliament will still be bound by the nature of the negotiated agreements (almost certainly inferior to present arrangements) that regulate and augment our trade with the world in the future. A member of the WTO, for example, is bound by independent quasi-judicial arbitration. More important still, the recent problems of our steel industry – exposed to competition from huge surpluses at knock-down prices from China – showed the economic limitations of national powers. That is true unless you opt for a degree of international protectionism that would impoverish us and other countries while it lasted, and break down inevitably as technology and greater mobility punched holes in it.

Overall, globalization produces threats and opportunities which individual countries (even the biggest), and therefore their governments and parliaments, cannot tackle on their own. This is the real world, from the environment and climate change to global health, from crime to the illegal arms trade, from sharing water resources to fighting terrorists. Individual governments cannot 'control' these issues themselves. They have to co-operate with others, sharing decision making, recognizing that sovereignty is not some pure, Platonic notion in order to overcome problems which they cannot solve on their own. Think again further, for example, about immigration, the most potent issue in the nationalist Brexit campaign – so potent that it left behind a nasty tinge of racism and a spike in hate crimes. This is not just a short-term issue for Britain and Europe, driven principally by the conflicts in Afghanistan and Syria, whose refugees, it was suggested, were about to land in their thousands on Britain's shores alongside millions of Turks. The real challenge posed by immigration is far bigger; it will affect the whole of Europe. England will not be saved by its Channel, which we must hope does not turn into a watery graveyard like the eastern and southern Mediterranean sea today. What does help us is the European mainland, which lies between us and the source of the problem.

During the nineteenth century as Europe's population grew from one fifth to one quarter of the world's total population, millions left their native countries for other continents. Between 1815 and the 1930s, about 60 million Europeans emigrated. Almost two out of every five people worldwide had European ancestry at the beginning of the First World War. Today, the balance has been completely reversed. Europe's population has fallen steeply to well below one tenth of the global total. As populations elsewhere sky-rocket, this fraction will fall much further. Moreover, the number of the economically active will decline in many countries, with older populations needing outsiders to do more of the hard work in their economies.

Over the last four decades, Egypt's population has increased from 39 million to over 90 million. During a comparable period, the population of Ethiopia more than tripled to 101 million. Nigeria, now home to more than 180 million people, has followed a similar trajectory. Its population is predicted to rise to a half-billion by 2050. During the first half of the twenty-first century, the population of Africa as a whole is expected to grow from just over one billion to 2.5 billion. The world's poorest countries, many but not all of them in Africa, are experiencing the fastest population growth. They have the youngest populations, and all too often are among the most likely to see a breakdown in governance. Failing states, as we have learned, export their problems and their populations.

The resulting flows of people will put developed countries under extreme pressure – nowhere more so than in Europe. Erecting more razor-wire fences will not come close to being an adequate response. The seas around our shores are cemeteries for some but barriers for only a few. Britain will not be able, island though it is, to meet the migration challenge on its own. There will have to be a long-term programme agreed across Europe (and with the United States if possible) which co-ordinates foreign, security and development policies in order to prevent uncontrollable, unmanageable migration – a phenomenon that will lead to many migrant deaths, will stoke xenophobia and will enable politicians on the far right like Marine Le Pen and Nigel Farage to flourish. We will need to agree on how to deal with failed states and help to put them back on their feet. We will have to use our development assistance strategically to help poorer nations to grow and provide their citizens with a reason for staying at home. We also need more aggressive policies to help tackle people-smuggling, supported where necessary by UN Security Council resolutions. We also need to deploy more naval resources in the

Mediterranean (and, in time, in the English Channel) and spend more on border security. This is what 'taking control' should look like in a sensible country: 'taking control' by working effectively with others.

English nationalists have concluded that the institution in which they have hitherto worked most closely with others infringes their liberties and places unnecessary burdens on their shoulders. The gains of EU membership, both those more and less easy to calculate, do not apparently overcome these negatives. There are some elements to this mood which match a rising spirit elsewhere. Most nation states find it easier and more comfortable to identify with and feel loyalty towards their national institutions than with and to those created specifically to manage shared sovereignty and to make the decisions taken in its name more accountable. The 'demos', the popular will in European countries, is based on the nation state; it does not run across borders from Finland to Spain, Poland to Ireland. So nationalists may feel more comfortable with the Brexit vote behind us. It would be easier to be sure about this if we knew what Brexit actually meant. For some time we had to make do with the proposition that 'Brexit means Brexit', which was sufficiently tautological to repel comprehension at every point. 'Breakfast means breakfast' – café crème and croissants, or the full English fry-up with a mug of builder's tea? Even now we will not know what will satisfy nationalists until we have negotiated something whose only known characteristic is that it should not be membership of the EU.

Those who think that parliamentary sovereignty, traduced and undermined by Brussels, can only be restored by leaving the EU will harbour anxieties during the Brexit negotiations about anything that involves compromise. Hardliners in the Conservative Party will not be satisfied by much less than full rupture of our EU relationships. Compromise is not an option. There will be more McCarthyite hunts for public servants who want a deal that meets the national interest rather than right-wing fictions about the way the world works. Whatever the outcome, our Parliament, in which trust has plummeted in the recent past, will be tied up for years dealing with the legislative consequences of departure. I wonder whether our tabloid press will encourage us to look the other way when we discover how little we can actually do on our own.

The government that has to decide what sort of breakfast we want to eat, what sort of Brexit should determine our future, is led today by a Prime Minister who has placed the most enthusiastically dogmatic Brexiteers in the key positions to negotiate our European departure. They will doubtless enjoy their own discoveries of reality. Their work will be no short-term fix, but instead will go on and on, with half a dozen interlocking sets of negotiations. We will first have to negotiate our divorce, and after that the economic ties – presumably some sort of Free Trade Area (FTA) – that we would like to have with the huge European market. Then we will have to work out with the EU the interim arrangements before that FTA comes into force. After that we will need to negotiate national membership of the World Trade Organisation; let us hope that Russia or some other country does not hold up this process. The deal to cut after this will be with the fifty-three countries that currently have FTAs with the EU. Finally, we shall need to work out our ties with the EU on co-operation in areas like policing, aid and foreign policy. EU negotiations are going to be a growth industry in Britain; I hope it will not be the only one.

To guide us through all the complexity and waffle surrounding the years of talks that lie ahead, we should be clear that Theresa May concluded that what the British public had voted for in June 2016 was control over EU immigration and release from any jurisdiction by the European court. There are consequences: not punishment by its remaining members for leaving the EU but a future trading relationship with our biggest market which is bound to be on worse terms than at present. That much at least is clear. We cannot possibly enjoy in future outside the EU a trading relationship as good as, or almost as good as, the one we enjoyed when we were members. The real cost we will pay for leaving the EU is as yet unknown but that it will have to be met is undeniable.

While we attempt to secure the best possible terms for the UK with our biggest market, we will find ourselves arguing a very different unionist case to discourage a Scottish vote for independence in a referendum north of the border. In Scotland, English unionists will be arguing that the country cannot exclude itself from its biggest market and the rule-setting that goes with it. Meantime, the same unionists will be saying that Britain can escape its own biggest market without damage. It does not take great perspicacity to see the contradiction here.

Will the outcome of negotiations close the British divide? What deals will be required to get the trade terms we need that will work? Will the EU give us whatever we ask for – all British take and no give? I doubt whether at the end of the process the blazers will feel that they have got their sepia-tinted country back, whatever that means and whatever that country was. There will be no emergency lever to pull, stopping the world so that the English can get off. There will be no sudden conversion of their children's generation, with its greater enthusiasm for Europe and the wider world, to their own older, grumpier, doleful view of foreigners, or abroad, or of the future.

What of the alienated workers? Will foreigners still be taking the jobs that natives are disinclined to do in England? Will low-productivity, low-paid jobs have been transformed? Will public services be delivering what the blue collars want? Will a probably less prosperous Britain be just what they required? Will national prosperity, national hope, national pizzazz, have been redistributed from London and England's biggest cities to older industrial England? And if not, what next? What sort of populist politics will slouch out of the shadows? What sort of national identity will that represent?

This is a subject which I approach with some foreboding. Look again at the crucial relationship between nationalism and immigration – and, by extension, race and community relations. Two speeches illustrate my argument. The first was Enoch Powell's to the City of London branch of the Royal Society of St George in 1961. He argued that, within Britain, England and the English were the principal focus. Praising English values and history, he set out with a romantic and very literary flourish the case for English nationalism, with its 'roots' in English earth, the earth of England's history. We should seek from our ancestors memorialized in brass and stone 'in many a village church . . . some answer from their inscrutable silence'. He went on, 'Tell us what it is that binds us together; show us the clue that leads through a thousand years, whisper to us the secret of this charmed life of England that we in our time may know how to hold it fast.' He noted that Herodotus reported the surprise of the Athenians, returning to their city after it had been sacked and burned by the Persians, finding one sacred olive tree flourishing among the ruins. Perhaps amidst 'the fragments of demolished glory' the English would find 'one of her own oak trees, standing and growing, the sap still rising from her ancient roots to meet the spring. England herself.' It was a remarkable speech – grand, romantic with patriotic sentiments from the sublime to the ridiculous, but did not set the blood of taxi drivers or West Midlands car workers racing. As a call to a sense of nationalist identity, it was pretty harmless.

Seven years later Mr Powell made another speech, in Birmingham. Again there were classical allusions, this time most notably to the Sybil's prophecy in Book 6 of the *Aeneid*, 'I see wars, horrible wars and the Tiber foaming with much blood.' Why so? Because of mass immigration. And this time the sentiments were heard far and wide. They echoed from factory floors to docks to council estates to saloon bars and gentlemen's clubs. This time Powell had hit the political jackpot. No more olive trees or English oaks. This time the talk was of 'excreta pushed through letter boxes' and 'grinning piccaninnies'. As far as Powell was concerned, what bound the English together now was not memorialized in brass and stone, it was an indigenous people under siege in their own homes.

Is that not invariably true, in our country and in others? Beleaguered nationalism rises up to smite 'the other' – in some countries Jews, in others different minority religious or racial groups, in others still immigrants in general. The outsider both threatens and partly comes to define our identity, and as that begins to happen we lose our foothold on a slippery slope. Values that we thought really did define us now seem tiresome luxuries that are too expensive and damaging to cherish and espouse. Lines that were once drawn with determination suddenly acquire an elastic flexibility. That is how it begins, the erosion of our civic humanity. That is how it begins everywhere. But where, for heaven's sake, does it end?

Perhaps we are about to discover in America. As a self-confessed pessimist, I am surprised to find myself moderately optimistic, that the nationalism which accounts for much of President Trump's support as it did for the Brexit vote, is not (whatever the tone of the inaugural address) going to turn America into an introverted, dangerous force in the world, both economically and in security terms. Nationalism in Britain would be bad for Britain; nationalism in America would be bad for the world as well as for America.

Brexit and Trump do have roots if not in precisely the same ground then certainly in adjoining plots. Will nativism make America great again? America is great already. America can only be enfeebled from within. Any decay and decline will be home grown. The real question is whether America forgets what has made it great: the values of freedom and the rule of law that shaped it and helped it to shape so much of the history of the rest of the world; the culture, technology and scholarship which took humanity to the moon and the masses to the movies; the military and diplomatic powers which gave the world leadership through both storm and tranquillity. America is the only country that matters absolutely everywhere. With American leadership things can get done and sorted out, as they were thanks to Marshall Aid, the Atlantic Charter, NATO and the WTO. Still today there is so much for other Western democracies to work out with Washington. What, for example, should be the relationship (if any) between the values that America and other free societies place on human rights and the day-to-day conduct of foreign policy? Where is force acceptable to deal with a common problem and what legitimization does it require? How best can we deal with failing states, which pose great dangers to us all? When the rest of the world chooses to ignore a problem, can America and its Western allies ignore it too? Without American leadership – as Europe and others should recognize – it will be much more difficult, if not impossible, to solve any of the big problems in our world. And that will hurt America as well as the rest of us. America needs to remember that it cannot go home – not without losing an essential element of its identity and weakening and demeaning itself.

On Britain's side of the ocean, enthusiastic Brexit supporters will surely need to reflect in due course whether we may be buried next to our old friends rather than grow together alongside them. As 'global Britain' quits the EU (its biggest market) it inevitably becomes more dependent on large countries elsewhere, above all America. But this is an America whose government presently stands four square against so much that Westminster still needs and says it wants, from free trade and effective international institutions to a strong EU, albeit one without Britain. The rest of Europe inevitably sees Britain anxious to play lickspittle to President Trump. This is surely not the best way of winning friends in Europe at the outset of a difficult negotiation. But then, we appear these days to be happy to sacrifice European goodwill in return for a supportive tabloid headline or some partisan advantage. Events as much as design have seen Britain apparently give up what has been for decades the centrepiece of our definition of our national interest – holding out one hand to Europe and another to America.

How much this balancing act will be affected by the outcome of the 2017 election will be for some time unclear. But the reasons for calling the election were, as I have suggested, rooted in more domestic considerations, above all the management of the Conservative Party. No one really knows whether Mrs May had been motivated principally by the desire to strengthen herself in standing up to right-wingers who wanted a hard Brexit or in managing more moderate critics who hoped for a more accommodating outcome. What tended to be overlooked in Britain's customarily introverted debate was that the other twenty-seven member states were in the driving seat in the negotiations and had their own domestic politics to take into account.

11

Poobah

Behold the Lord High Executioner
A personage of noble rank and title –
A dignified and potent officer
Whose functions are particularly vital!
Defer, defer
To the Lord High Executioner!

W. S. Gilbert, *The Mikado*

'Il Magnifico'

Title of the Rector of a university in Italy

I was first called a Grand Poobah – indeed one parliamentary sketch writer called me the Poobah's Poobah – when I became Chairman of the BBC Trust in 2012. The intention was to suggest that I had so many exalted offices (though they did not actually include being Lord High Executioner or Lord High Admiral) that I could not possibly give the required time to beating up the lefties at the BBC. There was also a suggestion that this particular post was bound to be held by an establishment figure with metropolitan, liberal sympathies who would connive at the BBC's corruption of the nation's morals and distortion of its politics. It was true that if you aggregated all the things I have done in my life it is, to borrow again from Gilbert and Sullivan, quite a 'little list'. But most of these things – advisory roles, chairmanship of occasional weekend conferences and so on – did not prevent me putting in three to four days a week at the BBC for three years. For a Catholic, as my wife explains, I have been bitten deeply by the Protestant work ethic. It is, for example, a failing that I do not really take weekends off, though I go away for proper holidays during which I usually write, walk or garden.

The Poobah tag was probably most relevant because of a subsidiary meaning originally intended by W. S. Gilbert: it was meant to mock those who take jobs that have impressive titles but do not carry much real authority. That has never really worried me: the jobs have been worth doing even if they packed little executive punch. The one exception was the post which triggered the joke, chairmanship of the BBC Trust, and that was because everyone else thought I could do more than was in fact possible. Actually, I was of the same opinion, as I will shortly describe.

As a constituency MP, I became interested in higher education because we had a first-class new university in Bath. In Hong Kong my interest in universities deepened. As Governor, I was Chancellor of about nine universities, including two that are today in the world's top fifty. This was naturally a great honour, but I thought it was rather an absurd one. I had to remember which cap and robes went with each institution; and luckily only turned up in the wrong outfit once. More importantly, it seemed to me to make more sense to allow universities to choose their own ceremonial heads. But they were not having it. There was a suspicion that I would give up most but hang on to one or two, implicitly creating two divisions of academy. So I left things as they were, did degree-awarding ceremonies at each university every year, and much enjoyed seeing the role that universities were playing as a part of the rite of passage for Hong Kong's youth. Typically, half or more of the students graduating came from families that lived in social housing, and a great number of them came from recent immigrant families. Given the number of those to whom I gave degrees in those days and subsequently I reckon I may have distributed more degrees than any other human being, sometimes in football stadiums, sometimes in a Victorian hall or Wren theatre; there must now have been nearly a hundred such occasions.

When I came back to Europe, it was not long before I was gowned again. Our eldest daughter had been very happily a student at Newcastle University. As a result I had been to the university several times and had given one or two lectures there. In 1999, I was invited to become Chancellor and responded enthusiastically.

University chancellorships differ enormously. One thing common to all is that the Chancellor does not actually run the university. As Harold Macmillan, one of my predecessors as Chancellor of Oxford, used to say, 'Everyone knows that the Vice-Chancellor actually runs the university, but if you didn't have a Chancellor you couldn't have a Vice-Chancellor.' The role begins with ceremonial functions like presenting degrees. It ranges far and wide beyond that from chairing committees, to fund-raising, to endless speech making to alumni and others, to giving general advice.

Newcastle is an excellent research-based university, one of the prestigious Russell Group of twenty-four British academies which together earn about two thirds of all UK research grants and contract income. Newcastle itself is a tough and handsome city; its university has a number of very strong research areas (like medicine) and plays an important role in promoting the north-east of England, which has had to adjust to wave after wave of generational change in industry. The high point of every year for me was the graduation ceremonies, which mostly took place in July, invariably in the sort of weather which has so many Geordies heading for holidays anywhere that can guarantee sunshine. At the end of each ceremony, held in the rather gloomy main hall of the university, I would give a little speech to the new graduates and to their families and friends who had come in their summer-best outfits to celebrate the success of their children. My speech usually referred to the underfunding of higher education in Britain, despite which, I noted, we had the second-best system in the world. The general enthusiastic support for these remarks contrasted with the continuing low priority given to higher education and research in the allocation of public funds. We had paid for the massive and welcome expansion of higher education, especially after the Robbins Report in 1963, by reducing the funding for each student. Universities managed by depressing salaries – traditional informal comparisons with the civil service were simply abandoned. At the same time, workloads were increased and facilities degraded. The Treasury called all this an increase in university productivity. Given the importance that families attached to higher education, I never quite understood why universities had not been more successful in putting their case for more support. Talking to the students who were graduating, I was struck by the large proportion who were still the first in their family to go on to higher education.

One of the additional tasks taken on by universities in the last few years has been to go out to schools, in and beyond their own regions, to try to broaden access, persuading young people from poor backgrounds and indifferent schools to apply for university. Newcastle did a lot of this: for example, with well-run summer schools every year. Those who passed through these special courses were able to enter the university with slightly lower qualifications than would otherwise have been required. The scheme worked well: those who benefited from it generally did excellently in their university studies. The biggest problem for the university was the poor quality of much of the secondary education in the north-east of England and the low aspiration levels of school leavers. There was an additional problem for Newcastle in my years there which made it difficult to meet the government's target for social balance at the university (with bad attendant publicity). Newcastle had an excellent classics department. There were more former private than state pupils studying classics precisely because the availability of A Level teaching in classics in state schools was so limited. It would of course have been madness for Newcastle for this reason to run down or close a first-class department in the university. Though if it had done so, it could easily have met the government's social-balance target.

Newcastle faced the same financial challenges as other British universities. There are four ways that universities can be funded – by taxpayer support, by private benefaction, by research and grant income, and by contributions from students. We now use all four methods. As taxpayers we are less generous to higher education and research than the USA (and several other OECD countries) and private philanthropy is of course much less than in America. Our universities are excellent at earning research income, though this may now be threatened in the medium and long term by our departure from the EU. While the evidence is mixed, the increase in student fees does not seem so far to have discouraged young people from poorer backgrounds from applying to go to universities; indeed, it looks as though proportionally more deprived youngsters from England have applied for university than from Scotland, where university education for local pupils is free. But whether the huge loans that students have taken out will ever be repaid in full, or anything like it, seems rather doubtful.

Newcastle had a more simple political culture than Oxford. The Vice-Chancellor could (with some diplomatic care) make decisions, pull levers and get things to happen. At Oxford, one of the greatest universities in the world, there is a very different political culture. I became Chancellor in 2003 after the death of Roy Jenkins, and until 2009 looked after Newcastle as well with no conflict of interest but a lot of work. I was approached to stand for the post at Oxford by two eminent Balliol Fellows, Adam Roberts and Dennis Noble, who I think had heard me give a lecture at the university not long before. They asked if I would throw my hat in the ring in what is these days a contested election in which all graduates of the university can vote, choosing someone to do the job for life. (I used to say 'like the Pope and the Dalai Lama.' Nowadays, after Pope Benedict's resignation, I can only mention a comparison with Tibet's spiritual leader, which probably further annoys the easily annoyed Chinese foreign ministry.) Adam and Dennis put together an impressive list of supporters and, come the two days of voting (in person only), I felt fortunate to win against a distinguished field of opponents. It was a serious campaign. One of my opponents had a PR firm in tow. All four candidates had websites and we all subjected ourselves to a lot of press and university interest. The campaign was more about personality than policy, though there was a side debate about tuition fees.

Oxford democracy does not end with the election of the Chancellor. Indeed, it barely starts there. University politics can be a complex and bloody pursuit as those who have combined public service and academic careers often attest. Henry Kissinger was always clear that Harvard, where he had been a professor, had been a very good training ground for Richard Nixon's Washington. Before him, Woodrow Wilson, when he retired from the presidency of Princeton University to run for the governorship of New Jersey (he later became President of the USA), announced his resignation with the statement that at his age he thought it was time to give up active politics. Oxford University even more than most other universities depends on the mobilization of consent among a community of scholars, some of whom inevitably view any deviation from what has happened in the past with suspicion. They are not always wrong. The old Oxford joke – 'How many Oxford dons does it take to change a light bulb?' 'What do you mean, change?' – is unfair. The university usually gets to the right runway eventually, though the journey sometimes involves a great deal of circling the desired destination first, sometimes in heavy cloud. But the question, 'What do you think the university's strategy should be?', has first of all to deal with the primary question for some academics of whether it is appropriate for the university to have a strategy at all.

Dealing with exceptionally clever people, many of them naturally holding strong opinions, requires an exquisitely sure touch – and occasionally, just to get some essential decisions taken, a Vice-Chancellor has to risk breaking some crockery. What makes the governance of this democratic academy more difficult still is that the university consists of almost two score of independent colleges with (in many cases) centuries of history, their own treasure chests and their own institutional personalities, from people's communes (think of Paris in 1871) to guided democracy to theocratic state. There would be no university without the colleges, autonomous as they are, and they usually recognize that the reverse is also true. They provide a home and a real community for undergraduates and resident graduates. This is vital but the cost only amounts to about 10 per cent of overall university financing. Yet the colleges have great authority, not least as the principal repository of alumni memories and often affection. So Oxford, with its very strong colleges, is one of the few institutions where power does not necessarily follow the money. The colleges and the university have to work very closely together, and a university leader has to twist the Rubik cube this way and that in order to align the various parties.

My predecessor, Roy Jenkins, used to say that the chancellorship (in which, as he put it, 'impotence was assuaged by magnificence') took up a quarter of his time and gave him half his enjoyment. I would marginally increase these figures. My principal preoccupations have not changed much in thirteen years. First, we still have to make the liberal as well as the utilitarian case for higher education.

We tend to forget about the former and argue the case for spending on universities and research almost entirely in terms of alleged GDP effects, a proposition which is often risible. We pay too little attention to the learning experience of students. The government even appears to think that you can apply a matrix, which they have designed, to measure learning. They often act as though the aim of pedagogy was simply to transfer information. This was presumably the aim at Trump University, now defunct, which offered courses in asset management and wealth creation. But universities are for learning, not 'credentialing', or enhancing future earning capacity. Students are not simply customers in an academic supermarket. As for research, pushing back the frontiers of knowledge may (almost certainly will) improve our national competitiveness. We do not, however, regard the seminal achievements of the Cavendish laboratories as a central part of our national story in Britain primarily because they raised Britain's growth rate. We are not proud about the development of penicillin in the laboratories of the Radcliffe Infirmary because of the money it brought in. The twenty volumes of the *Oxford English Dictionary* are not scored in the national accounts. All these examples of scholarship help make us a civilized society and play their part in the improvement of the quality of life everywhere. Our scholarship is a central part of our national achievement and legacy.

Second, given the constrained public funding of higher education, we have to raise more money from philanthropy in order to fund the best research and to give the maximum help to students from poorer backgrounds so that access to what we can offer is genuinely needs-blind. In philanthropy we still lag far behind the United States. The same is true of public support for research. Harvard gets 80 per cent of its research income from government; Oxford receives 40 per cent and this is part of the highest research income of any European university. We are getting much better at attracting private generosity; particularly gratifying is that the support from old members has increased steeply. Since we began our serious public appeal for funds a decade ago we have netted – colleges and university together – well above £2.5 billion. We shall need to be even better at this fund-raising if we lose access to EU research grants, as well as the disruption of research collaboration after Brexit.

Broadening access without lowering entry standards is a third priority. Universities should not be persuaded that degrading their own standards is the right response to the problems of parts of our secondary education system. They should accept their share of responsibility for promoting social inclusion in order to give all young people the opportunity of as full an education as can benefit them, redressing disadvantage and tapping the potential of the whole community. Yet it would be demeaning to have two sorts of students, those who got their university places on merit, others who were chosen on the basis of postal code selection. Oxford like other universities – more than most others – has a far-reaching programme to try to overcome the poverty of aspiration in some secondary schools and to help prepare students from indifferent schools for admission to our courses. We can and will do even more, helped as we are by imaginative donors like Michael Moritz and Harriet Heyman. But lowering the quality in Britain of what are still some of the best universities in the world would not do anything to reduce inequalities in our society which are a political, social and moral reproach to us all.

Fourth, we should firmly reject the treatment of the humanities at our universities as an optional add-on indulgence. We must support the humanities not because of some alleged addition to our national GDP but because they provide us with a fuller understanding of our world and of one another. Because they enable us to think creatively and critically. Because they inform our moral sense. Because they teach us to love jazz and Beethoven, Raphael and Cézanne, a Shakespeare sonnet and a Flaubert novel. Because they teach us about life and beauty and love and death. Because we are human.

Fifth, the controversy on some American and British campuses in recent years about freedom of speech and about the bounds of intellectual inquiry make it imperative to make again and again the case for universities, as important institutions in free and plural societies, bulwarks against the humbugging forces of populism and identity politics. Universities must themselves act as purveyors of liberal values, encouraging free speech, free inquiry, open debate and tolerance within the usual bounds of legality, decency and mutual courtesy. They should not allow their students and teachers to live within silos which enable them to avoid challenge and debate. The academy is not, as I have said, an educational supermarket, nor is it a collection of safe havens where inquiry and debate are prohibited lest they cause offence. At Oxford, we had forceful arguments about these issues in the context of the money left to the university for the support of international students by Cecil Rhodes, the buccaneering imperial adventurer whose views on race and whose commercial rapacity were deeply unpleasant but pretty typical of his times. Nelson Mandela had worked with us at Oxford to broaden the support from these funds to help more black African students. It did not seem sensible to him or to us to put the opinions and career of Cecil Rhodes centre stage in an age which should comprehend them but would (quite rightly) never condone them. I am wholly in favour of understanding history from the broadest and best-informed point of view; I am not in favour of rewriting it from a stance of contemporary prejudice or political opinion.

It has been a privilege to be associated with at least two British institutions – Oxford and the BBC – which are world-class. We do not have so many such institutions in Britain to brag about as to be careless about their continuing welfare and vitality. When I was approached in 2011 about becoming Chairman of the BBC Trust several friends warned me that it was an impossible job because of the governance structure that had been put in place after the uproar over one broadcast during the Iraq War. The irony is that this was just about the only occasion during the build-up to that awful nightmare when the government was correct and the media wrong. I recalled that some well-meaning friends had also advised me against going to Hong Kong, to Belfast to chair the Policing Commission and to Brussels to be a European Commissioner. Why should I listen to them this time, having greatly enjoyed all these jobs which they had thought would up-end me? I am stubborn and love challenges, and have always been inclined to heed Ronnie Knox's advice to 'do the most difficult thing'.

In any case, I was in love with the BBC. It was where I'd hoped to begin my career. It was and is one of this country's greatest institutions. Merely to rattle off a list of its overwrought and ubiquitous critics is to make a very powerful case for defending it to the death. The BBC developed organically, becoming a central part of the public realm without being part of the state, a position Edmund Burke would have celebrated. It is not a way of making up for market failure, as some contend, but a core part of our civic humanism and of our shared, multi-ethnic and multi-racial citizenship. Its role is underpinned by a common British set of values and a shared sense of mutual responsibility. It is a key part of the dialogue in our common British conversation and a great global asset, with polls suggesting that its World Service (operating on too tight a shoe string) does more for Britain's image overseas than anything else we do apart perhaps from royal ceremonials and the occasional deployment of our armed forces. The Trumpification of news ('alternative facts') should encourage us to invest a lot more in its invaluable news service. Aung San Suu Kyi, the Burmese democrat, is not the only world leader who has enthused to me about its importance in her life. At the UN in New York, many of the diplomats turn on the BBC World Service first thing when they get up in the morning.

There have always been problems of governance at the BBC, partly I suspect because it was primarily the creation of one huge, egotistical figure, Lord Reith, who was not prepared to be managed by anyone. During the Second World War the controversy often concerned what Penelope Fitzgerald in her lovely novel about the BBC, *Human Voices*, described as its responsibility for 'the strangest project of the war, of any war, that is telling the truth'. For years the BBC operated under a Chairman and Board of Governors. They were sometimes a bit rum; a list of them was a roll call of British establishment history in all its exotic tribalism. In the 1980s the caftan-wearing George Howard, owner of the castle of the same name, was succeeded as Chairman by Stuart Young, a chartered accountant and director of Tesco, so it was a broad church. But, by and large, the governors protected broadcasters from external interference with only occasional blood baths and calamities. With just the odd blip (usually an editorial slip in the news organization), the BBC maintained a fine record. It was widely viewed and listened to and it was trusted; and BBC independence was unquestioned. A consequence of this was that BBC executives occasionally displayed an ingrained reluctance to accept any higher authority at all; even the Holy Trinity – for some, especially the Holy Trinity – would probably have been deemed insufficient.

To try to improve alleged failings in governance when the BBC's

Charter was revised in 2007, the governing body and the executive were formally separated. This seemed a good idea to many, though not all, at the time; it should be a reminder that institutional changes should always be approached with considerable care. There is usually a good reason why things which have been around for some time are still there. The BBC Trust was set up to regulate the broadcaster and to represent those who paid the licence fee. It was to press for higher standards and greater distinctiveness in programming. But there was a confusion of roles. Was the Trust a regulator or a cheerleader? This was partly a matter of rhetoric. It was supposed to be both. If the BBC did well, the Trust said so; if not, it pointed this out. No problem surely? Well, it was not quite so simple. There was also a bigger difficulty. The Chairman of the Trust could call herself or himself Chairman of the BBC, but was she or he really in the Chair? Actually, no. The Chairman of the Trust was neither an executive nor a non-executive chairman of the whole organization. He or she was chairman of the regulator. The BBC itself had an executive board with its own chairman, the Director-General. But if anything went wrong the Trust's Chairman tended to be in the firing-line. It was a very straightforward governance muddle. To make the position clear about the supposed separation of powers, the Trust was housed separately from the rest of the organization. So, among other things, Trust members missed out on the gossip and informal exchange of views so important if you wanted to know what was going on. A friend of mine calls such communications latrine-ograms. Moreover, as I have noted, the government had been persuaded – by whom? – that the Director-General should also be allowed to chair a BBC board, containing both executives and non-executives. So where did the buck stop, and did the place at which it stopped correspond to where authority really lay? Who decided editorial issues? The DG – absolutely correctly. Who decided on money and broad strategy? This was surely rather an important question given the Trust's remit to represent the licence fee payers and public controversy about levels of BBC pay.

The DG's board had a remuneration committee chaired when I went to the Trust by a distinguished financier who also chaired Barclays, a bank whose views on the subject did not encompass frugality.

At my first lunch meeting with the executive board at Canary Wharf (for which I arrived by Tube, which seemed to slightly discombobulate some of these directors) I raised the question of both the pay and the number of senior BBC managers. Noting the salary of the outstanding director of the British Museum (it was at that time, I think, about £180,000 a year), I asked how many BBC executives were paid this or more and how this could be justified, given the extraordinary achievements of the comparator whom I had mentioned. There was general horror at this Maoist remark. The Trust had for some time been fighting to contain pay awards (the scale of which was a hangover, I suppose, from the previous governance structure) and to cut costs. While it could say 'yes' or 'no' to the aggregate budgets, its say over how they were built up was confused. Eventually the Trust got a reasonable grip on pay and budgetary matters; we introduced, for example, a cap on the multiple of top pay to median salaries. We were still, however, blamed for past sins. This confusion was later used rather cynically, but effectively, to discredit the Trust in front of the Public Accounts Committee of the House of Commons.

In retrospect, the BBC Trust model of governance would have worked better had the Trust avoided drilling down into too much detail about what the executives were doing and had the executives not run for cover behind the Trust when stormy weather arrived. In the meantime the Trust did some excellent work (especially on programme quality and competition issues) and had hard-working and always harassed staff and a director who behaved (to my great pleasure) like an old-fashioned Permanent Secretary. Nicholas Kroll was also funny, well-read and reasonable almost to a fault. I think that we might have been able to make all this work quite well if the later Director-General, Tony Hall, had been there when I arrived. But I did not have a particularly close relationship with Mark Thompson, the DG on my arrival. It is not in anyone's interest to exchange tittle-tattle about what went wrong. There is no shortage of such books by former BBC executives and overpaid clapped-out divas. Sometimes relationships just do not work out, which is one reason why I have always thought them more important than institutional tinkering. I reckoned that Mark Thompson was very clever; he clearly believed that he was the cleverest person at the BBC. I knew, everyone knew, that BBC executives had undermined my predecessor, Sir Michael Lyons, and I was reluctant to go the same way. The DG was plainly the operational boss of the organization in every possible respect, dominating meetings and discussions. But I never discovered who knew about, or was responsible for, things when they went wrong. Macavity – and there is no one like Macavity – was never there. A controversial programme was broadcast, for example, or commissioned and then dropped; casualties mounted; Macavity knew nothing about it. Whatever the turbulence in the atmosphere, Macavity always – lucky fellow – landed on his feet. This doubtless took skill as well as good luck. Anyway, it was a pity that Mark and I could not make things work better.

Mark Thompson's successor, George Entwistle, chosen unanimously by the Trust, was an exceptionally decent man and a broadcaster with a fine record. Unfortunately he was swept away by the tornadoes that blew through the BBC when the dreadful activities of Jimmy Savile were revealed and controversy blew up over whether the BBC had self-censored a programme opening up this dark chapter in its history. This row was exacerbated later by an appalling error in a *Newsnight* programme on child abuse. One aspect of this affair is worth noting, an example of the problems which a Chairman would have faced even under previous governance arrangements, and which certainly arose when there was an explicit bar to the Trust's Chairman having any editorial role. During the morning on the day of the broadcast, one of my staff saw in the blogosphere that *Newsnight* intended to allege that a former Conservative Party treasurer, Alistair McAlpine, was going to be named as part of a paedophile ring in Wales. I was told about this wholly implausible story and said that I must phone the DG to get him to intervene in the editing of the programme. I was quickly persuaded that this would be quite wrong, and the news that I had stopped a programme – an ex-chairman of the Conservative Party, about a former treasurer – would be leaked very rapidly. This was wholly convincing. In the event, I telephoned George to ask whether he was happy that *Newsnight*, which had lost its editor (over a dropped programme on Savile), was being properly run under adult supervision. He assured me on this, giving the names of the two senior executives who were looking after the programme. It went ahead, and was a disaster. George fell on his sword, without any discouragement from the Trust. As is often the case with inquiries, the media turbulence over the setting up of those into Savile was far greater than attended their findings. (Much the same seemed to be true later over the Chilcot Inquiry into the Iraq War). George was the principal casualty of the whole business, a largely innocent party in a grisly affair. I had never known such a media storm, partly a consequence of the inherent horrible newsworthiness of the stories and partly of the commercial interest of some of the print media concerned, which were taking a hammering at the time over phone tapping. The BBC quite properly faithfully reported all the 'ins' and 'outs' of these matters, and George was mercilessly interrogated on its *Today* programme. This was its job.

After George's departure, we rapidly turned to Tony Hall, and managed to persuade him to leave his job running the Royal Opera House. He quickly restored calm, continued to cut excess and reduce overheads to one of the lowest figures in the public sector, and presided over a Corporation that broadcast an extraordinary range of superb radio and television programmes for a fraction of the money that goes to other major broadcasters. The BBC Board would have been sensible to appoint him when he first applied for the job in 1999–2000.

These were not, then, my happiest days. The job was ten times more difficult than I ever thought it would be – a sort of non-chairman Chairman, Poobah cheerleader for (so it was claimed) a bloated lefty organization. How could one explain to its vociferous critics that it was still regarded by the British public as one of the institutions of which it felt most proud? Its trustworthiness as a news organization was and is as embarrassingly large as a Warsaw Pact election result, so much greater than that of any of the newspapers that attack it and therefore of course unreported by them. In 2016–17, the government decided to recast the governance structure, passed the regulatory function to the telecoms regulator OFCOM, and established a unitary board under the banker Sir David Clementi, who had himself proposed this model of management. The biggest problem that he and his colleagues will face is the extremely tough financial settlement within which the BBC is going to have to operate. This will put it at an increasing disadvantage with its commercial competitors: for example, the online broadcasters and content creators such as Netflix. An early challenge will be whether the BBC can hang on to sports coverage, given the amounts spent on it by commercial channels and the limited BBC budget. At precisely the time that we need a public service broadcaster ever more, the financing of the best one in the world will be under greater threat. The Russians, Chinese, Murdoch–Foxes and others must think we are mad, and are doubtless smiling quietly.

Walking to my BBC office in the spring of 2014 from the Tube station at Great Portland Street, I found myself increasingly having to stop for breath. (I would sometimes regret that I had given up my chauffeured car, not least since, when I surrendered it to save money, it was immediately snapped up by a senior BBC executive.) Even mild exertion was tiring me. I decided that I must report this at my next medical check-up. Well before this I was rushed into the A&E Department at the Chelsea and Westminster hospital in the middle of the night, and saved from a serious heart attack by a beautiful philosophy graduate turned doctor from Somerville College, Oxford. I was then transferred to the Royal Brompton hospital, where I had angioplasty for the second time (the first had been over twenty years before in Hong Kong). I also had a coronary bypass operation using keyhole surgery. (If only such meticulous science had been available when my parents could have benefited from it.) This was the NHS at its best, great British doctors and a team of paramedics and nurses almost entirely drawn, as it happened, from the rest of the EU. Was my condition caused by stress? Partly, it seemed. 'Stress isn't necessarily bad for you,' said one doctor, 'unless you are not enjoying it.' I wasn't enjoying it. I resigned from the BBC Trust in May 2014 and got my life back.

There was one other Poobah experience, one with a clerical dimension. In this case, though, there was no doubt where authority lay, at least in theory. In the late summer of 2014, after some wonderful months of recuperation in France, I had a telephone call from the office of Cardinal Pell, an Australian archbishop brought to Rome from Sydney by Pope Francis to clean up and reform the finances and management of the Vatican. This was no small task, like trying to cut back one of those huge garden brambles which colonize another plant. Others had tried their hand at it in the past. Pope John XXIII concentrated on a religious renewal of the Church, opening its windows to the twenty-first century. He simply bypassed senior members of the Vatican court, listening to and following the advice of outsiders. He was both holy and wily, and took with him to St Peter's throne a huge amount of experience accumulated as a Vatican diplomat. His successor, Pope Paul VI, an intellectual sufficiently liberal to have been denied his cardinal's hat by Pope Pius XII, originally considered just moving out of the Vatican and operating as Bishop of Rome from the cathedral church of St John Lateran. Alas, he was persuaded against this idea. Pope Paul was a Hamlet-like figure, a tortured liberal who was torn to shreds by critics as he tried (successfully) to avoid schism in the Church. On the receiving end on one occasion of a long lecture during an audience from Graham Greene, he leant forward, touched the author on the knee and said politely, 'But Mr Greene, I too am a Catholic.'

No pope should be expected to embrace spreadsheets and organograms. Pope Francis turned to Pell, a good and tough manager with nothing to lose. Cardinal Pell asked me whether I would contribute to his work by chairing a committee to reorganize the Vatican's media, an operation which is large, expensive, of variable quality and not obviously focused on delivering news in the way that most people receive it today.

I had had some experience of working with the Vatican before when David Cameron asked me after the election in 2010 to take over the co-ordination in Britain for the visit of Pope Benedict later that same year. At an early meeting at Buckingham Palace, he had picked up (doubtless from officials) that the arrangements were in a bit of a mess. Gordon Brown and Tony Blair had persistently invited Pope Benedict to visit Britain, but when he agreed to do so they seemed to lose interest in seeing that the visit went smoothly. A very good and decent Scottish Labour minister, Jim Murphy, was nominally in charge but had to work through a committee of ministers, with no agreed budget and with insufficient input from the very professional civil servants in the Foreign Office who normally organized official visits. Pressed by Downing Street to agree to take on the task myself, I initially declined or at least begged for time to consider the offer. The next day I was telephoned to be informed that the Queen had been told that I had agreed to do it. Thus bounced, I made three conditions: first, that the hierarchy in England and Scotland were happy about this arrangement; second, that I could do it on my own, with no committee of ministers, answerable only to the Prime Minister; and, third, that I could have a modest budget which I would not exceed. David Cameron agreed immediately and was as good as his word. I worked with an excellent team of officials, including the capable Foreign Office visits team, led by an outstanding Permanent Secretary, Helen Ghosh.

In the event, Pope Benedict's visit – to Edinburgh, Glasgow, London and Birmingham – went well, despite the criticism that preceded it and some of the complexities of organization. This was partly because the Pope's own gentle nature and the intellectual quality of his sermons and talks were so impressive. The pontiff whom people actually met – a gentle and courtly intellectual – was very different from the tough authoritarian whom the media led them to expect. Negotiating one or two issues between the Vatican and the First Minister of Scotland (Alex Salmond) was painful, and not because of anyone in Rome. Success was pretty well guaranteed as soon as the Pope was greeted by enthusiastic crowds in Edinburgh. For me, the high point was an Evensong in Westminster Abbey, with a Church of England liturgy at its best, the Pope and the Archbishop of Canterbury, Rowan Williams, leading a procession down the aisle as the great ecumenical hymn 'The Church's One Foundation' thundered out. I enjoyed some Vatican officials' bemused and rather belated recognition that Britain was not a God-less zone and had a diverse, active and joyful faith community, including the Catholic component. National stereotypes are interesting; perhaps the British have an equally stereotypical view of the Irish, or Italians.

With this experience to encourage me, I gave a quick affirmative reply to Cardinal Pell. The job was not particularly challenging intellectually. Cardinal Pell had been given a very rational and sweeping set of proposals for media reform by McKinsey's. The trouble was that they envisaged cost savings by extensive redundancies, not something which Pope Francis would contemplate. McKinsey's showed both the good side and the more questionable side of consulting work, but they provided a sense of the direction in which we should move. We duly provided a well-constructed plan after just over a year of regular monthly meetings by a group which comprised some insiders with a majority of very good outside experts from the wider Church. We proposed pulling a compartmentalized organization into a modern media operation targeting news gathering and reporting through the channels which audiences actually used.

Visiting Rome every three or four weeks was a particular bonus. I enjoyed seeing Vatican officials at prayer and even at work. Like all bureaucracies, the Vatican has its own culture, which was denounced in a galvanizing lecture by the Pope at Christmas in 2014. One of his milder criticisms was that it suffered from 'spiritual Alzheimer's'. My own three principal observations were, first, that there are parts of the Catholic Church's civil service that work conspicuously well. This is particularly true of the Church's diplomatic service, which is linguistically far more gifted than those of most nation states and with a wealth of experience of some of the world's most dangerous hot spots. If you want to know the position in an African war zone or the human rights situation in a Latin American country, you will not get a much better read-out than from these diplomats. There are others working elsewhere in the Vatican who are very professional. The secretary of my working group was an Irish monsignor, now a bishop in the Culture dicastery. Paul Tighe is an expert on social media, full of insights into what is going on in Rome, extremely competent and proof that you can be amusing company while also being teetotal. Paul helped make my time in Rome especially enjoyable and reminded me that some of the best diplomats and European officials I have worked with over the years were from Ireland. Working with him also made me realize, once again, that you go on making friends deep down the years.

Second, the Vatican works for the whole Church; it has of course done so since the beginning of its existence in Rome. It would be surprising if the Italian ambience did not impregnate almost every aspect of its existence. I know little of Italian bureaucracy, too little to generalize. But I have never heard anyone, not even an Italian, praising it, though we have often been told that Benito Mussolini made the trains run on time.

Third, as an enthusiastic supporter of Pope Francis and his efforts to get the Church to behave, as he has suggested, more like a generous, forgiving pastor and less like a stern, finger-wagging authoritarian, I was keen to see him close at hand, something that literally happens if you stay or work in the Vatican hostel – the Santa Marta – that he has made his home. It is simple, though not austere, a newish building, white walls, holy pictures, no sign of a television, a beautiful chapel for the Pope himself, and little noise save the swish of passing habits. Visitors were regularly surprised to have breakfast or lunch in the canteen there and be confronted by the large figure of The Man in White. What of the others there – the assembled hierarchy of the international Church? It would be a surprise if some of them were not biding their time, riding out this Franciscan storm, hoping that things will return to the 'status quo ante' once age or infirmity take their toll of this remarkable man. 'Basta,' he said to the archbishops who were trying to drape the fur-lined stole around his shoulders when presenting him to the crowds in St Peter's Square after his election. 'The carnival is over.' Scolded by his bodyguards for accepting a drink of the South American herbal drink *mate* from a group of pilgrims in St Peter's Square one day on the grounds that it could be poison, Pope Francis responded, 'What's the matter? They were pilgrims, not cardinals.' We do not really anticipate Renaissance behaviour from the Curia, yet the Pope must know how much opposition ending the carnival has engendered. I do not myself think that turning the clock back to pre-Franciscan days of rigid certainty and ubiquitous scolding is an acceptable option for most Catholics. Pope Francis is a man who displays enormous simplicity and humility in face-to-face meetings, and on more public occasions hugely impressive grace and authority.

What happened to Cardinal Pell and to our report on reforming the media organization? The cardinal, a very clever man with right-wing views on most issues, has been pushed to one side, weakened by the way he allegedly handled child abuse allegations in Australia in the past and by his candid and too public assessment of the quality of Italian management. While not agreeing with all of his opinions, I admired his intellect and thought he provided exactly the sort of heavy construction equipment that you always need to get any change in organizations where the bureaucratic cement has been setting for centuries. As for our report, it was accepted in full by Pope Francis and his inner circle of cardinals. Implementation was then given to a team of Italians. I hope to be pleasantly surprised. *Que sera, sera.*

I have focused in this chapter on the public sector responsibilities that I have taken on. I have also enjoyed working with a number of not-for-profit bodies, particularly Medical Aid for Palestinians and the International Crisis Group, a conflict prevention organization where I enjoyed my role as a co-chairman for several years. This excellent team was led by the veteran US diplomat Tom Pickering and the intelligent and tireless former Australian Foreign Minister Gareth Evans. We had a small team of clever foreign-policy experts, who added a wide range of insights to the work of conventional diplomats.

My experience in Rome, Oxford and the BBC taught me that they have nothing new to learn about politics from Westminster. Indeed, I suspect there may be a higher proportion of herbivores in the latter than in any of the other three. I have certainly worked in more danger-ous environments than the House of Commons. These days, as a member of the House of Lords, the Elysian fields of the British Consti-tution, I do not feel threatened by anything except the voluminous evidence of the imminence of mortality.

12

Violence and Faith

Alexander died, Alexander was buried, Alexander
returneth to dust, the dust is earth; of Earth we made loam;
and why of that loam whereto he was converted might they not
stop a beer barrel? Imperious Caesar, dead and turn'd to clay,
Might stop a hole to keep the wind away.

William Shakespeare, *Hamlet*

What after all is a good Catholic? One who keeps the observance of course but then? . . . there are times, I must confess,
when I think there can be too much faith. Faith excludes
humanity. I have seen faith elevated and distorted, so that only
the Church was remembered and Christ forgotten.

Alan Massie, *A Question of Loyalties*

I am a part of all that I have met;
Yet all experience is an arch wherethro'
Gleams that untravell'd world whose margin fades
For ever and forever when I move.

Alfred, Lord Tennyson, 'Ulysses'

Whatever our identity, or our shoe size for that matter, we all have
one thing in common. Sooner or later, like Alexander and Caesar,
and of course poor jesting Yorick, we are all dead and 'turn'd to
clay'. Serb and Croat, Christian and Jew, Sunni and Shia, president,
pope, pauper and pandar: for all it is the same – dust to dust, ashes to
ashes. Without being excessively morbid, one tends to think about
this rather more as one strides (or is wheeled) beyond the Psalmist's

'three score years and ten'. A friend of mine turns first every morning in the newspapers to the obituary columns, not to check that he is still alive but to have a look at the average ages of the recently departed. On a good day, there is a comfortable gap between his own age and the deathly median. But sometimes he has to concede that by that day's tally he should have been dead for years. When I sent a copy of my last book, *What Next?*, to the Duke of Edinburgh (who was the Chancellor of Cambridge University while I had the same office at Oxford), he wrote back, ' "What Next?" When you are my age there's only one answer.'

The answer can take a long time to arrive, though arrive it surely will. Some wish to speed the process, others to delay it for as long as they can; most probably try not to think too much of the train running inexorably towards the most terminal terminus of all. No leaves on the line, no snow on the points, can long delay the train's inevitable arrival.

Bette Davis once said, 'Old age ain't no place for sissies.' True enough. Many reckon, as I do, that if I'd known before what I know now about the bits of me that no longer work so well, I would have taken better care of them – knees and shoulders that creak from tennis, a paunch that threatens to bring on diabetes. Nevertheless, modern medicine – in my case cardiac surgery and statins – keeps many of us going longer than was once the case, and these days we most likely have our own teeth, no longer the in-and-out variety of our parents' and grandparents' day. I recall the mug on my grandmother's bedside table with its white frothing liquid and a row of dentures lurking like a shark's fin just below the water line.

As medicine and our health service keep us on the right side of death's door, many of us worry whether we will know who we are all the way to the end. There are 850,000 people with dementia in the UK, over 5 million in the USA, nearly 44 million in the world. This is not just a modern preoccupation. Juvenal called dementia 'worse than all physical loss – forgetting slaves' names, or the face of a friend who came last night to supper, the children one parented and named'. Jonathan Swift reckoned much the same when thinking about his decline, in 'Verses on the Death of Dr Swift':

Besides, his memory decays,
He recollects not what he says;
He cannot call his friends to mind;
Forgets the place where last he dined . . .

My wife sat next to the distinguished neuroscientist the late Lord Walton at a university dinner. He told her about a new test to check whether a patient was suffering from the early stages of Alzheimer's. He told her what the questions were. 'And what are they?' I asked her the next day. 'I've forgotten,' she replied.

Maurice Ravel, attending the recording of one of his own works after losing his memory, asked anxiously, 'Remind me of the composer's name.' Cicero thought that you could work away at keeping your wits in reasonably good order, like Tony Benn writing his voluminous diary. That approach produces all sorts of planned retirement occupations, some of which we may be better at than others. A brain surgeon explained to Margaret Atwood that he intended to take up writing on retirement. 'What a coincidence,' she replied. 'When I retire I'm going to be a brain surgeon.'

How much does the imminence of death terrify us? The very idea of propinquity should not, I suppose, be part of the question. Death is always imminent, as Somerset Maugham reminded us in one of his most absorbing stories. A Baghdad merchant sends his servant to market. The servant returns terrified. Death had jostled him in the crowded marketplace. The servant borrows his master's horse so he can take refuge for the night in Samarra, well away from Death. The merchant then goes down to the market and scolds Death for making a threatening gesture at his servant. 'It wasn't threatening,' replies Death. 'I was just surprised to see him in Baghdad because I have an appointment with him tonight in Samarra.'

My mother died of a heart attack in her sleep, my stepfather too. My father died of a heart attack as well, but after a car crash. They were not very old and would not have expected their appointments in Samarra. Now, if I wake in the night from time to time with chest pains, I first reach for the indigestion tablets; when they work I know that my own appointment is not yet due. It worries me, but I don't panic. I suppose this is partly because of my lifetime's comfort blanket. As a Christian, I believe in an afterlife. I admire the bravery of those who do not have this to sustain them, who may have allowed, even encouraged, their rational faculties to shred this hopeful mystery. It has been my solace from childhood to old age. So, though not at all Welsh, I sing with gusto:

> When I tread the verge of Jordan
> Bid my anxious fears subside,
> Death of death and hell's destruction
> Land me safe on Canaan's side.

And this is a part of my identity – a fundamental part – which does make me and others who believe in the same thing different. We believe in the Christian promise, that life is not the end of the story. So we all die, a universally shared experience, but not everyone thinks: 'That's it then.'

I have friends who cannot comprehend how I can possibly hold this view with a child-like acceptance of its comprehensive authority. One of the reasons for their disbelief is their contention that it is so totally at odds with much of what I say, write and have done about identity and violence. After all, they argue, religion itself has been a major cause of war, violence and suffering. They point particularly at the great monotheist religions of the Book – Christianity, Judaism and Islam. Have they not been primary reasons for violence? Well, yes and no, but mostly no.

In the agrarian communities and civilizations before these religions took hold of the imaginations and lives of so many, violence was systemic. When the Hebrews began to tell their tale, Cain the farmer killed Abel the herdsman. As it happens, herdsmen were historically the enemies of farmers, and sometimes suffered the consequences. Jesus was born during a period of Jewish uprisings following Herod's death, as the *Pax Romana* was brutally enforced by violence. The Roman Empire was built and maintained by the sword. But Jesus preached forgiveness and turning the other cheek. Of course that does not seem to be reflected later in the launching of the Crusades, which was the first cause of the sense of victimhood felt among Muslims at the hands of the West. But knightly ideals (going beyond Christian virtues) mixed with northern European testosterone also played their part, alongside religion, in bringing about this assault on a civilization that in many respects had surpassed Western Christendom. It had of course also set out over several centuries to conquer not just the outposts of Christendom but its heartland as well. That other crusade in the thirteenth century (against the Albigensians), in the Languedoc, a part of France I know well, was as much about the assertion of temporal authority as the stamping out of heresy. So religion may sometimes be a contributory factor in war and violence, but it is rarely the only or the primary motor. Even the Thirty Years War, which devastated Europe and appeared to pit Catholics against Protestants, was far more complicated than that. Catholic generals fought for Protestants against Catholics, and the reverse was also true.

Moreover, what do we learn from the secular age beginning perhaps with the French Revolution? Did attacks on organized religion – beginning in the 1790s, and continuing into the slaughter and imprisonment of its adherents by the totalitarian regimes of the twentieth century – show the peaceful side of mankind's nature? The industrialization of violence against humanity outdid in wickedness and brutality anything that happened in the days when Christian life fell woefully short of what Christians and other religious groups purported to believe. When the twentieth century turned out to be just as bad as Nietzsche had predicted, was this because God was alive or because He was dead? Or was it because humanity's moral compass was engulfed by events, by economic change, by technology and by societal breakdown? Yet it is certainly true that the gullible can always be persuaded that their own religion is their principal defining characteristic and is under assault, and that the only acceptable response is counter-attack and the search for vengeance.

Religious fundamentalists are often blamed for violence, but fundamentalist sentiment in the monotheist religions does not necessarily incubate or lead to it. Fundamentalists usually feel threatened by the world around them. It crowds in on their efforts to practise their religion with the concentrated purity which they deem essential. Modern technology brings challenges to their way of life but it also links them to fellow believers. Christian fundamentalism in the United States has thrived on its use of television and social media. Generally, the world outside, however, becomes 'the other', the enemy. Jewish,

Christian and Muslim fundamentalists always appear to be frightened and defensive. Science assaults their religious certainties: for example, evolutionary theory and modern physics, not only in the case of Christians. They are intolerant of other religious opinions. I once went to a Southern Baptist church in Texas to feel the power of a really hot sermon at scalding temperature. The pastor did not disappoint. Jews and Muslims came from the pits of hell. Catholics were led astray by Satan. I was not sure whether the Catholic fate was better or worse than Jewish and Muslim origins. Fundamentalists like that pastor take their intellectual sustenance from the simplest and often the crudest religious texts. Fundamentalist Christians are unlikely to pay much attention to St Matthew's Gospel and its account of the Sermon on the Mount, when Jesus preaches about forgiveness and generosity of spirit. (Indeed one Baptist who endorsed Donald Trump was quite explicit about not supporting any candidate who was offering 'Sermon on the Mount' policies.) They seize instead on the Book of Revelation with its apocalyptic prophecy, and its rejection of attempts to make accommodations with the rest of society. Jewish fundamentalists turn first to the Old Testament Book of Deuteronomy with its strict laying down of the law, and do not spend much time studying the rabbinical teaching that examining holy texts should lead to charity. Muslim fundamentalists ignore the calls in the Qur'an for tolerance and peace and focus on texts that justify violence. For all these fundamentalists the enemy is anyone who stands outside or disagrees with their own vision of the true faith.

Christian fundamentalists, especially in the United States, are usually strong supporters not just of the safe existence of the state of Israel – a proposition that many of us would readily accept – but of the most aggressive extension of Israel's borders. They interpret the Bible as telling us that Jesus will return to earth, the second coming, once the Jews have all returned to Israel. There will at this point be a great battle at Armageddon or, to use its modern, local name, Megiddo, a town in northern Israel. The battle will pitch Christians against the Anti-Christ. It is not clear where the Palestinians will be at this time, nor for that matter the Jews. Since the assumption is that they will ultimately accept Jesus as their saviour, maybe they will be locked in the struggle against the Anti-Christ. But this story unhappily ends without Jews; they all have to become Christians, according to the fundamentalists. The Christian right has played a part in steadily subordinating American policy making on the Middle East to increasingly right-wing Israeli interests and opinions.

Muslim fundamentalists used to cite Israel and Palestine as principal drivers of their violent extremism. I think this is usually more a pretext than a cause. Many Arab countries have been less generous to Palestinians than they should have been. But can we say that Muslims, whose fundamentalism came later than that of Christians, are inherently more violent than Christians, or is it really a matter of them having experienced a more bruising introduction to modernity?

Amin Maalouf, novelist and analyst of identity politics, wrote a book over thirty years ago examining the crusades through Arab eyes. Paradoxically, he argued that the failure of the crusades marked the beginning of the ascent of Western civilization and the death knell of the civilized Arab world partly because of the divisions opened up during the fighting between Turkish military commanders and Arab civilians, between Sunni and Shia. But the memory of the crusades still left its mark centuries later. When a Turk, Mehmet Ali Ağca, tried to shoot the Pope in 1981, he wrote: 'I have decided to kill John Paul II, supreme commander of the Crusades.' Western imperialism in due course helped to further brutalize Muslim attitudes to the West in the Arab world, and in more recent days the West has usually seemed – at least until the so-called Arab Spring – to be on the side of Arab autocrats. 'The war on God, on his message and on the Muslims' is often said to have begun with the Sykes–Picot agreement of 1916. Britain and France divided Arab lands between them and in the following year the Balfour Declaration urged the creation of a Jewish homeland in Palestine. This appeared to be the beginning of a Christian–Jewish alliance against Muslims. It was followed by the collapse of the Ottoman Empire, and then (so it is claimed) decades in which the Christian–Jewish alliance used weak and compliant Arab rulers, the United Nations, multinational companies and the media to surround and strangle Islam.

The sense of a shameful suffocation was armed with more dangerous weapons by events in Afghanistan (during the 1980s) and then Iraq (from 2003 to 2011) and Syria (after 2011). I recall, as Britain's

Development Minister, visiting Peshawar near Pakistan's border with Afghanistan in 1987. I went with the British ambassador to one of the camps for Afghan refugees from the war with Soviet forces in their country. A large number of very fierce men greeted us by firing their Kalashnikovs into the air. The West (principally the United States) was arming the tribes who were fighting and defeating Soviet troops. The ambassador sagely observed that Afghanistan was being flooded by weapons and that the conflict was sucking in sympathetic Muslims from elsewhere. Sooner or later, he opined, the Soviets would have to withdraw, humiliated. Afghanistan would be left with guns, rockets, warlords and opium. The world would be left with a lot of young Afghans, Saudis and Egyptians radicalized in the fight against these godless Russians. 'I don't know who they will fight next,' he said. 'But I doubt they will become doctors and architects.' The ambassador's insights proved all too accurate, and Western policy made things worse. After the terrible Al-Qaeda terrorist assault on the Twin Towers in New York in 2001 came the 'war of choice' in Iraq, the changes of regime in Egypt and elsewhere in North Africa, the destruction of Syria, and the stand-off between Sunni Saudi Arabia and Shia Iran with their proxy governments, armed factions, terrorists and bandits – throughout the region. Metastasized from all this is the Islamic State organization Daesh, bringing unimaginable horror to the lands of the world's first great civilization.

Is what these gangsters do a manifestation or expression of Islam? Do they cut heads off, bury men and women alive, drown them in municipal swimming pools and throw them off tall buildings because of their religion, or because of some more ghoulish, psychopathic sense of who they are and what they think they should be doing? Why are they willing to risk dying to bomb or burn down a cinema, mosque or church? Why do they run the gauntlet of drones and airborne attack? Why do they fight regular armed forces? They have no real defined and negotiable political aim. They do not seek national independence or a proper nation state of their own with its factories, power plants, a new capital, parade grounds, tanks, warplanes and platoons of well-drilled Muslim soldiers. The satisfaction they crave is to see others suffer and die, to see them humiliated, to know that they caused the humiliation, that they had the power in that moment to do it. They want to know that they can summon destruction 'on the wings of avenging angels', set the heavens ablaze engulfed in flames, destroy and then destroy some more. Vengeance, they tell themselves, is what Allah wants for His believers. That is what is really meant by divine justice: revenge for the West's cruel dominion; revenge for the unfairness of modern history; revenge for cultural assault; revenge for poverty when others are rich; revenge for a crummy job in a crummy flat in a crummy suburb in a Western city; revenge for not being anyone much or anyone special. They believe this is revenge ordained by a God who wishes it for each one of them, but this is not religion: it is the release of the basest impulses of humankind, the perversion of religion and humanity. As Karen Armstrong points out, 'IS [Islamic State] is no more authentically Islamic than the British National Party is typically British or the Ku Klux Klan genuinely Christian.' She reminds us that before their journey, two wannabe jihadis who left the UK for Syria in May 2014 ordered *Islam for Dummies* from Amazon: a cooked-up identity if ever there was one, but utterly deadly for all that.

For plural democracies in Western Europe and North America, the greatest worry is how these sentiments can be harboured by young Muslims in our own communities, sentiments so strongly held – or found – after years or a whole young lifetime in our countries, that they leave to participate in the slaughter of Syria, or stay home to slaughter their neighbours. What have we got wrong? Is there really no easy way of sharing a Western home with Muslims?

The fact that we even ask the question is partly caused by the seeming normality of some of the terrorists. They often appear well-integrated, and sometimes not very Muslim. The four young men who killed over fifty people in London in 2005 with bombs planted on public transport included three who, while of Pakistani heritage, had been born in Britain. They would have seemed to any outside observer to be well-integrated into British society, without giving up their identity as Muslims. One, for example, was a highly regarded teaching assistant at a primary school; another was a sports science graduate. Two of them were married with children. They may have been radicalized by local mosques, by madrassas and other contacts on the trips three of them made back to Pakistan. Was there more that their own British society should have done to help develop their resistance to the poisonous teachings which presumably converted them to evil? How did they become so alienated from their community? Looking at other terrorist identities, including some in France, it is clear that young Muslim culture does not always follow Muslim social or moral teaching. Smoking, drinking, promiscuity, both hetero- and homosexual, were parts of the lifestyle of several of these murderers. In some of these cases there was also obviously a deep strain of economic and social alienation, very apparent if you ever drive through any of the social housing high-rise suburbs of Paris or other French cities.

There are about 2.7 million Muslims in Britain, about 4.5 per cent of the population. It is difficult to get accurate figures for France because government policy since the nineteenth century has not allowed official statistics to distinguish between people on the grounds of race or religion. A Pew survey puts the figure at 4.7 million rising to 6.9 million in 2030; other estimates give higher figures, estimating that up to 11 per cent of the population may be Muslim already, the majority from North Africa and the Middle East. In Britain, Pakistan and Bangladesh are the principal originating countries for this diaspora. A significantly higher Muslim population in France has created greater social and political problems with a recent satirical novel, *Submission* by Michel Houellebecq, predicting the election of a Muslim president and government in 2022, supported by the traditional much-weakened parties of the left and right in order to shut the National Front out of government. There is just about sufficient plausibility to Houellebecq's description of the steady curtailment of civil liberties and the introduction of legalized polygamy, highly unlikely though it is, to make the book extremely unsettling. It underlines the crisis of liberal values in Western Europe, the lack of a self-confident assertion of our civic pluralism and solidarity.

This is surely even more important than some of the other measures we must take to tame or cage what Amin Maalouf calls 'the panthers' of identity politics, Muslim and other. Naturally, we need better policing intelligence about the organization of extreme anti-social radicalism; we should ban and arrest those who preach hatred and violence in mosques or elsewhere; faith schools – including Christian and Jewish ones – should be monitored to ensure that their curriculum is broad and outward-looking; economic and social policies should seek to mop up pools of alienated youth through training, education and housing policies. All these are often already part of the approach to governing the national communities of minorities to which most of us belong. What we must not try to do is sign up to a form of incoherent multi-culturalism which in effect behaves as though Britain (or any other country) could be a sort of federation of identity groups. All identities – racial and religious – should be treated with the same respect, but that respect should be enveloped in a common set of values which we insist all should esteem and to which all should subscribe. This is not tantamount to telling women what swimming costumes they should or shouldn't wear: nudity good, cover-up bad. But a plural society in Europe or North America operates under the rule of law which is made by an accountable, democratically elected parliament. It respects human dignity. It tolerates pretty much everything except intolerance. It protects freedom of speech. It does not allow minorities to attack behaviour which the whole community has agreed to accept and may even regard as a hallmark of a civilized society. Women have the same rights as men; sexual and religious preference is a matter for the individuals concerned. We are all individual members of a national community. Our identities are subsumed, but not buried, in a broader national civic order. I am not a Catholic who refuses to accept the standards and values of the broader community in which I live, even if I may wish to change them. I believe in rule by the representatives of a majority while still believing that the majority, if it is wise, should not simply trample over the point of view of the minority. That, in a way, is the formula that has brought peace to Northern Ireland. But even there, after almost two decades of relative peace, the relations between the communities seem delicately poised with the future of the power-sharing Executive constantly questioned or in doubt. I am not sure that this unsteady balance gets sufficient attention from senior ministers in London. As we know, it is easy to forget about Northern Ireland.

These ideas should naturally affect the approach of a host community to immigrants and of immigrants to the country in which they want to live. An immigrant should know about the life, culture and values of the country in which he or she wishes to make his or her home. It often follows that the more immigrants know about their new home of choice, the more they find out about the culture and identity which they brought with them. This was evident in the Polish community with which I grew up in West London after the Second World War. Most of the Polish boys with whom I played rugby – Sikorskis and Komerowskis – knew the words of 'Red Poppies on Monte Cassino', the song about the battle in which so many Polish soldiers had been killed. They also sang 'Jerusalem' lustily.

I imagine such an attitude was also true of my great-grandparents and grandparents, making a new home for their families during years when political turmoil and violence in Ireland must occasionally have made them nervous about the views that their host community might have about them. Earlier, I wondered how my grandparents would have felt during the Easter Rising of 1916. If I can do a reverse genetic test – thinking of my gentle father for example and going back another generation – I suspect that (as would have been the case with him) they would have deplored the violence. Their Catholicism was the part of their Irish identity to which my father too held fast, firmly but undemonstratively. And so, as I have written, it has been a central part of my own identity too, through thick and sometimes thin, through occasional bafflement and concern at the Catholic Church's reactions to a changing world, through serious doubts about the way in which it has sometimes exercised the central authority it claims, through its frequent tendency to place the enforcement of a narrow doctrine above the effort to help people live their lives while holding on to spiritual beliefs. Despite all that, I am proud to be a Catholic and I love this congregation and its ways even when they sometimes bewilder me. When Cardinal Consalvi, the brilliant and reformist Vatican Secretary of State at the turn of the eighteenth and nineteenth centuries, was warned that Napoleon wanted to destroy the Church, he replied, 'Not even we have succeeded in doing that.' The Catholic Church has somehow managed to survive its mistakes and its sins.

Naturally, like many other Catholics, I have to overlook some occasional absurdity, even pernicious absurdity. When in 1928 Al Smith became the first Catholic to run for President of the United States, he was questioned about some of the hostility to democracy in papal documents. He replied that like many other Americans he had never heard of them. The great English and Catholic historian Lord Acton, whose remark about the tendency of power to corrupt its holder was penned in the context of writing about the Inquisition, was a strong critic of the ultramontane pretensions of the papacy. He did not believe that popes were always wise and right. He even questioned the decisions made by Rome over the divorce of that terrible old tyrant, Henry VIII. There is indeed a good case to be made for arguing that both Pope Clement VII and Pope Julius III handled the Tudors so badly that they contributed significantly to the schism between Rome and England and the establishment of the national Church. The Blessed John Henry Newman made himself unpopular in Rome and with some in England like Cardinal Manning with his views on the authority of the Church's leadership. At a time when the Vatican seemed to believe that the modern world was an enemy, Newman argued that the Church and by inference the Pope as its head needed to change. 'To live is to change, and to be perfect is to have changed often.' Others were prepared to speak out about Rome's opinions. G. K Chesterton, for example, argued forcefully that there was a difference between heresy and criticism.

If my parents had been lapsed Catholics, if they had not been Catholics at all, I hope that luck would have led me to a faith group which would have provided me with some ordered way of expressing or discovering a sense of the spiritual. I find myself comfortable in the Church of England, whose services, music and language reflect some of the most enduring and admirable aspects of our national culture, not least its commendable tolerance. At the beginning of the service of Evensong in Westminster Abbey during the visit of Pope Benedict to Britain, which I mentioned earlier, I swelled with patriotic pride as the great procession of Anglicans – accompanied by the Pope – moved down the central aisle under the flags and banners of the national Church. They carried in the procession the illuminated Gospels of St Augustine, sent by Pope Gregory in 599 or 600, sometimes regarded as the foundation book of the Anglican Church. I also find admirable the religious practices of good evangelical churches, whose music and worship seem to touch their mixed congregations very personally and directly. 'Happy clappy,' people sneer. But why not be happy about what you believe? Why not clap what you reckon is very good news? Making fun of this exuberant form of worship should be put in the same category as deriding 'do gooding', as though 'do badding' must by definition be clearly preferable.

For all that, I remain a Catholic, with a profound sense of the importance of ecumenism and the hope that one day my wife will be able to take communion in Catholic churches, because Catholicism is a definable part of who I am.

Some right-wing Catholics – I have not called them fundamentalists – are unashamed in their embrace of double standards. They regard anything said by a pope with whom they agree as beyond criticism. But they get left high and dry when a pope is elected who tries to change a rigid line of teaching. When Pope John XXIII launched the Second Vatican Council and wrote his encyclicals, particularly *Pacem in Terris*, addressed to the world and advocating freedom of con-science, many opponents in the Church were horrified. Could it really be true that salvation, as was now asserted, could be found outside the Catholic Church? When this saintly old man died, the Vatican's theological enforcer, the head of the doctrinal praetorian guard in the Holy Office, Cardinal Ottaviani, said that he could now die a Catho-lic. But for many of us Pope John and the Vatican Council were what the Catholic Church should be; for me, John XXIII was a reason for being a Catholic. He and the Council gave us the sort of hope and inspiration as Catholics that kept us actively in the Church. They helped us to live as Catholics. Today, some of those who attacked Catholics who were critical from time to time of two of Pope John's successors – Pope St John Paul II and Pope Benedict – themselves denounce Pope Francis for his attempts to return the Church to a more sympathetic and forgiving pastoral approach than was evident in their leadership of the Church.

So I have not been pushed into abjuring my Catholicism when I have occasionally disagreed with Rome's behaviour during my life-time, but am easily enthused whenever what Rome is saying sounds like the New Testament. Nor, on the other side, have I been particu-larly troubled by the secular fundamentalists. Why should I stop believing in God because of Darwin, for example, whose own faith was not demolished by natural selection (though it was certainly affected by the death of his daughter Annie and his doubts about eternal damnation)? The attempt to use science to discredit religion often assumes that science itself is infallible. After the work of Einstein, I tend like others to agree with Karl Popper's view, 'We don't know anything.' Religion and science are separate domains, or *magisteria* as churchmen would argue. Science deals with empirical issues. What is this made of and why does it work? How can we improve some physical object or functioning? Religion embraces values and morality and deals with issues of meaning; it stands in the middle of the circle of final questions where believers seek inadequately and incoherently to act on God's presence. These domains of religion and science are not in conflict. Max Planck, one of the great scientists of the twentieth century, was one of those who argued that the two were quite compatible. Science doesn't only depend on reason. Intuition matters, and faith as well. This is one reason why science, like religion, uses aesthetics and metaphor. If something is a mystery how should I describe it? How do I express my sentiment on listening to Strauss's *Four Last Songs*? How can I, no poet, best put in words my reaction to the delicately coloured bloom of a white hibiscus in my garden or the aeronautical wonder of the butterfly which alights on it? How do I explain exactly why I believe in a soul and an afterlife? I use metaphors, just as cosmologists do with their talk of dark energy, dark matter and black holes.

So, with only a moderate sense of embarrassment, caused by the inadequacy of my life as a Christian, and with no intellectual shame at all, I declare my Christian beliefs, my Catholicism, as a fundamental part of who I am. They do not crowd everything else out. They do not exclude all the other things I have written about in this book – British patriotism, liberal Toryism, internationalism, the knowledge that I am a European, sport-loving, dog-loving, book-reading, Francophile (a proud *Commandeur* in the *Légion d'Honneur*), cautious, lucky, hard-working and besotted by my family. All those things are what make up 'me'. They make me different from, not necessarily better or worse than, you or anyone else. And it is the Christian and family parts of my identity which I hope will be with me right down to the wire.

But that is years away, isn't it? After all, I have read Somerset Maugham and have absolutely no intention of going anywhere near

Samarra. I hope I continue to be as lucky as I have been now for over seventy years. I have led, to seize the nearest available cliché, what you might call a charmed life. As I have written here, I had a happy home, loving parents, a good education and a set of religious beliefs which have helped me to find my way through life's maze. What Machiavelli called *fortuna* – by which he meant more than luck – led me into politics. Then one thing followed another, never really planned. I tumbled from job to job and was never bored. Some things that I did turned out well, others didn't; I think I left a mark. Maybe some bits of the world through which I passed were better off because of what I helped to do there. But that is a judgement better made by others, and perhaps one day will be.

What is success and what is failure? Philip Roth, who writes so often about identity, suggests in one of his novels that men and women leave 'a stain . . . a trail . . . our imprint' and that this has nothing to do 'with grace or redemption or salvation'. Maybe success is leaving a mark or imprint which encourages people to cheer up, to cope with life a bit more happily and successfully. Maybe your mark should give others hope, make them smile, and give them the confidence and understanding to know that in ways large or small they can make their world and our own a slightly better place. Did I transform anything – leave in a blaze of glory? Certainly not. All you can really do – to sound like a headmaster's speech at a prize-giving – is your best, not hurting people, muddling along through and around life's predicaments and hoping to emerge relatively unscathed at the other side, where naturally there is another thicket of predicaments awaiting you. In democratic politics, where I spent most of my time, you have to learn patience and remember that life is not always fair, that you will not always win even when you are sure you are right. The only great regret I have at this stage of my life is the result of the EU referendum and what it tells us about the populist perils that ambush liberal international values here, elsewhere in Europe and alas in America too. I worry about what all this portends for the future of my country, whose Prime Minister today seems to doubt whether you can be both a British citizen and a citizen of the world. I hope for the best for Britain, Europe and America.

Not the smallest part of my good fortune has been to live with a loving family through what must have been one of the most peaceful, prosperous and increasingly tolerant periods in our island's history. If our luck holds as a country, we will somehow avoid becoming poorer and meaner as a result of Brexit. If my own luck holds (fingers crossed and count to nine) there will be a few years yet knowing who I am – more walks with Lavender and our dog in the Parks at Oxford, more Saturday morning visits to the farmers' market in Barnes, more evenings sitting in my vegetable garden in the Tarn in France while the tomatoes ripen, watching the sun go down in a blaze of pink, orange and yellow glory over the wooded hills to the west, a glass of wine in one hand and a good book in the other. Perhaps my children and grandchildren will be somewhere nearby, the grandchildren scouring the strawberry beds and raspberry canes for something to pop into their mouths. Not a bad life for them; not a bad life for me.

Acknowledgements

Like Caesar's Gaul, my expression of gratitude is divided into three.

First, this book would never have been started without the encouragement and support (as ever) of my agent and friend Michael Sissons. We have been in harness now for twenty years; lucky me. The book would not have been finished without the magisterial editing of Stuart Proffitt and the help of the superb team at Penguin. I am one of many authors who know that Stuart is the best, and that we are fortunate to benefit from his wise, intelligent and extraordinarily well-informed professionalism.

Second, this has been a family effort. My wife, Lavender, chivvied, read, reminded me of things I had forgotten and, as always, supported. This is her story as well as mine. Kate brilliantly uncovered my family history. Laura gave me expert Pilates lessons to keep me, most of the time, on the road. Alice typed and re-typed the book and gave me very smart advice on what I was writing. I could not have written this book without her. I hope she will help me again. I was also, once again, the happy beneficiary of the support of my friend and wonderful PA Penny Rankin.

Of course, mistakes and inadequacies are my own responsibility.

Third, I would like to thank those who have kept me going over years – my cardiologists and their colleagues. Laura Corr and Jonathan Clague and Anthony de Souza (with all their great staff at the Royal Brompton Hospital) have kept me away from Samarra. I am very conscious that my parents would have lived longer if all this medical attention had been available to them. These doctors and nurses are the NHS at its best, a service on which we spend too little money and which depends so much on expertise from the rest of the world.

I enjoyed writing this book; I hope others will enjoy reading it.

Photographic Acknowledgements

Every effort has been made to contact copyright holders. The publishers will be pleased to make good in future editions any errors or omissions brought to their attention. Numbers refer to plates.

Alamy: 15, 20, 26, 29, 31, 32, 33, 35; Balliol College Archives: 10a (photo by Gillman & Soame), 11 (photo by Ramsey & Muspratt), 12; Ealing Local History Centre: 5; Getty Images: 17 (photo by David Montgomery); © L'Osservatore Romano: 34; © National Portrait Gallery (photo by Bernard Schwartz: 16; PA Photos: 27; Rex Shutterstock: 10b, 21; South China Morning Post: 23; © 1997 Time Inc. All rights reserved. TIME and the TIME logo are registered trademarks of Time Inc. Used under licence: 28; TopFoto: 18, 30 a & b.

All other photographs are from the collection of the author and the Patten family.

Index

Heiser, Terry, 121
Hennessy, Peter, 65
Henry VIII, 294
Heseltine, Michael, 151, 171, 193
Hewitt, John, 159, 163–4
Heyman, Harriet, 269
Hill, Bridget, 56
Hill, Christopher, 50, 55–6
Hobsbawm, Eric, 56
Hong Kong: after 1997, 201–2; Basic
  Law, 186, 189–90, 200; CP as
  Governor of, 6, 148, 183–4; and
  democracy, 185–95,
  200–202, 210; and Edward Heath,
  138; idenitiy of, 202–3; Umbrella
  Revolution (2014), 201–2, 210
Houellebecq, Michel,
  Submission 291
Housman, A. E., 1
Howard, George, 271
Howard, Michael, 124, 246–7
Howe, Geoffrey, 146, 151, 252
Hu Jintao, 195
Hua Guofeng, 207
human rights, and China, 199–200
Hume, Basil, Archbishop of
  Westminster, 116–17
Hurd, Douglas, 101, 130, 132,
  150–51, 174, 192
Hussein, Saddam, 152

Ibrahim, Anwar, 196
immigration, and Brexit, 240–41,
  243, 251, 254–6
India, 198, 205–7
IRA, 167, 176
Iran, 90
Iraq War (2003–11), 92, 100,
  122, 288
Ireland, Republic of, 164–5

Irving, Denys, 58
Islam, and violence, 288–92
Islamic State (Daesh), 289–90
Ismay, Hastings (Lord Ismay), 89
Israel, and Palestine, 234–6, 287–8
Israel Defence Force, 235

James I, King, 159, 163
Jay, Peter, 149
Jenkins, Roy, 58–9, 131, 134, 153,
  227, 266, 267
Jiang Zemin, 195
John Paul II, Pope, 129, 288, 295
John XXIII, Pope, 35, 277, 295
Johnson, Boris, 96, 241, 245
Johnson, Lyndon, 75, 82
Johnston, Robert, 166
Jones, Owen, 64, 65
Joseph, Keith, 109, 119–20, 140–41
Jowett, Benjamin, 52
Joyce, James, *Portrait of the Artist
  as a Young Man*, 39
Judt, Tony, 4
Julius III, Pope, 294
Juvenal, 283

Keegan, John, *The Mask of
  Command: A Study of
  Generalship*, 128
Keen, Maurice, 53–4
Keilor, Garrison, 239
Kennedy, Bobby, 86
Kent, Bruce, 97
Keynes, Maynard, 142
Kim Dae-Jung, 196
Kincora Boys' Home, 173
King, Martin Luther, 80, 81
Kinnock, Neil, 153, 219
Kipling, Rudyard, 74, 140
Kissinger, Henry, 266

McCormick, Neil, 59
McGahern, John, 15, 164
McGuinness, Martin, 178
McKinsey (management
  consultant), 278–9
McQuaid, John Charles,
  Archbishop of Dublin, 164
Medical Aid for Palestine, 235
Mellor, David, 96
Mencken, H. L., 239
Merkel, Angela, 226, 240, 248
Mesopotamia (student magazine), 60
Millar, Ronnie, 132, 149
Milne, A. A., 1, 95
Milner, Alfred, 1st Viscount
  Milner, 52
Milošević, Slobodan, 232–3
Mintoff, Dom, 184
Mitchell, George J. (US Senator), 176
Mitterand, François, 102, 224
Modi, Narendra, 206
Monti, Mario, 218
Moore, Charles, 140
Moritz, Michael, 128, 269
Mortimer, Edward, 59, 69, 72,
  78, 84–5
Mosley, Oswald, 15
Mossadeq, Mohammad, 90
Moussa, Amr, 235
Mowlam, Mo, 175–6, 180
Murphy, Jim, 277

Nash, Ogden, 172
Nasser, Abdul, 90
National Economic Development
  Office, 100
National Trust, 123
NATO, 89, 253
Needham, Richard (Earl of
  Kilmorey), 110, 112, 118, 170–71

New York, 85–6
Newcastle University, 263–6
Newman, Cardinal John Henry,
  46, 294
Nietzsche, Friedrich, 286
Nixon, Richard, 82, 90
Nkrumah, Kwame, 82
Noble, Dennis, 266
Nolan, Annie (CP's grandmother),
  16, 17
North Korea, 212, 229
Northern Ireland: background to
  the Troubles, 159–64; and Brexit,
  250; CP as Minister for, 166–75;
  government attitude to, 158;
  housing in, 169, 170; policing,
  176–81
Notre Dame University, Indiana, 74

Oakeshott, Michael, 99, 105
Obama, Barack, 76, 83
O'Connor, Frank, 38
Oklahoma, University of, 73–4
Olsen, Paul, 48, 50
Omagh, Ulster, 178
O'Neill, Terence, 161
O'Neill, Tip, 72
Open University, 134
Orange Order, Ulster, 163
Organ, Bryan, 109
Osborne, George, 108, 247
O'Toole, Cathy, 176
Ottaviani, Cardinal, 295
Our Lady of the Visitation (primary
  school, Greenford), 41–2
Oxford University, 57, 266–70; *see
  also* Balliol College, Oxford

Paisley, Ian, 163, 168, 170
Palestine, 234–6

Parris, Matthew, 108, 115
Pataudi, Mansoor Ali Khan
  (Nawab of Pataudi), 60
Patten, Alice, 7, 166, 167, 173
Patten, Angela (CP's sister), 19,
  20, 32–3
**Patten, Christopher Francis, Baron
  Patten:** family background, 6,
  16–21; childhood, 21–9, 213;
  schooling, 24, 41–3, 46–51; in
  Cadet Corps, 97; at Balliol
  College, Oxford, 52–61; travels
  to USA on Coolidge Fellowship,
  68–73, 77–8, 80–83; mayoral
  campaign in New York, 6, 85;
  works for Conservative Research
  Department, 96, 106, 107–9; in
  the Cabinet Office, 106; political
  assistant to chairman of the
  Conservative Party, 106; fights
  Labour seat in Lambeth, 109;
  MP for Bath, 110–11; Northern
  Ireland Minister, 118, 158,
  166–75; Department of
  Education and Science, 118–20;
  Overseas Development
  Administration, 120–21;
  Secretary of State for the
  Environment, 121–2; Chancellor
  of the Duchy of Lancaster, 122;
  Conservative Party Chairman,
  152; defeated in 1992 election,
  153, 182–3; Governor of Hong
  Kong, 6, 183, 189–94, 263; EU
  Commissioner, 6, 83–4, 194,
  213–38; chairs Independent
  Commission on Policing in
  Northern Ireland, 175–6;
  Chancellor of Newcastle
  University, 264; Chancellor of

Oxford University, 266–70;
  Chairman of the BBC Trust,
  262–76; co-ordinates Pope
  Benedict's visit to UK (2010),
  277–8
personal life and characteristics:
  Catholicism, 6, 7, 34–40, 168,
  284–5, 292–6; cultural tastes, 8;
  health, 34, 276; interest in
  football, 28–9; love of cricket,
  26–8; love of literature, 42–3, 49;
  marriage and family, 7, 112–13,
  297–8; superstitions, 51
views and opinions: on American
  politics, 75–83, 86–94, 103–4; on
  Asian values, 187, 195–200; on
  the BBC, 270–71; on the Brexit
  referendum, 7–8, 11, 122, 124–5,
  130, 215, 243–53, 256–61, 297;
  on Britishness/Englishness,
  215–17; on the Catholic Church,
  38–40; on China, 204–5, 207–10;
  on class and the Establishment,
  63–6; on death, 283–5; on
  defence, 253; on Donald Trump,
  242; on education, 41, 43–5,
  47–8; on Edward Heath, 130–33,
  138–9, 189; on the euro, 224–7;
  on Europe, 130, 214–15, 220,
  222–4, 236–7, 249–55; on
  globalization, 254; on higher
  education funding, 264–70; on
  homosexuality, 107–8; on Hong
  Kong, 187–96, 200–204; on
  identity politics, 8–11, 13–14,
  157, 172–3, 291–2; on
  immigration, 251, 254–6, 258–9,
  292–3; on Islamic terrorism,
  289–92; on John Major, 153–6;
  on Margaret Thatcher, 133,